Whispers

THE GIFT BOXED LINGERIE SHOP

15 HEPWORTH'S ARCADE

SILVER STREET
HULL
HU1 1JU

TEL: (01482) 326457

Briefs, Bodystockings, Bodies

Basques, Suspender Belts, Thongs

Teddies, Cami-Sets, Menswear

and Much Much More

ALL GARMENTS GIFT BOXED

FREE OF CHARGE

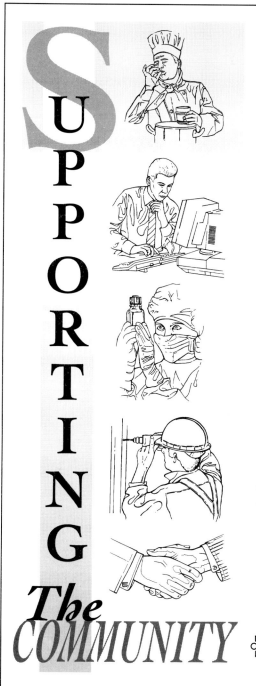

HEPWORTH'S ARCADE: ONE HUNDRED YEARS OF TRADING

by

GRAHAM HARDY

HUTTON PRESS
1996

Published by

The Hutton Press Ltd.,
130 Canada Drive, Cherry Burton,
Beverley, East Yorkshire HU17 7SB

Printed and bound by
Clifford Ward & Co. (Bridlington) Ltd.,
55a West Street, Bridlington, East Yorkshire
YO15 3DZ

ISBN 1 872167 84 5

DEDICATION

This book is dedicated to both my wife Debbie for her love and understanding in the time that we have been together and her patience and encouragement during the past two and a half years whilst I have been researching and writing this book, and to my parents Alan and Jean Hardy for all of the support they have given me over the years.

Thank You.

CONTENTS

The Publisher and the Author wish to thank Next Plc, Hull City Council Leisure Services, Hull Economic Development Agency and Hull City Council Technical Services for their generous financial support in the production of this book; also all the businesses who supported the book with advertisements.

Much of the information contained within the book has been obtained from the memories and recollections of many individuals. In some cases it has been possible to verify the facts supplied, but in others it has not. The author and publisher cannot accept responsibility for any errors resulting from information accepted in good faith.

PREFACE

During the course of my research for this book I have been told on numerous occasions that the Centenary of the Arcade with which it has always been my intention to coincide the publication would be in the year 1994 and not 1995 as I have maintained throughout that research. I therefore believe that it is necessary to explain my reasoning as to why, in my opinion, the Arcade reached its centenary year in 1995. Prior to attempting to establish when the Arcade should celebrate its centenary it should first be verified whether the date which is to be accepted as being 'day one' should be a) when the site was first cleared, b) when the first brick was layed, c) when the first shop opened or d) when the final lick of paint was applied and the whole Arcade was complete and ready to open for business. The above decision is particularly relevant considering the construction of the Arcade was undertaken in Victorian times when such a project would not be completed in a few months and indeed probably spanned at least two years which could create a differential of anything up to twenty-four months between dates a) and d).

For the purpose of this project, I have chosen option d) as, I believe, it would not be correct to celebrate the centenary of the Arcade at a time when some of the shops would only be 99 years old. Therefore, in my opinion, any celebrations should take place one hundred years from the date the construction was completed.

According to the Victoria History of the County of York, East Riding, Volume One published in 1969 (which I believe was the reference source used by the Hull City Council prior to the manufacture of the signs dated 1894 which hang above both the Silver Street and Market Place entrances) the Arcade was built for Leeds Tailor J. Hepworth, designed by W. H. Kitching and opened in 1894.

It should therefore, I feel be pointed out that the date quoted in that publication, although not clearly defined as such in the text, must be the date on which the first of the shops to be completed actually opened for business. That date was, I believe, probably more than a year before the construction of the remainder of the Arcade was completed. Whilst I have much respect for the publication and the information obtained within I also feel that it is necessary to clarify what is, I believe, an error in the name of the party responsible for the design of the structure.

William Henry Kitching, although an accomplished Architect with numerous projects to his credit, was not responsible for the design of the Arcade. The credit for that goes to the local firm of Gelder and Kitchen and it is conceivably the similarity in the surname of Alfred Gelder's partner Llewelyn Kitchen and that of Mr. Kitching that has caused the confusion. Furthermore it is interesting to note that, from the copy plans that it has been possible to view, the only set that are actually signed by the architect bear the signature of Alfred Gelder.

The information from which I have concluded that the Arcade was not completed until 1895 is as follows:-

1. Despite the fact that one set of plans for the Arcade dated January 1893 has been uncovered, plans of the site prior to the construction dated as late as January the following year (as described in greater detail later in this book) would suggest that the building of the Arcade did not commence until the beginning of 1894 at the earliest. Taking that information as being correct and allowing for the fact that it is highly unlikely that a project of this size would be completed in less than one year, it can safely be assumed that the completion date would have been during 1895.

2. Although it is known that Joseph Hepworth and Son Ltd. did open for business at no. 8 Silver Street at the end of November 1894, it has also been established that, just prior to the move, the company was still occupying its previous premises at nos. 60 and 61 Market Place. That property was later demolished to accommodate the building of the Market Place Arm of the Arcade.

3. Advertisements placed in the *Hull Daily Mail* by Andrew King, watchmaker and jeweller whose premises at 62 Market Place were next door to those previously vacated by Mr. Hepworth offer further evidence that the building work continued into 1895. In those advertisements which appeared regularly until June 1895 Mr. King makes reference to the great structural alterations in the New Arcade adjoining his premises which caused much inconvenience to his trade.

4. It is noted that although the Cook's Directory which was published in March 1895 lists four businesses as occupying shops within Hepworth's Arcade (all incidentally situated in the section leading from Silver Street to where the Arcade now bends hereinafter referred to as the Silver Street Arm) the Arcade itself is not listed. Indeed the street section of the same publication refers to 'Arcade building' between numbers 59 and 62 Market Place.

In conclusion I suggest that the Arcade was built in two stages. The first being the Silver Street Arm with emphasis having been given to completing the two shops fronting Silver Street, one of which was intended for Mr. Hepworth's own concern. This would enable Joseph Hepworth and Son Ltd. to continue trading from 60 and 61 Market Place with only a minimal interruption in trading when their new shop at 8 Silver Street was complete and the fixtures, fittings and stock had to be transferred. The second stage which I believe could not have been started until the final months of 1894 or the beginning of 1895 being the section leading from Market Place to meet up with the section previously completed (hereinafter referred to as the Market Place Arm) again with emphasis being given to the 'front' shops facing Market Place. It is known that one of those 'front' shops was occupied by the beginning of August 1895 but no evidence has been uncovered on any of the other shops in the Market Place Arm of the Arcade having tenants until December of that year.

I therefore conclude that December 1895 is the earliest date on which it can be categorically declared that Hepworth's Arcade was completed and fully open for business (although perhaps not fully occupied) and subsequently the date from which the Centenary and any subsequent celebrations should be calculated.

Graham Hardy,
Spring 1996.

INTRODUCTION — EXPLANATORY NOTES

Throughout the past one hundred years and long before the advent of the modern day Shopping Centres, Hepworth's Arcade has served the people of Hull as a place to call and shop for a variety of goods whilst remaining under one roof. It has survived two World Wars, numerous floods and the demolition man's hammer to become one of the few remaining pieces of Victorian Architecture in the City. It is thankfully now covered by a preservation order ensuring its continued existence for the enjoyment of the future citizens of Hull as it was by their forefathers.

During the past century the Arcade has housed a variety of businesses ranging from tobacconists to tea dealers and from coal merchants to artificial teeth makers and for many years has been known as the home of the City's only joke shop. It is the intention of this book to try to recollect on the Arcade and the businesses within it from its opening in the days when Queen Victoria was on the throne through the reign of five different monarchs to the present day, and whilst the details listed may be far from complete every attempt has been made to create an accurate account of the comings and goings over the past hundred years in Hepworth's Arcade.

In order to make this book a little easier to understand both an old plan of the Arcade (circa 1920) and a more recent one (circa 1990) showing the section recently altered are included.

As the Arcade forms an 'L' shape around the corner of Market Place and Silver Street it is difficult to make clear reference to any part of it whilst avoiding confusion and therefore, for the purpose of this book, the following guidelines have been followed:-

a)   The section of the Arcade which leads from between numbers 60 and 61 Market Place is referred to as the Market Place Arm.

b)   The section of the Arcade which leads from between number 8 and 9 Silver Street is referred to as the Silver Street Arm.

c)   The side of the Arcade on which the shops with even numbers begin behind number 8 Silver Street and continue through to number 61 Market Place is referred to as the North/East Side.

d)   The side of the Arcade on which the shops with odd numbers commence behind no. 9 Silver Street and continue through to number 60 Market Place is referred to as the South/West Side.

e.g. No. 18 is situated on both the Market Place Arm and the North/East Side and similarly no. 7 is situated on both the Silver Street Arm and the South/West Side

15

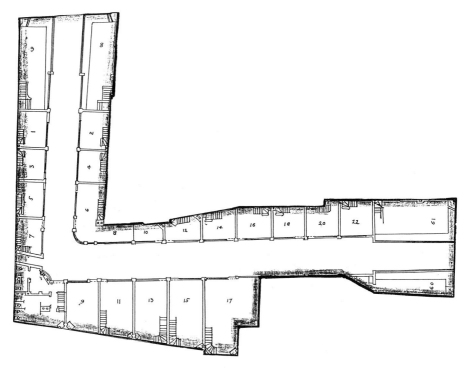

Hepworth's Arcade 1920.
Courtesy of Hull City Council Archives Department.

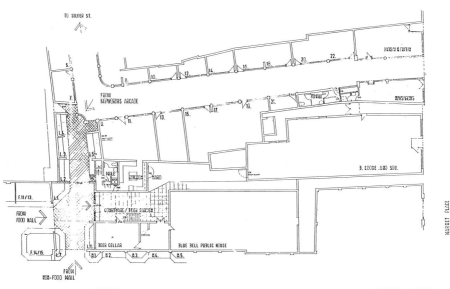

Hepworth's Arcade 1990.
Courtesy of Hull City Council Planning Department.

CHAPTER ONE
BEFORE THE ARCADE

When Joseph Hepworth first opened for business in Hull in 1888 having purchased the properties of numbers 60 and 61 Market Place the district around his shop was the principal commercial area in the city. The Directory of Hull for the year lists in Silver Street and Market Place alone 5 jewellers, 6 grocers and tea merchants, 4 chemists and no fewer than 22 clothing and footwear retailers. The main Post Office was situated on Market Place practically opposite Mr. Hepworth's shop and further south around the Holy Trinity Church the open market was held as it had been for centuries before. In addition to an array of milliners, hatters, hosiers and shoemakers Silver Street also included the offices of the Imperial Russian Consulate and within 400 yards of Mr. Hepworth's shop were situated over seventy licensed premises only 13 of which now remain.

The land on which the Arcade was later constructed was occupied by a number of buildings in and around a walkway by the name of the Spread Eagle Entry. An entry is a courtyard or in some cases merely a passageway flanked with buildings and situated behind the properties facing a main street or thoroughfare. It is accessed by means of an alleyway or covered passage passing between or through those 'front' buildings. This particular 'entry' which presumably took its name from the public house contained within it led off Market Place from between numbers 59 and 60 in a westerly direction before diverting to the south and terminating in a courtyard behind the properties on Trinity House Lane.

It is along the westerly route that the Market Place Arm of the Arcade now stands and it has been established that sections of some of the buildings that stood in the entry were retained as part of the new structure. The practice of preserving parts of buildings being pulled down for use in the construction of their replacements was apparently very commonplace at the time and such an explanation would possibly also account for the unusual shapes and varying sizes of the shops in the Arcade. A small section of the covered passageway that led into the entry from Market Place is still in existence and can be seen in the photograph. Regrettably a great part of the courtyard at the end of the entry has since disappeared following the construction of the Market Hall in 1904 and the small portion that does still remain is sadly now used for the storage of dustbins.

The public house or inn from which the entry took its name was an unusual establishment, peculiar because of the fact that it occupied two completely separate and unconnected buildings. The first which is named on the Ordnance Survey Map of 1853 as the Spread Eagle Public House was at the east end of the entry and adjoined Market Place whereas the second titled on the same map as the Spread Eagle Inn was some forty or fifty feet further down the entry. In

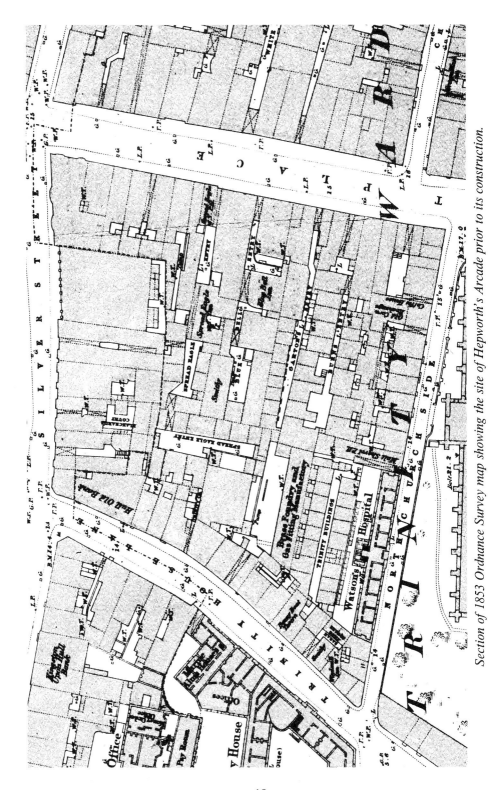

Section of 1853 Ordnance Survey map showing the site of Hepworth's Arcade prior to its construction.

addition to the public house and inn the entry also contained ten other one and two-storey buildings which, although probably only used for storage purposes in the years immediately prior to their demolition, were originally built as dwellinghouses. It is known that around the middle of the eighteenth century, whilst residing and operating his business from numbers 58 and 59 Market Place, Henry King, founder of the Hull ironmongers and planemakers firm of King and Company, provided six cottages behind his premises in which he housed some of his tradesmen. As most of the dwellinghouses and tenements in the Spread Eagle Entry were situated directly behind nos. 58 and 59 Market Place and the access to the entry itself is through that building

The remaining section of Spread Eagle entry.
Photograph by Graham Hardy.

it is very possible that it was those cottages that were amongst the premises that were later demolished to accommodate the building of the Arcade. Although it has been established that the cottages were at one time in the ownership of Mr. King it has not been possible to verify whether he was responsible for their building and the following extract from the *History of Hull* by George Hadley published around 1788 (over forty years after Mr. King took up residence in Market Place) in which the author appears to be writing an eye witness description would suggest that this was possibly not the case and reads as follows:-

'The house known as the Spread Eagle in the Market Place is a very ancient building, in the front of which is ANNO DOMINI 1587. The houses backward have much the appearance of having formerly been cloisters for nuns, as they all communicate one with another.'

Assuming that the premises to which Mr. Hadley makes reference are the same as those in which Mr. King once housed his tradesmen and of course that the properties were not demolished and rebuilt during the following one hundred years it is very feasible that the buildings later removed by Mr. Hepworth were, at the time, over three hundred years old.

The census of 1891 confirms that the eight houses listed were home to 23 people and that only two of those, nos. 8 and 9, had three or more inhabited

19

rooms with two of the properties, nos. 1 and 2, being single room occupation only. It also confirms that the final proprietor of the hostelry which is listed as the Spread Eagle Hotel, was Herbert Guest, aged 57, originally from Kidderminster who lived with his wife Emma 22 and son Herbert 3 months. Eliza Clark, a barmaid, aged 22 was also shown in residence at the hotel.

¯ The other buildings that had to be removed to make way for the Arcade were numbers 8 and 9 Silver Street and Mr. Hepworth's own premises at 60 and 61 Market Place. No. 8 Silver Street which was occupied at the time by Thomas E. Kirkness, milliner, fronted Silver Street and was bordered to the east by a covered passageway belonging to the Charterhouse and being part of no. 7 Silver Street. Although unnamed it is very possible that the passageway, which is still in existence to this day and gives access to the hairdresser's premises to the rear of no. 7 Silver Street, also at some time led into the Spread Eagle Entry. To the rear of the property were additional spacious premises which also extended to the rear of both nos. 7 and 9 Silver Street (to which they were connected) and led out onto the Northern side of Spread Eagle Entry. Those premises apparently housed the kitchens and restaurant section of a confectionery business operated under the name of Robert Ostler and Co. from no. 9 Silver Street that had reportedly been established for in excess of seventy years and was described as the principal confectioner's and wedding cake business in Hull.

Unfortunately very little topographical evidence of the site prior to the Arcade being built is available and the only examples that have been uncovered are in the form of two sketches by the Victorian Hull street artist F. S. Smith. The first of the two drawings vaguely shows the entrance to the passage leading into the entry although it is highly probable that Smith's intention, when he did the sketch in 1887, was to focus on the Post Office opposite which later became the Customs House and is now a bar, restaurant and offices. The second drawing, which Smith created some seven years later in 1894 after the work on the Arcade had commenced, depicts the gap created in Silver Street by the demolition of numbers 8 and 9.

Illustration of Market Place 1887 by F. S. Smith.
Courtesy of Hutton Press and Hull City
Museums and Art Galleries.

Illustration of Silver Street 1894 by F. S. Smith.
Courtesy of Hutton Press and Hull City Museums and Art Galleries.

CHAPTER TWO
TO BUILD THE ARCADE

The first steps taken by Joseph Hepworth towards the building of the Arcade were made in January 1888 when the property of number 61 Market Place was purchased by him from William Elliot Martin, seedsman (seed merchant) of Hull. Mr. Martin had, until the time of the sale, occupied the premises himself but later moved his business across the road to no. 20 Market Place. The following month Mr. Hepworth made a further acquisition purchasing the neighbouring property of number 60 Market Place from Sarah Stoker, widow of Hull. Those premises had previously been in the occupation of Charles Campbell, chemist who had earlier vacated the property in favour of a shop further south along Market Place at no. 50. At the time of purchase of the two properties, both of which included ancillary buildings and land to their rear, it is likely that Joseph Hepworth was merely securing premises for a branch of his

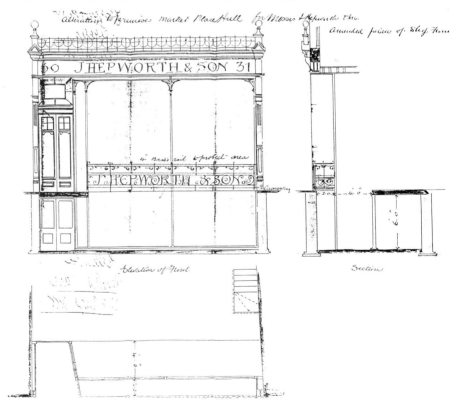

Illustration of proposed alterations to Joseph Hepworth's premises in Market Place.
From the archives of Hull City Council Records Office — Reference OBL/M/8139.
Courtesy of Hull City Council.

own business which was, at the time, expanding and probably had no thoughts or intentions of building an Arcade.

In September of the same year approval was sought for alterations to the premises which probably involved joining the two properties together to make one larger shop. The drawing which formed part of that application gives an artist's impression of the appearance of Mr. Hepworth's premises on completion although it is noted that the shop numbers have, in error, been shown as 30 and 31.

As stated in the previous chapter Mr. Hepworth's business was in the centre of the principal commercial area of the City and in 1890, after two years of trading in Hull, Joseph, obviously recognising this fact, saw the potential of the near derelict properties to the rear of his shop and made the first moves towards their purchase.

The properties at nos. 60 and 61 Market Place although originally purchased outright had been mortgaged in July 1888 and by taking out a further charge against that mortgage Joseph raised the necessary capital and, following negotiations with the parties concerned, the following sales were agreed on 23rd August 1890:-

1. The Spread Eagle Tavern including the ground floor dramshop situated at 59 and a half Market Place along with numbers 1, 4, 5, 6, 7, 8, 9 and 10 Spread Eagle Entry from Thomas Connell, Tanner of Sunk Island in Holderness.

2. No. 8 Silver Street and property to the rear of nos. 8 and 9 Silver Street from Henry Preston, Confectioner of Hull.

3. No. 9 Silver Street from Fanny Anne Preston, Spinster of Hull.

At the time of sale most of the property owned by Thomas Connell was reported as being in the occupation of Henry Bentley and Company or their under-tenants. Henry Bentley and Co. were a firm of local brewers who no doubt managed the Spread Eagle Tavern and sub-let the tenements surrounding it to a number of individuals and families although it is noted from the electoral registers that a Joseph Elsom also operated a business from premises within the entry. Nos. 8 and 9 Silver Street and the property behind them were occupied by Thos. E. Kirkness, milliner, and Henry Preston who operated a confectionery and restaurant business under the name of Robert Ostler and Co.

Following the purchase of the properties by Mr. Hepworth in 1890 the premises at numbers 8 and 9 Silver Street were vacated and re-let to Mark Feldman, pianoforte dealer but there appears to have been little immediate change in the occupancy of the other buildings within Spread Eagle Entry. It has, however, been noted that the licensee of the Spread Eagle Tavern who was listed in the 1889 directory as being Joseph Bird had, by 1891, changed to Herbert Guest. By 1893 it would appear that the public house had closed, Joseph Elsom had relocated his business into Blue Bell Yard and that all of the tenants with the exception of one Henry Tagg, a tallyman who occupied a single room at no. 1 Spread Eagle Entry, had left.

As it was the intention of Joseph Hepworth not only to erect an Arcade on the land created by the demolition of the buildings that he had purchased but also to utilise part of the entry itself it was also necessary for him to reach agreements with many other parties who, through the position of their properties, had right of way through the said entry. Therefore, on 31st October 1893 agreements were made with:-

1. Arthur Henry Eastern.
2. William Allison, Henry Godolph Rooper and John Rooper.
3. Francis Richard Pease.
4. The Reverend Edward Thomas Mortlock of St. Leonards in Sussex and The Reverend Edward Mortlock of Hastings in Sussex.

that, in return for forfeiting their right of way (and that of their heirs, servants, workmen and others) over and along the Spread Eagle Entry to and from their properties as shown on the following plan, Joseph Hepworth would grant a similar right of way through the newly constructed Arcade. It is possible that the two Reverend Mortlock's, who it is believed were father and son, drove a harder bargain than the other parties affected by the new Arcade as it is noted in the document which outlines the agreement with the two gentlemen that, in addition to granting a right of way as indicated above, Joseph Hepworth also agreed that the new drain that was to be laid beneath the Arcade could also be used by the premises of Messrs. Mortlock and would be connected to their property at his own expense. Furthermore he gave up all rights as beneficial owner to the remaining section of the Spread Eagle Entry leading off Market Place to the gentlemen and agreed that, should they wish, a door or gate could be fitted across the access to the entry enabling the property to be secured and that such a door or gate could be fastened to the wall on the north side belonging to Mr. Hepworth. It is interesting to note that this part of the entry still, to this day, remains and the gate with which it is sealed off from Market Place is attached to the northern wall of the entry at the rear of no. 60 Market Place. It has also been established that, at some point in time, a small section of 9 square yards of land between the rear of the Spread Eagle Tavern and Blue Bell Yard was also given up to the Mortlock's. Both that piece of land and the remaining section of the entry now form part of the premises of 58/59 Market Place currently owned by B. Cooke and Son Ltd, but at the time the Arcade was constructed belonged to the Reverends Mortlock. Some of the rights of access along the Arcade that were granted to the various parties over one hundred years ago are still applicable to this day to the buildings now occupying the sites on which the various premises then stood.

The various plans of the site which accompanied both sales of properties and grants for access from which the following plan has been produced and a further example prepared by Messrs. Gelder and Kitchen dated 31st January 1894 all show the existing buildings and further confirm the theory that construction of the Arcade did not commence until February of that year at the earliest. It is, however, worth noting that none of the plans which made reference to the rights of way included the premises of 8 and 9 Silver Street which could suggest that the properites had already been demolished although it is possible that, as those buildings bore no relevance to the purpose of the plans, they were purposely omitted.

The Market Place 'arm' looking east taken from the balcony.
Photograph by Tony Ward of Topcolour.

It is known that work on the Arcade had definitely begun by July 1894 as during that month a dispute which had arisen between Mr. Hepworth and The Charterhouse of Hull who owned (and still actually own) the property of no. 7 Silver Street, was settled. According to the agreement which was later registered with the authorities, Mr. Hepworth's builders had, following the demolition of no. 8 Silver Street, proceeded to erect a wall to a height of 23 feet 10 and a half inches which exceeded the height of the wall which was being replaced by over eleven feet and, according to the Charterhouse, therefore lessened the supply of light and air to their property at no. 7.

It was eventually agreed that, in consideration of a payment of one hundred pounds from Mr. Hepworth, the Charterhouse would grant permission for the part of the wall at that height that had already been completed to remain but also that the section still to be built must not exceed 16 feet nine and a half inches. They also stipulated in the agreement that Mr. Hepworth must accept responsibility for the legal and surveyor's costs incurred by them which had amounted to ten pounds and that he should also make arrangements for the glass roof of the passage belonging to no. 7, which had apparently been damaged by the builders, to be repaired. This agreement explains why a small part of the roof on the North/East side of the Arcade has, like the whole of South/West side, a central peak (see picture taken from the roof of Holy Trinity Church), whereas the majority of the remainder of that side slopes from the Arcade roof downwards to a substantially lower level and the rear of the ceilings of the shops numbered 4 to 18 inclusive are lower than those in the rest of the Arcade.

The roof of Hepworth's Arcade as viewed from the roof of Holy Trinity church.
Photograph by Graham Hardy.

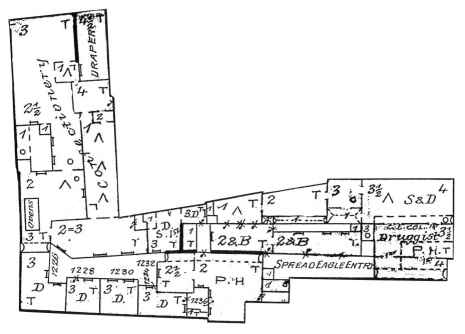

A section from Goad's insurance plan of 1886.
Courtesy of Chas. E. Goad Ltd.

Although several sets of original plans have been uncovered (all slightly different from one another) none of those identifies accurately with the Arcade as it is today or those which were produced to accompany a mortgage on the property in 1895. Also shown is a copy of the relevant section of the Goads Insurance Plan of 1886 which, although failing to align exactly with those of the completed structure, hopefully gives an idea of the similarities in the positioning of some walls prior to and following construction of the Arcade.

As discussed in the previous chapter it was apparently common practice during the period in which the Arcade was built to try to re-use parts of buildings being demolished in the construction of their replacements and although it has not been possible to establish if this procedure was adopted in other parts of the Arcade structure it is highly likely that the wall at the rear of the shops on the south side of the Market Place Arm, or at least part of it, is the same wall that formed the rear of both the public house and the dwelling houses on the southern side of Spread Eagle Entry. In recent years the majority of that wall has been covered over with concrete but a small section of the rear wall to no. 17 is still exposed and the brickwork appears to date back a lot longer than that used on the rest of the Arcade. During the recent extension to the café at nos. 9 and 11 Hepworth's Arcade it was reported that the section of wall removed was reportedly much older than the majority of the Arcade structure and was described by Mr. John Whittaker of Hull City Council Planning Department as being almost medieval. This would appear almost certainly to confirm that, as suggested in the previous chapter, although the Arcade is only now due to celebrate its centenary, parts of the

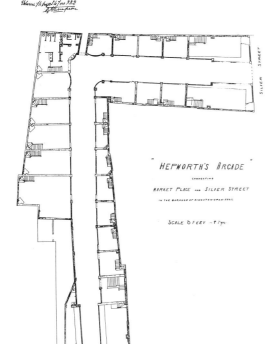

Hepworth's Arcade 1895.
Courtesy of Hull City Council
Archives Department.

actual structure date back feasibly as much as four hundred years.

Although it has been noted that on one set of plans, which included an artist's impression of the Arcade, the name of Victoria Arcade appears no doubt in honour of the reigning monarch it would seem that this title was later forgotten when Mr. Hepworth obviously decided to use his own name. The idea of businessmen naming Arcades after themselves was, however, by no means a new one with Thornton's Arcade in Joseph's home of Leeds having, at the time, been established over twenty years. It is, however, vaguely possible that the title of Hepworth's Arcade may have prompted an idea by Joseph's business rival Montague Burton as nearly fifty years later the George and Dragon Yard off Briggate in Leeds where Mr. Burton had premises became known as Burton's Arcade.

As previously mentioned the Arcade was, during the year of its completion, mortgaged although this was obviously only as a temporary measure as just two years later the mortgage was settled.

The following extract is taken from an 1897 publication entitled *Kingston Upon Hull Illustrated.*

'Mr. Hepworth is to be congratulated for removing, at considerable cost (for the building of this arcade involved the acquiring of many lots of property, and of various vested interests, including a public house and giving up of the license) this unsightly and decayed property, and erecting in its place such useful and ornamental buildings.'

The article went on also to commend Mr. Gelder who it suggested:

'has utilised a difficult site to considerable advantage.'

'The Arcade,' the publication reported,

'is lighted by electricity, and forms a very pleasing retreat from the busy thoroughfares which it connects, and where purchasers can pass along and inspect the goods in the shop windows under cover of a neat glass roof.'

28

CHAPTER THREE
THE STRUCTURE

Hepworth's Arcade is situated between Silver Street and Market Place in the heart of Hull's Old Town and forms a link between the two thoroughfares. Just two hundred yards from the Silver Street entrance lies Whitefriargate, one of Hull's busiest shopping streets, and a little further south from the Market Place entrance is the Holy Trinity Church and the golden statue of King William the third. To the south and south-west of the Arcade stands the Indoor Covered Market behind which the open market is held three times a week.

The majority of the Arcade is constructed to two storeys with each of the individual shop units having a first floor although the properties at each end on Silver Street and Market Place are of three storeys plus attic and also span the Arcade. At the outer 'bend' in the Arcade, at the junction where the Silver Street Arm meets the Market Place Arm, is situated a covered walkway leading to the Market Hall above which is a balcony overlooking the Arcade. The roof, often unnoticed due to being hidden at street level by the surrounding buildings erected to a greater height, is one of the finer features of the structure and comprises of two glass barrel vaulted sections with cast iron ribs leading down the two 'arms' of the Arcade and meeting at an octagonal glazed dome topped with a small glazed cupola. At each end of the Arcade where the two-storey levels join with the higher premises fronting Silver Street and Market Place is an elliptical arch with the name of the Arcade on a panel above it. The individual shops are separated at ground floor level by pilasters with each unit having three first floor windows divided by half-columns. On the Southern side of the Market Place Arm where there are no shop units the style has been continued for consistency and at ground floor level is a Victorian painted advertisement for J. Hepworth and Son, Tailors and Clothiers which probably dates back to the opening of the Arcade.

To the exterior at the Market Place end the property is fronted with 2 two-storey bay windows with cornices. To either side of these is a single window with round headed sashes to the first floor and segment headed sashes to the second. The third or attic floor has a pair of dormers each with two glazing bar sashes under ornate gables topped by swan necked pediments. On the ground floor an off-centre segmental archway with iron gates and decorative cast iron grille leads into the Arcade.

At the Silver Street end the first and second floors each have a central two-storey bay window with cornice with three single windows to either side. The single windows to the first floor having round headed sashes, those above having segment headed sashes and all having marble shafts between and flanked by panelled pilasters. The third or attic floor has a central dormer with two glazing bar sashes flanked by pilasters under an ornate gable topped with a swan necked pediment. On the ground floor is a central Arcade opening with gates and decorative cast iron grille.

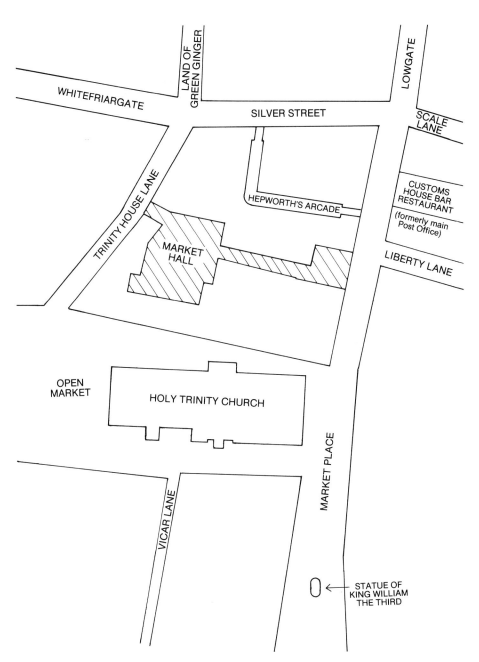

Plan of streets in locality of Arcade showing Holy Trinity, King William statue and indoor/outdoor markets.

CHAPTER FOUR
OWNERSHIP OVER THE YEARS

Although Hepworth's Arcade has stood for one hundred years it has only, during that period, been in the ownership of six different parties.

As discussed in the previous chapters the original owner was Joseph Hepworth who also gave his name to the construction. When Joseph died in 1911 the Arcade which would have formed part of his estate was included in his will and one of his sons and one of his sons-in-law were made exors and trustees of the estate with the instruction that the property was to be sold as soon as those gentlemen saw fit.

For simplicity the status of ownership of the Arcade in chronological sequence is listed below:

1. From completion of building until his death on 17th October 1911 —
    JOSEPH HEPWORTH

2. 17th October 1911 to 10th May 1920 —
    HERBERT MORTON HEPWORTH, Clothier of Leeds (Son) and
    WILLIAM ALFRED IBBITSON, Gentleman of Leeds (Son-in-law) as exors and trustees to the estate of Joseph Hepworth

3. From 10th May 1920 to 20th November 1946 —
    SOLOMON COHEN, Bedding Manufacturer of Liverpool
    HYMANN GRAFF, Gentleman of Liverpool and
    ISAAC HARRISON, Clothier of Liverpool

Isaac Harrison died in 1929 and Solomon Cohen in 1934 which left the ownership of the Arcade to Hymann Graff. When, in 1942, he too died, the Arcade was bequeathed to his two daughters Sadie Eppel and Dora Harrison and Dora's husband Harry. Consequently when, in 1946, the property changed hands again the names of the vendors shown on the records of the sale were:

HARRY HARRISON, Estate Agent of Liverpool
DORA HARRISON, wife of above
SADIE EPPEL, formerly wife of Isaac Eppel but now single woman of Liverpool

4. From 20th November 1946, to 31st January 1949 —
    JOSEPH AARON LITTMAN, Gentleman of London

5. From 31st January 1949 to 1st September 1961 —
    KAYAR INVESTMENTS LTD., of London

By September 1961 Kayar Investments Ltd. were in liquidation and the appointed liquidator of the company, Howard John Henry Greenacre, Chartered

Accountant of London, agreed and oversaw the fifth and most recent sale of the Arcade.

6. From 1st September 1961 to Present Date —
    THE LORD MAYOR, ALDERMEN AND CITIZENS OF THE CITY AND COUNTY OF KINGSTON-UPON-HULL also known as The Corporation but today better known as Hull City Council.

CHAPTER FIVE
THE TENANTS

Although the tenants of Hepworth's Arcade during the last century have included several businesses which have developed, since their occupation, to such great proportions that it may seem hard to believe that the business ever operated from such humble surroundings the majority of ex-tenants have been, as they are today, smaller local businesses. Many of the ventures that have been undertaken in the Arcade throughout the past one hundred years have been one or two-man outfits or family concerns several of which have passed down from father to son. Whereas it has been the intention to acknowledge the achievements of the larger and more successful concerns in attaining such progress in the difficult world of retailing the true purpose of this chapter, and perhaps the book itself, is to give some recognition to the 'little man' who would otherwise, in time, become no more than a distant memory and eventually be forgotten.

Although the accomplishments of some of the businesses included in this chapter may never have been outstanding with some failing to even progress out of their infancy, all of them, big or small, success or failure, were no doubt founded with the same determination, spirit and hope and for that reason an attempt has been made to give each and every one of them their 'five minutes of fame'.

Because, as previously stated, some of the individual businesses that have occupied the Arcade had an ephemeral existence sometimes lasting no longer than a year or two it has regrettably been difficult to uncover much information on them. It has however been possible to establish a few details on the great majority and in some cases what could perhaps be described as a 'mini company history'.

As the occupancy of the individual shops in the Arcade has, throughout the past century, altered over an irregular time span it would not be possible to list the tenants in a combined chronological order. It has therefore been decided that each of the separate premises should be given a dedicated section tracking the occupation of it throughout the last one hundred years.

Because many tenants, both past and present, occupied more than one shop in the Arcade sometimes concurrently, and on other occasions not, although each business has been credited with their individual tenancies under the appropriate shop number the article on the business itself has been included under the section covering the premises in the Arcade with which they were first attributed. On some occasions where occupation of two or more shops commenced on the same date the article has been included under the lower of the shop numbers. As the main source of information regarding dates of tenancy has been the Hull Directories which were not published every year it is highly possible that, in some instances, the dates of tenancy may be inaccurate

The Silver Street 'arm' looking north.
Photograph by Tony Ward of Topcolour.

The Silver Street 'arm' of Hepworth's Arcade looking south towards the balcony.
Photograph by Tony Ward of Topcolour.

The Silver Street entrance to Hepworth's Arcade.
Photograph by Tony Ward of Topcolour.

The Market Place entrance to Hepworth's Arcade also showing entrance to the remaining section of Spread Eagle entry.
Photo by Tony Ward of Topcolour.

35

with the business covered having occupied the premises both prior to and following the dates given and it should therefore be noted that the years shown are those during which it has been possible to verify that the venture occupied the shop or shops. For some businesses occupation dates have been further defined through the use of electoral registers, newspaper advertisements and in later years telephone directories, but again, although establishing that the venture was in occupation at the time of publication, the information obtained from these sources, in most cases, remains inconclusive when trying to establish the opening or closing dates for any business.

The dates given alongside each entry are those in which the business occupied those particular premises and not the lifespan of the concern itself. Similarly the business description given for each of the ventures is that with which they were attributed in the directories when they first took up occupation of the premises. For simplicity and to highlight further the instances where one business occupied two or more consecutive shops the premises are not listed in immediate ascending or descending numerical order. Instead a route has been followed starting at no. 8 Silver Street and following the sequence of shops with even numbers up to no. 61 Market Place at the other end of the Arcade. The Arcade is then crossed to no. 60 Market Place and the line of shops with descending odd numbers followed back towards the starting point and terminating at no. 9 Silver Street.

The photographs show the two 'Arms' of the Arcade as viewed from the balcony at their junction.

NO. 8 SILVER STREET

Number 8 Silver Street which is situated at the Eastern side of the Silver Street entrance to the Arcade was one of the original shops in the Arcade to be completed and occupied. As the plan shows the premises not only had a ground floor area which offered window space to two sides but also benefited from extensive extra space on the first, second and third floors which also span the Arcade itself.

Joseph Hepworth and Son Ltd., Wholesale Clothiers and Tailors, 1894-1910

Joseph Hepworth was born in Lindley, Huddersfield on 12th May 1834, the son of a shoemaker. At the age of ten he started work at a woollen mill in the village. Although described as a 'half timer' he worked over thirty hours a week for the princely sum of one shilling and sixpence (7½ pence) per week. Two years later he became a full-timer and at the age of sixteen moved to Walkers Wellington mill in the village as a teazle setter. During his time with that company he studied at the Lindley Mechanics Institute to such an extent that by 1853 he became a volunteer teacher.

When, in 1860, Walkers defaulted and Joseph was without work such was the high regard in the village for his voluntary work that he was made an assistant overseer at thirty pounds a year.

After three years he became a traveller for a woollen manufacturer a position which he maintained until 1864 when he took his first steps into his own business. It was in that year that he, along with his wife's brother, opened

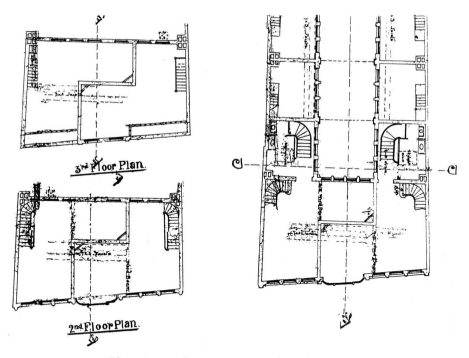

3rd Floor Plan.

2nd Floor Plan.

Plan of upper floors to nos. 8 and 9 Silver Street.
Courtesy of Gelder and Kitchen.

as woollen drapers from premises in Briggate, Leeds. His earnings for that year were around fifteen shillings (75 pence) per week.

The following year he set up on his own as a wholesale clothier in Bishopsgate Street in the city with seven sewing machines and twelve 'hands'. The business developed and by the early 1880's when he was joined in the business by his son Norris the company had works in Wellington Street and employed 500.

At this time the company was purely a manufacturer, supplying a string of small independent retailers, but following a series of losses caused by insolvent tradespeople they made the move that was to change not only the face of their own venture but that of the clothing industry throughout the country. Their decision to open their own retail premises and sell direct to the public caused the company to lose many of its existing customers against whom they would be competing, but regardless of that the venture was an obvious success and over the next twenty years one hundred and forty-three branch shops were opened.

It has been suggested that following 1891 when the concern became a private company under the name of Joseph Hepworth and Son Ltd. Joseph devoted less time to business presumably leaving the day-to-day running of the firm to his son. It is therefore possible that he, having worked very long hours throughout his life, found the need to fill his newly discovered 'free time' and perhaps saw the building of the Arcade as a suitable project with which to keep himself busy. On several documents relating to the planning and building of the Arcade is the signature of Joseph Hepworth which would indicate that he was very closely involved with the development. It should also be noted that the

Top: The Market Place 'arm' of Hepworth's Arcade looking west towards balcony.
Bottom: Painted advertisement for J. Hepworth and Son.
Photographs by Tony Ward of Topcolour.

The Silver Street 'arm' looking north taken from the balcony.
Photograph by Tony Ward of Topcolour.

Joseph Hepworth.
Courtesy of Leeds Central Library.

Arcade was built on behalf of Joseph Hepworth himself and not for his company as is common belief. He also spent more time with council matters having been elected onto Leeds City Council as a Liberal in 1888, and later in 1892 becoming an alderman and later still a magistrate.

In 1895 by which time the firm had also built up a substantial export trade to Australia and South Africa they suffered a major setback when their Prospect Works in Leeds was gutted by fire with losses estimated as high as £80,000 including the entire stock of patterns. Fortunately duplicates were soon obtained from the overseas subsidiaries and the factory was quickly rebuilt.

In 1905 in which year the company profits were £33,323, to celebrate his golden wedding anniversary Joseph awarded all 1200 of his employees a bonus dependant on years of service at a cost to the company of £2,000.

The following year at the age of 72 he was recalled from retirement by Leeds City Council to fill the highest civic office which could be offered to him and became the Lord Mayor of Leeds. As a life-long tea-totaller who often commented that his favourite beverage was water he soon made his presence felt. At the City Council meeting immediately after his election he announced his intention to replace the dinner, at which the chief magistrate normally entertained, with a breakfast and that he would be donating the £500 supposedly saved to a fund to provide meals for poor children.

In his final years Joseph divided his time between his home in Harrogate and the one in Torquay where he spent the winter months. After a period of ill health he passed away on 25th October 1911 leaving an estate of £168,218. He was survived by his widow Sarah, three sons and four daughters.

Under the leadership of Joseph's eldest son Norris the company continued to grow becoming a household name with branches in every major city in the country with the total number of outlets reaching 350 by 1945.

In 1986 following over ninety years of trading under the names of their founders a decision was reached by the board of directors that a change of name would be beneficial to the company image and J. Hepworth and Son Plc formally became known as Next Plc. Many of the premises now occupied by Next outlets were, like those currently occupied by the branch in King Edward Street, Hull, originally purchased by or leased to J. Hepworth and Son Limited.

The name of Joseph Hepworth, wholesale clothiers, first appeared on the streets of Hull in 1888 when the company opened the premises at 60 and 61 Market Place which they had purchased earlier that year.

Within four years of establishing themselves in the City a second branch at the eastern end of Hessle Road opened. Although different directories disagree on the actual numbers of the three shops occupied by Hepworth's it has been established that these were on the southern side of the road immediately adjoining the Vauxhall Tavern Public House.

Towards the end of November 1894 with work on the front shops at the Silver Street end of the Arcade completed the business vacated the premises on Market Place enabling them to be demolished and the second phase of the arcade started, and moved to no. 8 Silver Street. A William Francis Costell was the manager at the time and proudly entered the following advertisement in the *Hull Daily Mail*.

> 'Hepworth's, the Leeds XL Clothiers of Market Place are removing this week to their new and handsome premises in Silver Street, corner shop in Hepworth's Arcade. A magnificent lot of new goods will be shown in every department.'

By 1900 when Alfred J. Handley had replaced Mr. Costell as the manager of the Silver Street branch the second outlet on Hessle Road had been reduced to one shop — no. 5.

In 1911 possibly due to some persuasion by Stanley Bastow who wanted to take over the shop at 8 Silver Street (see 6 Hepworth's Arcade) Hepworth's

Plan of buildings occupying the site prior to the construction of Hepworth's Arcade.
Courtesy of Hull City Council Records Office. Graphics by Charles Roach.

The balcony in Hepworth's Arcade.
Photograph by Andrew Bolder.

Some of the current Arcade tenants making a toast to one hundred years of trading in Hepworth's Arcade 11th December 1995. Left to Right: Mike Fanthorpe (A. Fanthorpe Ltd.) Ken Furmage (Brantons), Graeme Knox (Hull City Council), David Baxter (Baxters), George Dinsdale (Dinsdales), Graham Hardy (Whispers), Debbie Hardy (Whispers), Graham Williams (Dinsdales), Andrew McDowell (A. Fanthorpe Ltd.), Larry Willby (Larry's), Gavin Gray (Top Pictures), Anthony Furmage (Brantons), Christine Martin (Doll's House).
Courtesy of Kingston upon Hull City Council.

Joseph Hepworth and Son premises at 8 Silver Street circa 1897.

vacated the arcade and opened new premises at both 59 Whitefriargate and 46 Prospect Street.

The branch in Prospect Street only lasted for the one year but that in Whitefriargate along with the outlet on Hessle Road was maintained until 1913 when unusually the company disappeared from the streets of Hull completely and did not return for nearly forty years.

When the first phase of the building of Queens House was completed in 1952 Hepworth's Tailors as the business was then known moved into one of the larger shops in the development at no. 1 King Edward Street. This shop which was built on or near the site of the Prudential Tower is still occupied by the group although, as previously mentioned, the trading name of the outlet was changed to Next in January 1986.

Stanley C. Bastow, Hatter, Hosier etc. 1911-1944

See no. 6 Hepworth's Arcade.

Leonard Silver, Tailor and Men's Outfitter, 1946-1958

The name of Silver in connection with gentlemen's tailoring in Hull can be traced back to 1914 in which year Leonard's father Alfred was first listed in the Hull Directories whilst living at 86 Francis Street West. He was at the time in partnership with Hyman Lipman the father of Hull Outfitter Maurice Lipman who for many years had premises on Monument Bridge and grandfather of actress Maureen Lipman. Alfred had, along with his wife, emigrated to this country around the turn of the century from Poland and worked with Hyman, who was also Polish, in the clothing industry in Hull prior to setting up in business with him. The two gentlemen operated under the name of Lipman and Silver from premises at 27 Sykes Street.

Alfred had a son by the name of Leonard and although the partnership of Lipman and Silver dissolved when Alfred passed away in 1931 Leonard who was only 18 at the time had obviously been trained by his father as in 1936 he had his own listing in the Hull Directory as a tailor living at 67 Freehold Street.

By 1937 Leonard had established his own business based at 63 King Edward Street. That building has since been demolished with the site currently occupied by Woolworth's.

Two years later the business had expanded and moved to new premises in Regent House, Paragon Street, but unfortunately for Leonard any further development had to be put on hold as the same year the war started and he was later called up to serve in the R.A.F.

During the war whilst he was stationed at Lindholme, near Doncaster, Leonard had arranged for the business to be managed by another tailor but on his return to the city after he was demobbed he discovered that the man he had entrusted with the job had somehow taken over the concern.

Despite that major setback in his career Leonard was soon on his feet again and in 1946 he once again set up in business taking over the empty shop at no. 8 Silver Street employing as an assistant Sergeant Sackville-Bryant under whom he had served in the R.A.F.

On 14th April 1947 he also took over the trade and goodwill of J. Blackburn and Company who were an established firm of Hull tailors whose origins in the City could be traced back some eighty years but had last been included in the directories in 1941 trading from no. 7 Silver Street, next door to Leonard's new shop.

As it is known that Leonard had very little money at the time it is feasible that he may have struck up an agreement with the owners of that business which it is believed had ceased trading by that time whereby he utilised their name in the hope of profiting from the goodwill attached to such an old established firm. It is possible that, in return, he may have paid a commission or a fee to be settled when his own business was up and running. It has been verified that for a period of four years from 1949 the telephone directories for the city listed both Leonard Silver and J. Blackburn and Co. at no. 8 Silver Street giving the same telephone number for both concerns.

Around this time Leonard was joined in the business by Bernard Holmes who brought with him a vast experience as a gentleman's outfitter thus enabling the business to expand from being only a tailors to become Leonard Silver, tailors and outfitters. It should perhaps, at this point, be explained that although in recent years the two types of retail outlets are generally classified together under the title of menswear shops, fifty years ago the situation was very different. Whereas a tailor would supply suits, jackets and trousers he would not normally be expected to stock shirts, ties, socks etc. as that was the domain of the gentleman's outfitter. Bernard who later became manager of the branch in Driffield, stayed with the business for over thirty years and can

Leonard Silver inside his shop at 8 Silver Street.
Courtesy of Eric Silver.

Leonard Silver's stand at Malton Show 1952.
Courtesy of Eric Silver.

be seen in the background of the photograph showing Leonard in his Silver Street shop in the 1950's.

In addition to the tailoring and gents outfitting sides to the business Leonard also expanded into what could perhaps best be described as 'country clothing' and later became local agents for Harry Hall breeches and jodphurs. Through his wife's father, who was a cattle dealer in the area, his name was introduced to the local farming fraternity and the name of Leonard Silver, Civil and Sporting tailors, was regularly represented at the many agricultural shows in the region. Such was the extent of the success of this branch of the business that in 1953 Leonard opened a second shop in Market Place, Driffield, to capitalise on the name he had made for the business in the area through the shows. The photograph shows the company stand at the 1952 Malton Show with Bernand Holmes in attendance.

In 1953 Leonard Silver took into his employ a young man by the name of Eric Beckwith. Eric recalls:

Ah! now here's something!

'Don't seem to see anything beautiful'.
'Not a girl you oaf! The suit that fellow's wearing.'
'Oh yes, I've got you.

Mm - very distinctive, I agree. I wonder whose it is ?'
'Glencarrick tweed I'll wager. It's got that look about it. Pure virgin wool, all finely spun with a two-fold warp and weft - and look at that close weave - no wonder it's thornproof.'
'And I bet suits like that cost a fortune ?'
'Not really. About fifteen guineas, and moreover, some forty patterns to choose from. Ah, here comes a taxi.'

Glencarrick REGD.
TWEED
PROBABLY THE WORLD'S FINEST THORN-PROOF

In a range of forty patterns
2-PIECE SUIT £15-15-0

exclusively tailored by

Leonard Silver
SILVER ST. HULL
TEL. 38623
AND AT DRIFFIELD

Hull Daily Mail advertisement for Leonard Silver 1955.
Courtesy of The Hull Daily Mail.

'I left school at 15 and started as a junior at Leonard Silver's shop at the end of Hepworth's Arcade. There were five staff plus the boss and I remember that one of my jobs was to go upstairs to the Trocadero Restaurant which was above Mr. Silver's shop and bring a meal for his lunch.'

By the mid 1950's Leonard's shop was known throughout the city as a supplier of 'quality' men's clothing stocking such names as Simon Ackerman and Glencarrick and advertised regularly in the local press. The advertisement shown is taken from the *Hull Daily Mail* of Thursday 20th October 1955.

After over a decade at no. 8 Silver Street Leonard decided that if the business was to expand he would have to move to a busier part of the city and in November 1958 vacated the shop and took over no. 19 Jameson Street. The same year the Driffield branch was closed and Bernard Holmes joined his employer at the outlet in Hull. In later years Leonard reflected on his days in the Arcade to his three sons recalling that he often stood at the door to his shop on Silver Street watching the crowds on nearby Whitefriargate wishing that they would venture just one hundred yards further to where his business stood.

In 1962 Leonard was joined in the business by his second eldest son Eric whom he eagerly taught the ins-and-outs of the retail clothing industry as his own father had taught him over thirty years earlier.

Sadly, in 1976, aged only 63 Leonard Silver passed away and the running of the business passed to his son Eric. In 1981 following 23 years at the premises in Jameson Street Eric uplifted the concern and moved around the corner to Savile Street taking over the unoccupied shop at no. 51.

The business continues to this day to trade from that shop with a second branch at 29 Saturday Market, Beverley having opened in 1987 with Eric and his staff maintaining the high standards of quality and customer service his father originated nearly sixty years previously.

Stardisc Music Company 1958-1981

Louis Saffer opened the first Stardisc Record Shop at no. 613 Holderness Road in 1958 and such was the success of the venture that later the same year he opened a second branch in the city centre at no. 8 Silver Street. Local entertainer Johnny Pat who worked for Stardisc after leaving school in 1958 recalls:

'When I first joined Stardisc there was just the one shop on Holderness Road above which Louis Saffer lived. When the Silver Street branch opened I was promoted to Assistant Manager and paid three pounds a week. I remember that the shop had previously been a tailor's and needed quite a lot of work to transform it into suitable premises for a record shop and Louis, keen to catch the weekend trade, worked continuously through one Thursday night so that he could open at 9.00 o'clock on the Friday morning. I only worked at the Silver Street branch for a few years before being made manager of the new branch on Hessle Road but I remember, whilst working there, being able to set my watch by the local traders, office workers, bank staff and cleaners who would pass through the Arcade at a specific time each day.'

The branch at 8 Silver Street is pictured in the early 1960's.

As recalled by Johnny Pat a third Stardisc branch was opened on Hessle Road in 1961 and the same year the company started also to sell musical instruments. Johnny Pat recalls:

'Before any shop could start selling musical instruments it first had to be a member of the Music Traders Association and I recall Pat Cornell being sent by the Association to vet Louis and the shop before approval would be given. The first ever bass guitar for sale in Hull was in Stardisc in Silver Street. It was a Framus Starbase as played by Bill Wyman and I remember Louis proudly displaying it in the window. Unbeknown to him, on many occasions after locking the shop at 6.00 o'clock I would return a couple of hours later and borrow the instrument to perform in a local pub or club taking care to polish and return it later the same evening.'

Both the branch on Holderness Road and that on Hessle Road closed, but in 1970, by which time he was assisted by his son Alan and daughter Sharron, Louis opened a second city centre branch at 20 South Street. Judi Crumpton who was manageress of the branch in South Street after starting her career with the company at the Silver Street shop recalls:

Stardisc shop at 8 Silver Street in 1960.
Courtesy of Hull City Council Records Office — Reference TP/5/772.

'I started working for Stardisc in 1970 and stayed with the business for seven years and recall that during my time there a number of celebrities including Mick Ronson, John Miles, Peter Wyngard and Ken Dodd called at the shop as well as complete groups such as Wishbone Ash, Sweet Sensation and the Humperdinks (Englebert's backing band).'

Johnny Pat continues:

'Rick Kemp who later found fame with Steeleye Span bought his first ever guitar from Stardisc.'

During the early 1970's the shop in Silver Street was given a 'facelift' when, presumably in an attempt to modernise the image, the exterior walls facing Silver Street and Hepworth's Arcade were covered in a patchwork of what were probably meant to resemble record sleeves made from formica. The photograph taken around 1975 shows the finished result and one can perhaps appreciate why the City Council who owned the Arcade were, reportedly, not very happy.

After nearly two decades the business of Stardisc was sold, Louis Saffer moved onto pastures new and is now living in Puerto Rico after having spent

Stardisc shop at 8 Silver Street in 1975.
Courtesy of The Hull Daily Mail.

several years in America. Although no longer under the ownership of its founder the venture continued to operate for several years and was last listed in the Hull Telephone Directory for 1979/80 still occupying the shops in Silver Street and South Street. By 1981 all entries for the business had disappeared although it is very likely that the name is permanently implanted in the memories of many people in Hull who, in their youth, albeit in the days of Rock 'n Roll, the Mersey Sound, Flower Power, Glam Rock or Punk, spent many hours flicking through the record racks at Stardisc.

A. Fanthorpe Ltd., Television and Hi-Fi Dealers 1981-Present Day

See no. 6 Hepworth's Arcade.

NO. 2 HEPWORTH'S ARCADE

Joseph Wroe, Tobacconist 1899

When Joseph Wroe first appeared in the Hull directories in 1899, in addition to the premises at 2 Hepworth's Arcade at which he was listed as a tobacconist, he was also shown as being a confectioner at 78 Princes Avenue which, according to the electoral registers in later years, was also his home address. Later the same year Joseph moved his tobacconist business to no. 4 in the Arcade and by the following year was listed at Princes Avenue as being, in addition to a confectioner, a wine, spirit and beer merchant. Joseph stayed at both 4 Hepworth's Arcade and 78 Princes Avenue until 1903 having also had premises at 102 Melrose Street for just one year in 1901 when he was listed as a confectioner. By 1904 the tobacconist business in the Arcade was owned by

Marion Bastow (see no. 4 Hepworth's Arcade) and it would be a reasonable assumption that Marion's husband Stanley (see no. 6 Hepworth's Arcade) whose business, at the time, occupied the shops at nos. 2, 6 and 8 in the Arcade, may have bought the tobacconist business off Mr. Wroe as a way of acquiring the lease of the shop separating the three he already occupied. The same year, in addition to keeping his outlet on Princes Avenue by which time he had added dairyman to his list of activities, Joseph opened another tobacconist at 475 Hessle Road. The success of this venture must be viewed with suspicion as by 1905 it was no longer listed and Joseph reverted to just one shop (Princes Avenue). It is quite possible that Joseph Wroe died in either 1905 or early 1906 as the Kelly's Directory for the latter year does not list him at all and attributes 78 Princes Avenue to Miss Josephine Margaret Wroe. It is of course equally possible that Mr. Wroe merely retired and moved away from the area. Miss Wroe, whom it is assumed was Joseph's daughter, continued to run the business for just one more year and by the time the 1908 directory was published the shop was credited to a Mrs. Charlotte Shinfield. Miss Wroe was last included in the Hull directories in 1909 whilst residing at 72 Blenheim Street.

S. C. Bastow, Hatters, Hosiers, Glovers and Outfitters 1899-1944

See no. 6 Hepworth's Arcade

During the occupation of S. C. Bastow Ltd., the walls separating the adjoining shops of 8 Silver Street and nos. 2, 4, 6 and 8 Hepworth's Arcade were removed to form one large premises. Also at some point in time, most probably during the occupation of S. C. Bastow Ltd. the stairs which led from the ground floor of 8 Silver Street to the upper floors which spanned the Arcade were removed. A doorway was created through the wall dividing the first floors of 8 Silver Street and 2 Hepworth's Arcade (which are unusually at slightly different levels) giving access to the upper floors of both shops through the ground floor of no. 2.

Following the departure of Bastows, to accommodate the Trocadero Restaurant, the section of the first, second and third floors spanning the Arcade and facing north towards Silver Street which were originally a part of the premises of no. 9 Silver Street were sealed off from that address and knocked through to join with the corresponding floors of 8 Silver Street. At ground level the shops were again split into individual units with numbers 6 and 8 also maintaining their upper floors. The first floor of no. 4 remained as part of the premises used by the Trocadero and accommodated the restaurant's ladies toilets.

The above facts explain why, in some years, the shop of no. 2 Hepworth's Arcade was accredited with being occupied by businesses which were far too large for premises only measuring 13 feet x 10 feet. Although the address of these businesses was often given as 2 Hepworth's Arcade this was merely the street level entrance with the actual situation of those businesses being the first, second and third floors of 8 and 9 Silver Street.

The Trocadero Restaurant 1946-1955

The address of the Trocadero Restaurant was listed in the Hull Directories as being no. 2 Hepworth's Arcade whereas the local telephone directories for the period show the business as occupying nos. 8 and 9 Silver Street. Unusually both sources were actually correct because, as previously mentioned, although the street level entrance was at no. 2 Hepworth's Arcade the actual restaurant itself was situated on the first and second floors of nos. 8 and 9 Silver Street with the third floor accommodating the kitchens.

The Trocadero was opened in 1946 by a Mr. Eric Greaves who was well known in the catering industry in the City having previously, in 1942, opened the Silver Grill in King Edward Street and two years prior to that the Regatta Tavern in Castle Street which later became the Princes Dock Canteen. Eric recalls:

'When I opened the Trocadero shortly after the Second World War all types of materials for decorating were in very short supply and I remember the walls on the second floor, which was the private functions suite, were decorated with the silk linings normally used for lining marquees. On the first floor which was the public restaurant we had a 'sprung' dance floor installed and the ground floor which was only very small merely accommodated the stairs and the gents toilet. The staircase leading from no. 9 was removed and the vacant stairwell adapted to accommodate the dumb waiter enabling the first and second floors to be served from the kitchens on the third floor. We were unable to buy tablecloths or even the fabric with which to make them and ended up buying big rolls of cloth used for manufacturing sails for boats which we bleached and had sewn up into tablecloths. Because of food rationing and the restrictions that the Government introduced to combat black marketeering we were not permitted to charge over three shillings and sixpence (17½pence) for lunch and five shillings (25 pence) for dinner although we were allowed to charge an additional fourpence (1.6 pence) for tea or coffee.

As the rationing did not finish until 1954 obtaining supplies was not always easy and we had to be pretty versatile to get around the restrictions imposed. I bought fifty chickens which I kept at my home in Portobello Street so that I could use their eggs in the restaurant. A friend of mine who lived in Dunswell bred pigs and in return for supplying him with pigswill free of charge he would, once every couple of months, slaughter a pig for the restaurant. Another friend was a funeral director and, in return for doing a spell of driving for him when he was otherwise stuck for a driver, he would loan me the hearse and a coffin when I needed to collect a pig from Dunswell. In those days there was often a police officer directing traffic at the crossroads where Beverley Road meets Cottingham and Clough Roads and it still amuses me to think of the number of pigs that must have passed that point in the back of the hearse only to be saluted by the constable on duty.'

Although the restaurant was often granted a special occasional licence which allowed it to sell alcohol at individual functions it was unable to obtain a license on a permanent basis. Eric managed to overcome this problem by making an agreement with the landlord of Ye Olde White Harte in Silver Street whereby any drinks ordered by restaurant customers would be collected from the pub by one of the waitresses and brought across the road and upstairs to the restaurant.

Eric continues:

'The restaurant was only open each evening up until 8.30 p.m. which enabled us, when we were also catering for a private function on the second floor, to clear the room to be used by the guests upstairs as a dance floor after their meal was finished. During the time the Troc' was open we were visited by many of the stars appearing at the New Theatre including Anna Neagle, Flora Robson and Wilfred Pickles who, during his visits to Hull, would even call on us for his breakfast.'

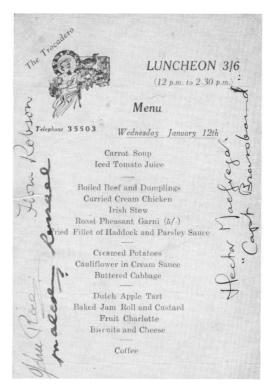

Copy of the Trocadero lunch menu from 1949.
Courtesy of Eric Greaves.

The sample menus shown from early 1949 include autographs which Eric managed to collect from some of the New Theatre stars who visited his restaurant including that of Flora Robson who later became Dame Flora Robson.

The venue also proved popular with the local business community and a table for six was reserved for lunch every day for a group of local estate agents including James Dufton (see 61 Market Place).

In 1951 David Whitfield, who in later years had a string of top twenty records including two number one hits, chose the Trocadero as the venue for the reception following his wedding to Sheila Priestman. David and Sheila are pictured greeting David's brother Ted into the Trocadero.

Regrettably, following the closure and demolition of the Silver Grill in 1954 and the expiry of the lease on the premises above the Arcade, the Trocadero Restaurant served its final meal in 1955 bringing to an end nearly a decade of night life in the Arcade which is probably well remembered by the thousands of customers who no doubt wined, dined and danced many nights away at 'the Troc'.

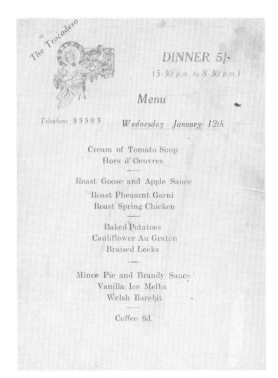

Copy of the Trocadero dinner menu 1949.
Courtesy of Eric Greaves.

David Whitfield at the Trocadero.   Courtesy of Bill Wilkins.

54

When the Trocadero Restaurant closed the premises were divided into a number of office suites, the occupants of which are listed below. No attempt has been made to research the history of those companies as it was decided (with the exception of the Trocadero) to concentrate on those businesses who traded from the Arcade at street level and that any tenants who only occupied office space above it would be excluded.

North British and Mercantile Insurance Co. 1958-1962

Fletcher and Co., Insurance Claims Adjusters 1958-1975

C. T. Bowring/Jowitt and Freeman Insurance Ltd., 1962-1970

John Watson & Carter, 1962-1970

Hull District Property Owners Association 1970-1975

Buckley, Hall and Devin, Accountants 1970-1980

Following the departure of Buckley, Hall and Devin, A. Fanthorpe Ltd. took over the premises of no. 2 Hepworth's Arcade to extend their 'run' of shops to four utilising the upper floors as a showroom and storage and office space.

A. Fanthorpe Ltd., Radio and Television Engineers 1980-Present Date

See no. 6 Hepworth's Arcade.

NO. 4 HEPWORTH'S ARCADE

Jap Surprise Stores, Fancy Goods Dealers 1897

See no. 6 Hepworth's Arcade.

Joseph Wroe, Tobacconist 1900-1903

See no. 2 Hepworth's Arcade.

Marion Bastow, Tobacconist 1904-1905

Marion Bastow was born in Howden in 1864 and married Stanley Clarke Bastow in the 1880's. It is not known if the couple first met in Hull or moved to the city together but it has been established that they were residents by 1888 when their first child was born. By the time of the 1891 census when they were living at 25 St. Hilda's Grove, Beverley Road, the couple

Marion Bastow.
Courtesy of Jack Bastow.

55

had two daughters and a son. It is likely that Marion assisted her husband in his own businesses both in the Arcade and whilst in partnership with John Holyman in Whitefriargate (see no. 6 Hepworth's Arcade — Stanley C. Bastow), but it was not until 1904 that her name received recognition in the town directories. In that year she took over the tobacconist business at no. 4 Hepworth's Arcade formerly owned by Joseph Wroe although it is likely that the take-over was ultimately to secure the lease on the shop itself as no. 4 separated the premises of nos. 2, 6, and 8, occupied at the time by Marion's husband Stanley. It can however be assumed that, as this was done in Marion's nane instead of that of her husband, it is probable that she actually conducted the business herself. In 1906 the tobacconists was moved around the corner in the Arcade to no. 10 to enable Stanley's business to extend to four consecutive shops and three years later had vanished completely from the Arcade. Marion however stayed and assisted her husband to build his business over which she commanded a watchful eye following the death of Stanley in 1921 until her own death in the late 1940's, by which time she would have been well into her eighties.

Stanley C. Bastow, Hatter, Hosier and Glover 1906-1944

See no. 6 Hepworth's Arcade.

N. T. Leslie, Antiquarian Bookseller 1946-1966

Norman Titley Leslie had gained much of his experience in antique books at Godfreys in York, a long established business, with whom he worked for some time up until the start of the war. Following the war during which he was a sergeant in the Army, Norman moved to Hull and opened an antiquarian bookshop at no. 80 Princes Avenue. In 1946 he opened a second shop at no. 4 Hepworth's Arcade, an address at which he would stay for two decades. During the occupation of Mr. Leslie no. 4 which was only a small shop with no upper floor was reportedly an historian's dream packed from floor to ceiling with hundreds of old and wonderful books and original maps of the East Riding and surrounding area. After twenty years Norman felt the need to expand the business beyond the confines of this tiny shop which was starting to

N. T. LESLIE

Antiquarian Bookseller
15 Hepworths Arcade, Hull
ENGLAND

Entire Libraries
Smaller Collections
of Books Purchased
I pay immediate cash &
remove without trouble
or expense to Vendor

'Phone   26457

Catalogues & Specialised Lists
of Books Issued and Posted
Free on request.
Books not in stpck Quickly
Located & Reported Free of
Charge or Obligation

Norman T. Leslie.
Courtesy of Peter and Michael Leslie.

feel decidedly cramped (it has been suggested that, at times, Norman could not get into the shop himself until he had pulled out the two large bookcases which he stood in the Arcade during opening hours). At the beginning of April in 1966 he moved the business to no. 15 in the Arcade which was a substantially larger shop with an upper floor. The previous tenant of no. 15, A. Fanthorpe Ltd. who at the time also occupied nos. 6 and 8 in the Arcade took over the lease on no. 4. It is very likely that the move had previously been discussed by the two parties as being mutually beneficial with Norman getting the larger premises he needed and Fanthorpe's being able to expand their business into three consecutive shops. Seven years later, shortly after expanding even further by taking over the neighbouring shop of no. 17, Norman retired and sold his business to Barry Kaye (see no. 15 Hepworth's Arcade). The name of N. T. Leslie which had, over the previous thirty years, become very recognised by collectors both in England and abroad, did not disappear immediately as Mr. Kaye continued to trade under that name until 1981. Norman Titley Leslie who in his later years resided in Hornsea died in 1982 aged 76.

Michael Leslie (Norman's son) recalls:

> 'I remember the shop at no. 4 as being packed floor to ceiling, wall to wall with books. If anyone wished to look at one of the books on the top shelves Dad had a long ladder which they would have to climb up (the walls are 12 feet high in the shops in the Arcade). I often remember collectors perched precariously at the top of that ladder studying the contents of an old book. A lot of orders were received from foreign collectors and Dad would parcel them up ready to send and keep them until the following Saturday when I used to go in to help. It was my job to carry those heavy parcels to the Post Office. He did a lot of business with California in the States and I recall on several occasions us receiving gifts from the customers there. They would send packages of tinned fruit and cake mixes which were always very welcome because those things could not easily be bought in England at the time due to rationing.'

Michael's brother Peter adds:

> 'Dad used to sell original John Speed Maps of Hull which are now worth over £150.00 for thirty shillings (£1.50). He often visited book sales and would, at times, return with an enormous amount of books — sometimes one or two removal vans full. It took months, sometimes years to sort through them.'

A. Fanthorpe Ltd., TV and Radio Dealer 1966-Present Day

See no. 6 Hepworth's Arcade.

NO. 6 HEPWORTH'S ARCADE

The Jap Surprise Stores, Fancy Goods Dealers 1895-1897/8

> 'FOUND AT LAST — THE PRETTIEST SHOP IN HULL — THE JAP SURPRISE STORES'

enticed the *Hull Daily Mail* advert in December 1895.

'APARTMENTS CAN BE IMPROVED AND BRIGHTENED
AT LITTLE EXPENSE BY VISITING THE JAP SURPRISE
STORES'

suggested another. The Jap Surprise Stores, not having been listed in any
previous Hull Directory, seemed to appear from nowhere and in the first year
that the Arcade was listed were shown to be occupying three shops — nos. 6, 8
and 10.

'MATRIMONY — YOUNG LADIES CONTEMPLATING
MATRIMONY WILL FIND THE PLACE TO MAKE A HOME
PRETTY AND BEAUTIFUL WITH SMALL EXPENSE IS THE
JAP, HEPWORTH'S ARCADE'

they boasted in yet another *Mail* advertisement and by the end of 1897 had also
taken over the occupancy of no. 4 giving a total of four consecutive shops
around the north-east bend of the Arcade. The business, which one would
assume sold small furnishings and ornamental items for the home, was owned
by a Harry Fisher. Although they may have proved popular with the people of
Hull at first, by 1899 in which year Mr. Fisher was operating under his own
name and was described in the directories as Fisher and Co., Toy and Fancy
Goods dealers, they had been reduced to just two shops, nos. 6 and 8. They
had, however, opened another branch at no. 48 Prospect Street which Cook's
Directory lists as The Jap and Kelly's attributes to Fisher and Co. It was
possibly the arrival of Marks and Spencer's in the Arcade which was
contributory towards the demise of this business or perhaps just a good idea
which didn't quite work out, but regardless of the reason neither the Jap
Surprise Stores or Fisher and Co. appeared in the directory for 1900 or
subsequent publications. No home address has been established for Mr. Fisher
so it is a possibility that this was a business from 'out of town' that failed to
achieve the success in Hull that it had experienced in its birthplace and it is
therefore equally feasible that it may have continued to trade elsewhere long
after it vanished from the streets of Hull.

Fisher and Co., Toy and Fancy Goods Dealers 1897/8-1899

See Jap Surprise stores.

S. C. Bastow, Hatters, Hosiers, Glovers and Outfitters 1899-1944

Stanley Clarke Bastow was born in Manchester in 1860. By the age of 20 he
had moved to Hull where he lived at no. 1 Dansom Lane and was working for
Wm. Harland and Co., hosiers in Silver Street from whom he presumably
learned his profession. In the early 1890's he left the employ of Harland's and
went into partnership with John William Holyman trading from premises at 62
Whitefriargate. The business which operated under the name of Bastow and
Holyman was described in the directories for 1895 as hosiers, glovers and
shirtmakers. It is not known what happened to the partnership but records
show that in 1900 when Bastow and Co. first appeared in the directories

Stanley Clarke Bastow.
Courtesy of Jack Bastow.

Hull Daily Mail advertisement, 1925.
Courtesy of the Hull Daily Mail.

as hosiers and ladies outfitters at nos. 2, 6 and 8 Hepworth's Arcade, the premises at 62 Whitefriargate were attributed to Mr. Holyman operating under his own name.

Stanley had commenced in business alone in 1899 as a hosier from nos. 6 and 8 in the Arcade but such, it would appear, was the success of his venture that later the same year he took over the premises at no. 2 and expanded into the business of ladies outfitting. As he presumably had little or no knowledge in this field he obviously thought it wise to employ someone who had and for this purpose engaged the services of a Mrs. Mountain who had, for a number of years, served with Mr. Lyne of Savile Street, an established ladies outfitters.

By 1901 the business had obviously expanded its lines and was described, in addition to being hosiers and ladies outfitters, as also being hatters and glovers. In 1904 in what one would assume was a move to secure the lease on no. 4 in the Arcade, then occupied by Joseph Wroe's tobacconist shop and at the time separating the Bastow shops at 2, 6 and 8, the Bastows bought the business in the name of Stanley's wife Marion. Later in 1906 the tobacconist, still under the

Stanley Frederick Bastow.   Courtesy of Jack Bastow.

name of Marion Bastow, was moved to number 10 allowing Bastow and Co. four consecutive shops. Three years later the tobacconists and the name of Marion Bastow had disappeared from the directories and no. 10 was credited, along with nos. 4, 6 and 8 to Stanley C. Bastow, hatter, hosier and glover. No. 2 was still occupied by the business but was listed separately as Stanley C. Bastow, ladies outfitter. During this time (in 1907) Stanley Clarke was joined in the family business by his son Stanley Frederick Bastow who is covered in further detail later in this chapter. In 1910, already occupying five shops in the Arcade but keen to add to those the prestigious 'front shop' facing Silver Street, Mr. Bastow approached Joseph Hepworth who, in addition to being the landlord, also occupied the aforementioned shop. Apparently Mr. Bastow took Mr. Hepworth who was visiting the Hull outlet from his base in Leeds across the road for lunch at Ye Olde White Harte. He explained to Mr. Hepworth evidently in no uncertain terms that, because of the similarity in their types of business, Mr. Hepworth's shop was having an adverse effect on his own trade and presumably vice versa. He added that it would therefore be to their mutual benefit for Bastows to take over the lease of no. 8 Silver Street. Whether it was this apparent forceful persuasion by Mr. Bastow who was described as a formidable character who liked to get his own way or if indeed Hepworths already had intentions of giving up the premises anyway is unsure, but regardless of this by the following year Bastow and Co. had extended their premises to include 8 Silver Street and maintained their number of shops at five by giving up the lease on no. 10. It is indeed possible that there may have been some animosity between Stanley Bastow and Hepworth's as it is noted that whenever the address of Bastows was used in advertising it was always shown as 8 Silver Street and 2, 4, 6 and 8 the Arcade, Hull. The use of the name of Hepworth's was always avoided even though, at the time, there were several different arcades in Hull each with a different prefix. Perhaps Mr. Bastow merely thought it unwise, in advertisements which his company was paying for, to promote the name of a competitor. The photograph of the premises in around 1913/14 shows how each of the windows was dedicated to a different part of the business (note the curving spotlights directed at each of the individual windows).

In 1918 towards the end of the war in conjunction with Welch Margetson and Company (shirt collar manufacturers) Bastows gave to customers calendars depicting, in addition to the variety of collars available, the Naval and Military medals awarded to the British Forces.

The business presumably continued to flourish under the leadership of Stanley Clarke who worked right up until his death at the age of 62 in 1922 when control was taken over by Stanley Frederick under the watchful eye of his mother Marion, a strict disciplinarian, who also stayed with the business until her death in the late 1940's. Apparently in the earlier years when Bastow and Co. also sold ladies-wear Mrs. Bastow would get the female staff to make fancy garters which were quickly snapped up by visiting seamen.

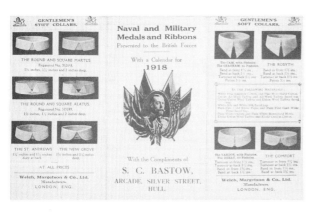

Stanley Frederick Bastow who joined the family business straight from school in 1907 fought for his country in both wars and was, whilst serving in the East Yorkshire Regiment in the First World War, held as a prisoner-of-war. He was a keen low handicap golfer and was a founder member of the Hull Golf Club.

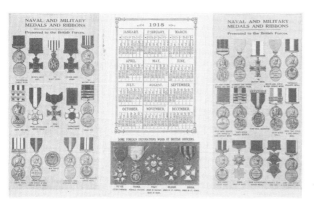

S. C. Bastow's Calendar for 1918.
Courtesy of Jack Bastow.

Advertisement circa 1913/1914.
Courtesy of Jack Bastow.

He was also president of the Old Hymerians Association and like his mother and father before him a strict disciplinarian. Apparently, as the shops had only one toilet, Stanley Frederick decided that this must be 'the bosses toilet' for use by him and him only and consequently all other members of the staff were instructed to use the one at Hiams Café in the Arcade. Another story was that when his son Jack Stanley Bastow joined the firm in 1937 and asked if he would be able to continue to play rugby for the Old Hymerians on a Saturday he was told that he would be permitted but only for home matches and that he was to return to the shop immediately after the match presumably thus avoiding the temptation of having a pint or two with his team-mates. Stanley Frederick also liked an occasional bet on the horses and, when telephoning the bookmakers, would use the coded name of Arcade A5 to place his wagers. Like his parents before him he remained active in the business until his death in 1964 at the age of 74.

In 1924 the business expanded to a second shop in Jameson Street and shortly after registered as a Limited Company retaining the names of its founder and becoming S. C. Bastow Ltd. The advertisement taken from a publication announcing forthcoming attractions at the Grand Theatre, George Street, Hull in Spring 1925 proudly mentions the new branch in *Daily Mail* Buildings.

By 1934 H. Samuel had vacated the premises at 9 Silver Street and moved to 28 Whitefriargate. Photographs show that just prior to the Second World War, probably due to the Depression, many of the shops in the Arcade were empty and it can therefore be safely assumed that Samuels, who had time remaining on their lease, would have found it difficult to re-let the premises. It is probably for that reason that an agreement between them and Bastows was made whereby Bastows could utilise the window space of the premises facing both Silver Street and the Arcade to display their merchandise. It is not known if this was legally binding or merely a gentleman's agreement, or indeed if any payments were made. However it has been established that one of the conditions of Bastows being allowed usage of the window space was that they would ensure that the clock bearing the name of H. Samuel which hung over Silver Street at the front of the shop was to be kept wound up and correctly set at all times.

In 1944 by which time the centre for shopping in Hull had moved more towards the area near the railway station and presumably because the Jameson Street branch of the business was proving to be the more profitable of the two, a decision was made to close the premises in Silver Street/Hepworth's Arcade and concentrate on Jameson Street. In the late 1940's Jack's brother Frank who had recently been demobbed from the army in which he served in the King's African Rifles joined the business. Shortly afterwards in the early 1950's a gentleman by the

Advertisement from the programme for the Grand Theatre, George Street, Hull, 1925.

name of William Roland Flewitt also joined the board of directors. William who stayed with the firm until his sudden death some years later was serving his second spell with the company having first been employed, as a boy in the late 1920's following a recommendation from a traveller who called at the shop.

S. C. Bastow Ltd. stayed in Jameson Street until 1982 when, under the management of Jack Stanley Bastow and his brother Frank, the third generation of the Bastows to take the reins of the family business, they moved to Newland Avenue. In 1987 after nearly nine decades of serving the public of Hull Bastows closed their doors for the final time. Following the closure of the shop Frank Bastow retired to Driffield and is reported to be fit and active. His brother Jack Stanley Bastow still lives in the Hull area and has fond recollections of his half-century with the firm.

Jack Stanley Bastow recalls:

'When I joined the family business in 1937 we sold a wide range of menswear from workers' overalls to dress tail suits at seven pounds ten shillings (£7.50). Amongst our other popular lines were Vantella shirts (complete with two collars) from ten shillings and sixpence (52½ pence), and a double-fronted shirt with three separate collars which we called the 'Filey' at seven shillings and sixpence (37½ pence) each or three for a guinea (£1.05). Raincoats were one guinea each or for the better off, with half fur lining, three guineas. Caps at

The Silver Street 'arm' looking south circa 1935.

Frank Bastow.
Courtesy of Jack Bastow.

half-a-crown 12½ pence), semi stiff collars at one shilling and sixpence (7½ pence) and Morley full length marl socks at one shilling and ninepence (9 pence) each had a full window of the shop dedicated to them. Because of the large amount of 'professional' people in the old town we sold a lot of stiff collars and shirts and many customers would bring their soiled shirts and collars in every week which we would send to Northern Ireland to be laundered. Maenson three-piece suits were three guineas, trilby hats fifteen shillings (75 pence) and bowlers twenty-one shillings (£1.05).

On the ground floor there were three doors which were open summer and winter even though the three gas heated radiators were quite inadequate. We also had six serving counters with serving fixtures behind. We had three removable showcases which were hooked on the pillars at the entrance to the Arcade during opening hours and brought in when we closed. On the first floor we kept stocks of hats, overcoats, suits, trousers and underwear and there was a room that was originally used as a tea-room for Mrs. Bastow but doubled up as a fitting room. The second floor was used to store evening and morning wear for hire and as a staff tea-room. This floor overlooked the Arcade to one side and Silver Street to the other. The third and top floor which had marvellous views over the old town was used by our tailor and for fittings, pressing, and alterations. Our opening hours were 9.00 a.m until 6.00 p.m Monday to Friday and on Saturdays we would be very busy from first thing in a morning until about 5.00 p.m when there was a lull until about 6.30 p.m when people used to pass through the Arcade on their way to the markets and the shambles. This meant that we often didn't close until 9.30 p.m and we were lucky if we managed a refreshing drink at Ye Olde White Harte before it closed at 10.00 p.m. Isaac Gardiner the Watchmaker in the Arcade was quite a character and due to his liking for visiting the local pubs and

Jack Stanley Bastow whilst serving in the forces.
Courtesy of Jack Bastow.

bookmakers one often had to wait a considerable time for a watch to be repaired. One customer we had who was a stallholder in the indoor market would buy a pair of black socks for one shilling and sixpence (7½ pence) every Saturday and wear them for the following week before throwing them away and buying a new pair the following Saturday.

Travellers from our major suppliers came from London twice a year for their main order and would arrive with a huge basket skip on a handcart which they had hired for the day (with pusher) from Paragon Station. Another visitor who came regularly was the owner of Swallow Raincoats who would arrive with his products loaded into his Rolls Royce (complete with chauffeur). I went into the Navy in the early part of the War but often visited the shop whilst home on leave and was sure to call on Mr. Gardiner who always knew when each of the surrounding pubs was due to receive its quota of beer. In those days you could buy a three-course lunch at Ye Olde White Harte for one shilling and sixpence (7½ pence) or if you were feeling flush you could select your own steak for the chef to cook for just half-a-crown (12½ pence). I remember the Hands sisters at the Singer Sewing Machine shop, the Canby sisters at the tobacconists around the corner in Market Place and of course Hiams Café.'

A. Fanthorpe Ltd., Radio, Television and Electrical Engineers 1945-Present Day

Arthur Fanthorpe started in business in 1939 in premises at nos. 190 and 206 George Street at which time he was shown as a wireless engineer. By 1940 he only occupied the shop at no. 206 and was described as A. Fanthorpe, Radio Repairs. During the Second World War Arthur served in the Airforce and on his return to Hull in 1945 resumed in the business which the War had interrupted taking new premises at no. 6 Hepworth's Arcade. In addition to repairing radios Arthur sold radio parts and accessories and a wide variety of War surplus purchased from Military sales. The business proved successful and was soon very popular with the growing 'Radio Ham' fraternity of Hull who quickly discovered that Arthur could lay his hands on some parts that were otherwise very difficult to obtain.

Ex employee Arnold Girling recalls:

'I worked for Arthur Fanthorpe for a couple of years in the late forties or early fifties. He would buy up large quantities of radio parts etc. from sales and word soon got around that he could get difficult to get parts at a good price. One particular incident I recall is of one delighted Radio Ham announcing over the airwaves that he had recently bought a new piece of equipment from 'Fanny's in the Arcade'. It was not of course permitted in those days to advertise in any way, shape or form 'on air' and within two days representatives from the Government Office had called on him and confiscated his radio set.'

Arthur did not, it seems, limit his purchases to radios and accessories and would apparently buy anything which took his fancy and which he thought he may be able to sell at a profit.

Arnold Girling continues:

'I remember Arthur returning from the sales with all sorts of stuff which we used to store in a warehouse that he had on Mytongate. It was behind an old pub and I think was originally the pub stables. He once bought a great stack of fluorescent light tubes which had been removed from a factory when they fitted new ones throughout. Some of course were dud but others were still working and it was my job to test each and every one of them and there must have been hundreds. Another memory that comes to mind was when we also had Bob Wildbore working with us. It was Saturday and Arthur was busy in the shop, the area was pretty crowded and there was myself and Bob in the middle of the Arcade cutting up these massive sheets of aluminium that Arthur had bought.'

By 1955 Arthur had expanded the business and was also dealing in and repairing televisions and eight years later in 1963 saw the opportunity to expand further when the occupant of no. 15 — Mrs. Holmes decided to sell up. It was apparently Arthur's wish to just take over the lease on the shop with the intention of using it to sell washing machines and other domestic appliances. However Mrs. Holmes who was retiring and also needed to dispose of her remaining stock refused to sell the lease alone and consequently, although not by his own choice, Arthur became the new owner of a toy shop. Arthur's wife Laura helped him in this business by running the toy shop at no. 15 with the original aim of selling off as much of the stock as possible before converting the premises into a sales outlet for domestic appliances as was originally intended.

The following year Arthur's son Michael left school with the intention of taking up a career in accountancy rather than joining his father's business. Arthur respected his son's decision and, through a personal contact, made arrangements for Michael to have an interview with a local company. That interview however never took place as, the evening prior to the appointment, Arthur passed away. Consequently Michael (or Mike as he prefers to be known) joined his mother Laura in the family business.

Fortunately for Mike who, as a youngster of just 16 had little knowledge of the business in which his father had been involved for twenty-five years, a long-time employee and friend of Arthur's Joe Little (also known locally as the Radio Doctor) was on hand to teach him the trade.

In 1966 following discussions with their neighbour Norman Leslie at no. 4 Hepworth's Arcade, who had for many years been a close friend of Arthur, the company agreed to vacate the shop at no. 15 which was still operating as a toy shop allowing Norman to take over the larger premises. In return Norman gave notice on his premises at no. 4 allowing the Fanthorpe shops at nos. 6 and 8 to expand giving the business three consecutive shops.

In 1973 by which time Mike had nearly a decade of experience under his belt he was joined in the business by his cousin Andrew McDowell and between them Mike and Andrew have developed the concern which Mike's father had started from a single shop nearly forty years earlier into one of the major independent dealers in electronic home entertainment in the city. They have, during the past twenty years, expanded the business from radios and televisions to include complete hi-fi systems, video recorders, camcorders and more recently Laser Disc Players whilst still catering for radio enthusiasts with a wide range of spares and accessories.

In the late 1970's they acquired the leases for the shops at nos. 3 and 5 from which they now sell secondhand equipment on behalf of customers and soon afterwards, in 1980, also took over no. 2 which included the complete upper floors of nos. 8 and 9 Silver Street. The following year Mike fulfilled a personal dream when, following the departure of Stardisc from no. 8 Silver Street, the business also took over those premises. It is often said that from little acorns large oak trees grow and it could be speculated that the business formed by Arthur Fanthorpe over half a century ago would go a long way towards justifying that statement.

NO. 8 HEPWORTH'S ARCADE

Although the shop at no. 8 Hepworth's Arcade was illustrated as being separate premises from that at no. 6 in the plans of the Arcade used when the property was mortgaged in 1895 the evidence available would suggest that the two premises were connected to create one larger shop prior to being occupied by their first tenants in 1895. Subsequent entries in the Directories show that, throughout the past one hundred years, each and every tenant of no. 8 has also occupied no. 6. It is therefore very likely that although it was probably the original intention of Joseph Hepworth to let the two properties independently, because of the small size of the units which would undoubtedly restrict the types of business which could operate from them, he later decided to combine the two addresses into one shop.

Jap Suprise Stores, Fancy Goods Dealers 1895-1897/8

See no. 6 Hepworth's Arcade.

Fisher and Co., Toy and Fancy Goods Dealers 1897/8-1899

See no. 6 Hepworth's Arcade.

Bastow and Co., Ladies Outfitters 1899-1944

See no. 6 Hepworth's Arcade.

A. Fanthorpe Ltd., Radio, TV and Electrical Engineers 1945-Present date

See no. 6 Hepworth's Arcade.

NO. 10 HEPWORTH'S ARCADE

Although one of the smallest shops in the Arcade no. 10 has experienced the greatest number of tenants during the past one hundred years having been 'home' to seventeen different businesses.

Jap Surprise Stores, Fancy Goods Dealers 1895-1897

See no. 6 Hepworth's Arcade.

Isaac Gardiner, Watchmaker 1900-1905

The business of Isaac Gardiner, watchmaker was first mentioned in the Hull Directories and was shown in that year and each year up until 1904 under the name of John Green Gardiner and later in 1908 as George Gardiner. It has nevertheless been almost certainly verified that there was only one Mr. Gardiner whose name was neither John nor George, but Isaac. It has been suggested that, as apparently was common amongst businessmen of his religion around the turn of the century, Isaac initially traded under the different names to avoid any connection being made with his Jewish faith which was not freely accepted by all at that time.

The electoral register for 1900/01 shows Isaac as residing nearby at no. 17 Market Place which further investigations reveal to be a butcher's shop under the ownership of Witty and Easterby Ltd. and it can therefore be assumed that Isaac was a lodger there. By 1903 he had moved to 72 Linnaeus Street.

The business remained at no. 10 until 1904 when Isaac also took over the slightly larger premises of no 16. Two years later in 1906 he gave up no. 10 to Marion Bastow and expanded the premises of no. 16 into the neighbouring shop (no. 14). It was around this time that he also changed residence moving to a large house at 188 Hallgate, Cottingham, which would suggest that the business was prospering. It is noted that, although it is known that Mr. Gardiner remained in that house for over thirty years, in many directories and electoral registers the address is not attributed to him but to a Mrs. Eliza Gardiner. As it is also known that Isaac did not marry until later in life there is a distinct possibility that Eliza was his mother. If this theory is correct it should be noted that although it has not been possible to trace Isaac in the 1891 census an Eliza Gardiner is listed as residing at no. 9 Market Place which was at the time a butcher's shop owned by a Mr. Henry Witty (later of Witty and Easterby). Mrs. Gardiner, then aged 50, was shown as being the housekeeper and a later addition to the entry indicates that she did have a son. This theory is further strengthened by the fact that Mrs. Gardiner originated from Wolsingham in County Durham and it is known that Isaac was also from the North East of England.

In 1912 Isaac gave up the tenancy of no. 16 and reverted to just one shop (no. 14). Those premises can vaguely be seen on the photograph of the arcade taken in the early 1920's.

In the late 1920's Mr. Gardiner took into his employ a young man by the name of William Robert Furmage. William (better known as Bob to his friends) was an orphan who benefited from a scheme to which Alderman Cogan of Hull had bequeathed a sum of money to pay the costs of setting the poor boys of the parish on indentures with tradesmen. (An indenture is an apprenticeship and in those days payments had to be made to the tradesmen to take on and train an apprentice). Bob presumably worked hard and after several years qualified as a watchmaker. Around this time Isaac employed a new female assistant by the name of Ethel Hutton who later courted and

Bob and Ethel Furmage outside nos. 3 and 5 Hepworth's Arcade.

Courtesy of Ken Furmage.

married young Bob and although she only stayed with the business until the mid 1930's before leaving to start a family Ethel was destined to be still involved with Gardiners Jewellers some sixty years later. Bob and Ethel are pictured.

In 1937 again wanting more room Isaac moved his business around the corner in the Arcade to the larger premises of no. 5, later expanding further still by taking over the neighbouring property of no. 3.

Bob Furmage continued to work for Mr. Gardiner for a further twenty years even though some weeks, perhaps due to lack of trade caused by the depression or maybe because of his love of a drink and a bet on the horses, Isaac was unable to pay him. On such occasions Mr. Gardiner made amends (in his own mind at least) by giving his employee shares in the business which had been registered as a limited company in 1930. Although the shares were presumably of equal value to the wages that were due these pieces of paper were of little use to Bob who had a wife and family to support, but as he was to discover they were to prove to be very much to his benefit in later years.

In 1946 Isaac took onto his staff another apprentice on the Alderman Cogan Charity scheme by the name of Geoffrey Smith. Geoffrey recalls:

> I started with Gardiners on a wage of twelve shillings and sixpence (62½ pence) a week and remember from day one that Mr. Gardiner always told me that I had my own corner of the shop and that I should work hard with the indication that I could one day own part of the business. I realised some time later that he had cleverly suggested this to all of his staff to ensure dedication to work without any real intentions of making any of us partners regardless of our efforts. I stayed with the business for only two years before leaving after a disagreement with Isaac (he hated that name) over the length of my hair. My hair was never really very long, but he was always sending me to get it cut and on one occasion I objected and pointed out that it was the length that i liked it and that it was not affecting my work. We disagreed and parted company shortly after that when I left Hull and moved to London where I completed my training as a watchmaker.'

Ken Furmage at workbench on first floor of nos. 3 and 5 Hepworth's Arcade.
Courtesy of Ken Furmage.

Bob and Ethel Furmage's son Ken joined the business as an apprentice in 1951 and although the system of paying for apprenticeships had by that time ceased his wages were only 27 shillings (£1.35) per week for the first year of his training. Ken is pictured busy at his workbench on the upper floor of nos. 3 and 5 Hepworth's Arcade.

Isaac Gardiner passed away on 17th September 1952 aged 80 and moves were made by the executors of the will to sell the business as a going concern until it was correctly pointed out by Bob Furmage that this could not be done as he had three shares in the company and should therefore at least have first refusal on purchasing the balance of the firm from the beneficiaries of the will. It later materialised that Bob was not the only one to whom Isaac had used shares as a form of payment and several other parties came forward as shareholders. Bob and his wife Ethel managed to raise enough capital to buy out the other shareholders and beneficiaries of the will and in February 1953 became sole proprietors of I. Gardiner Ltd. As the name of Gardiners watchmakers had been known in the city for over half a century there seemed little point in changing the name.

However all was not to be smooth sailing and in 1956 Bob discovered that, prior to his death, in addition to paying his debts with shares in the company, Mr. Gardiner had also raised capital by selling the lease on the two shops he occupied and that the business would be expected to vacate the premises by Christmas that year. Left with no alternative but to move, Bob and Ken uplifted the firm which had occupied the Arcade for nearly sixty years and relocated at no. 3 Anlaby Road, the premises of Brantons Ltd., another firm of

Bob and Ethel Furmage.
Courtesy of Ken Furmage.

Hull watchmakers and jewellers which they had purchased two years earlier. They continued to operate under the name of Brantons which was equally well known in the city and later in 1958 re-established the name of Gardiners at a shop in the Weir, Hessle, where it remains to this day. Bob Furmage who is pictured with his wife Ethel outside their shop at nos. 3 and 5 Hepworth's Arcade was later President of the Hull and East Riding Branch of the British Horological Society.

Following his father's retirement the business was taken over by Ken Furmage but has since passed to the next generation of the Furmage family — Ken's two sons Rob and Anthony and his daughter Janet, with Rob and Janet controlling the Hessle side of the business (see also Brantons Ltd. — 13 Hepworth's Arcade). Pictured is Bob Furmage in his shop in Hepworth's Arcade with George and Beryl Formby.

Mrs. Marion Bastow, Tobacconist 1906-1908

See no. 4 Hepworth's Arcade.

Stanley C. Bastow, Hatter, Hosier and Glover 1909-1910

See no. 6 Hepworth's Arcade.

G. Elvin and Co., Printers 1911-1914

George Elvin began trading as a printer in Hull in 1910 with premises at 47 George Street whilst residing at 21 Walmsley Street. The following year he took over the shop at no. 10 Hepworth's Arcade from Stanley Bastow where he

Bob Furmage with George and Beryl Formby.

stayed for three years during which time he changed his home address twice, first in 1912 to 116 De La Pole Avenue and one year later to 23 Desmond Avenue, Newland. In 1914 he moved his business to 26 Waterworks Street and the following year once again changed his home address moving just a few houses along Desmond Avenue to No. 2. The business stayed in Waterworks Street for 15 years although during this time, in 1921, the printers was listed at no. 26a which could be assumed was either at the rear or on the upper floors of the shop. As appears to have been the case with many of the past tenants of the Arcade George had decided to expand into another business enterprise and was listed in the year's directory at no. 26 as being a Fancy Goods Dealer. By this time he was domestically on the move again with the new location of the family home being Withernsea. By 1925 presumably with the Fancy Goods venture proving successful and having taken over the complete premises at no. 26 the printers was listed at no. 24a. 1929 saw George not only move the Fancy Goods side of the business to what were probably larger premises at 64-66 Jameson Street but also relocate his family home back to Hull moving into no. 17 Beech Grove. The following year also featured two moves for the Elvins —both the business and the family. No. 7 Dock Street was the new address for the printing business and 54 Claremont Avenue being the new home abode. This year (1930) was also the last year in which the Fancy Goods side of the business was listed in the directories. Although the printing business was to remain in Dock Street for eleven years until 1942 when it removed to no. 7 Waltham Street, during that time George moved his family a further three times first to no. 5 Berkeley Street, then to 11 Park Avenue and finally to 18 Danesway, Hessle. It is understood that the business, which some time prior to 1949 had become Elvins (Printers) Ltd., had been sold and was no longer under the control of the Elvin family but it is not known exactly when. In 1955 by which time the premises in Waltham Street, being in the city centre, were probably commanding a high rent because of their central position which was not essential for a printer, new premises in Grey Street were taken. Elvins the printers stayed at Grey Street until 1973 in which year they made their final move to Springfield Way, Anlaby. They are last listed in the Hull Telephone Directory in 1989 when it is known they were under the ownership of Northwaite Printing of Bradford. In that year their parent company went into receivership and the final premises at Springfield Way along with some other assets of the business were sold ending nearly eighty years of printing in Hull by Elvins.

E. Taylor, Confectioner (Sweets) 1920-1921

Ethel Taylor who, according to the electoral register for Spring 1920, resided in Beverley was the first in a string of four different confectioners to try to establish a business at no. 10. The photograph taken in the early 1920's shows the shop and the name of E. Taylor can vaguely be made out under the window. Ethel's term in the Arcade was however a brief one and although she was listed in the directory for 1921 as still being the tenant, by the time the Spring electoral register of that year was issued her name had disappeared.

Market Place 'arm' looking east from balcony circa early 1920's.
Courtesy of Basil King.

Mrs. Minnie Hall, Confectioner (Sweets) 1921-1923

Although Mrs. Hall was to have the longest tenancy of all of the confectioners at no. 10 little other information is known about her. The electoral rolls for the years 1921 to 1924 show her as the tenant and give her home address as 1 Chatsworth Avenue, Welbeck Street.

Chatterton and Porter, Confectioners (Sweets) 1923-1925

Chatterton and Porter, confectioners appeared in the directories for one year only in 1925 and consequently little solid information is available on the business. The electoral registers for 1923 and 1924 confirm that the owners were a James Chatterton of 2 Byron Street and John Porter of 21 Westcott Street. Further investigations in the directories show that 2 Byron Street was attributed at the time to a Walter Chatterton and 21 Westcott Street to a Mrs. Ann Elizabeth Porter. This evidence would suggest that both James and John were relatively young and still living at home with their parents. The close promiximity of their two home addresses (Byron Street leads off Westcott Street around the area of no. 21) would suggest that the two young men were friends who had possibly even grown up together. In the 1920's the Hull directories also list an Alfred Porter, manufacturing confectioner on Hessle Road and a Sidney

74

Chatterton, confectioner on Newbridge Road. It is possible, considering the similarity of both the names and of the type of businesses being undertaken, that James and John were in some way related to their namesakes although, as there is no concrete evidence of this, such an assumption would be only speculation.

Mrs. Florence Ashton, Confectioner (Sweets) 1926

Florence May Ashton, to quote her full name, first appeared in the Hull Directory of 1921 when she was listed as a grocer at 83 Walcott Street. By 1925 she was attributed with premises at 50 Market Place and described as a confectioner. This address was an unusual one as it was also credited to five other businesses and was therefore probably a large building that had at some stage been split into several individual shop units.

In 1926 in addition to the shop at 50 Market Place where Florence was described as a newsagent she also took over the premises of no. 10 in the Arcade from Chatterton and Porter and later the same year also moved into no. 60 Market Place. It has not been possible to establish whether the premises at 50 Market Place and 10 Hepworth's Arcade had been vacated prior to the opening of no. 60 Market Place, or if indeed all three outlets were operated concurrently, but by the time the 1929 directory was published Mrs. Ashton had just the one shop, a newsagents at no. 60 Market Place.

If it is possible to measure the success of a business by the area in which the proprietor resides it could be declared that Mrs. Ashton's was a prosperous one as during the 27 years that she operated the newsagents her home address changed three times. In 1926 when she first took over the premises at 60 Market Place she was living at 64 Melrose Street, in 1928 moved to 21 Marlborough Avenue and in 1937 to Kirkella. The last recorded home address for Mrs. Ashton was in the 1939/40 electoral register when she was listed as living in Anlaby. The business changed hands in 1946.

Louis Gabriel Colomb, Manufacturers' Agent 1928-1929

The name of Louis Gabriel Colomb was never actually shown attributed to Hepworth's Arcade in the directories and has only received a mention by virtue of an entry in the electoral register for 1928/9 in which he was shown as being the tenant of no. 10. Louis Colomb, whose name would suggest Italian origin, was listed in the Hull directories between 1928 and 1930 as a manufacturers' agent dealing in hairdressing sundries at no. 53 Market Place. His home address for the period was given as 238 Anlaby Road. Mr. Charles Linford who began his career with the Postal Service in Hull as a telegram boy in the Old Town around the same time as Mr. Colomb occupied number 10 recalls that a number of the boys with whom he worked used a barber's in Hepworth's Arcade and it is therefore very possible that, in addition to supplying sundries to the hairdressing industry, Louis himself also operated as a hairdresser.

George William Dinsdale, Gramophone Dealer, 1930-1939

G. W. DINSDALE "The Record King" boasted the business cards of George Dinsdale in the early 1930's. "First with the Latest" they added with

G. W. DINSDALE,
"The Record King"
FOR
COLUMBIA, REGAL ZON, REX,
DECCA and PARLOPHONE
— RECORDS —
First with the Latest.
10 Hepworths Arcade, Hull.
Send a P.C. for Dealer to call and let you hear a selection

George Dinsdale Senior.
Courtesy of George Dinsdale Junior.

the suggestion that a postcard should be sent for a dealer to call and let you hear a selection. George Dinsdale had originally trained as a barber but although he achieved the required qualifications was unable to settle in his chosen profession and took a stall on the open market in Hull from which he sold gramophone records. His mother Harriet Dinsdale was listed in the directory for 1926 as a general dealer at 25 Porter Street, but such, presumably, was the success of the venture in to the business of gramophone records that in 1929, the year before George first took over the shop in Hepworth's Arcade, his mother listed herself as a Gramophone Dealer. George took up occupation of no. 10 in 1930 although for some time apparently also maintained his stall on the market. Pictured are examples of the record covers which George had printed to promote the sales of his gramophone records.

The business was presumably successful and in 1935 he saw the opportunity to expand his horizons and, following the departure of Thomas Kenny, coal merchant from no. 12, took over those premises and opened up the shop as a cycle agent. Both of the shops can be seen in the photograph taken around 1935 and George himself is just visible, pipe in mouth, looking out of no. 10.

It is possible that George thought that he could succeed where the Myton Cycle Depot had earlier failed (see no. 20 Hepworth's Arcade) or maybe saw the opportunity to 'cash in' on the prosperity of Currys Ltd., a cycle accessory

Dinsdale's record sleeve.
Courtesy of George Dinsdale Jnr.

dealer established some nine years earlier around the corner in Silver Street and still prospering. Regardless of his reasons for starting it the cycle business failed to be a success and by the time the 1937 directory was published no. 12 was unoccupied. George did, however, still have two shops, having opened a second outlet for his gramophones and records at 119 Hessle Road.

During 1937 and 1938, obviously undeterred by his unsuccessful attempt as a cycle agent, George diversified again and began stocking novelties and fancy goods. This addition to his business was presumably a much more fruitful one as two years later in 1939 he took the brave decision to abandon the gramophone and records business that had given him a livelihood for over a decade and concentrate on novelties and fancy goods. He changed his shop in the Arcade for the slightly larger premises at no. 16 and was described in the directory of the year at no. 16 as a 'dealer in novelties' with the shop on Hessle Road being attributed to the sale of fancy goods. The fancy goods side of the business was only listed in the directories for one year and following the 1939 publication the address also ceased to be credited to George, but the sales of

The Market Place 'arm' looking west circa 1935.

9d

Box 6d   Best in Tube 9d

The Best 6d

Box of 5 1/3

Sample page from Dinsdale Joke and Trick catalogue circa 1945.
Courtesy of George Dinsdale Jnr.

of novelties which soon developed into jokes and magic thrived ensuring that the name of Dinsdale in Hull would be associated with those items by many generations of schoolboys in the future. In addition to selling from the shop George soon discovered that there was a vast market for his merchandise particularly the joke items, on the wider scale of mail order and consequently prepared catalogues and advertised nationally. A sample page from one of these catalogues issued just after the War is pictured and can be seen to feature the age old 'gags' of itching powder, fake dog dirt and exploding cigarette cartridges which are still as popular today nearly half a century later.

In 1953 George was joined in the business by his son George Junior who, in addition to working in the shop took up magic as a hobby. With easy access to the best and most recent tricks and illusions young George soon became very proficient and the hobby quickly developed into an additional source of income and he soon discovered that a one night appearance as 'Ricardo the magician' could easily earn him as much as a full week would working for his father. George junior as 'Ricardo the magician' is pictured, ably assisted by his girlfriend (later to become his wife) Shirley Williams who first met George whilst working in the Arcade for Selby Leedham and Co. (see no. 17 Hepworth's Arcade).

In later years George Senior put his foot down and told his son in no uncertain terms that he must choose between a profession as a magician and the opportunity to eventually take over the family business. Because of the difference in wage levels it was a difficult decision for young George to make but favouring the stability of a definite wage against the possibility of weeks without a booking he decided to opt for the shop and continued to perform magic on a less regular basis.

George Senior, assisted by his son, continued to run the shop and the mail order side of the business and, in the mid 1960's, some years later after the death of his first wife Lucy, married for a second time to Vera Wood the widow of Arthur Wood (see 12 Hepworth's Arcade).

In 1973 following the deaths of the two Miss Deans (see 18

George and Shirley Dinsdale as 'Ricardo and Assistant'.
Courtesy of George Dinsdale Jnr.

George Dinsdale senior in later years.
Courtesy of Shirley Dinsdale.

Hepworth's Arcade) George expanded the business to take over the neighbouring premises of no. 18. He retired from the business in 1974 and died in 1987 aged 84 and is pictured during his later years in the business.

His son George Junior was joined in the business in 1978 by his nephew Graham Williams and more recently by his daughter Stephanie. George Junior or George Alfred Dinsdale to give him his full title, his wife Shirley, nephew Graham and daughter Stephanie continue to operate to this day the business founded by his father over sixty years earlier which is probably one of the oldest established joke shops in the country and has itself become a landmark often referred to when directing people to the Arcade. Pictured is George Junior with his nephew Graham Williams in the shop around 1990.

'Maurice' Salon, Gents Hairdresser (Maurice Kauffman) 1946-1953

Maurice Kauffman served his apprenticeship as a gentleman's hairdresser in Hull prior to the Second World War during which he was a sergeant in the airforce stationed at R.A.F Leeming. Shortly after being demobbed he returned to Hull and opened his own salon at no.

George Dinsdale jnr. and Graham Williams inside their joke shop.

10 Hepworth's Arcade using his first name as the title for the business. The shop, like many gents hairdressers of the era, had the bottom half of the window blanked out. This was done in yellow with the name 'Maurice' etched out in navy blue. Following his departure from the Arcade in 1953 when he sold the business to Selwyn Clark, Maurice took over the barber's shop in Paragon Station from a Mr. Branski which was at the time

and still is reputedly the oldest barber's shop in the city and one of the oldest in England. Shortly after he added a salon on Spring Bank West and during the thirty-seven years from when he opened in the Arcade to when he retired in 1983 Maurice built up a chain of 48 salons throughout the country. Assuming the total number of establishments which a business operates can be used as a measure of its prosperity this venture was undoubtedly the most successful of all of those that can trace their origins and starter premises back to Hepworth's Arcade. Maurice Kauffman died in 1991 aged 74 but the name of Kauffman is still connected with hairdressing in this area as his son Raymond, himself a hairdresser of international acclaim, continues to operate from a salon in Beverley.

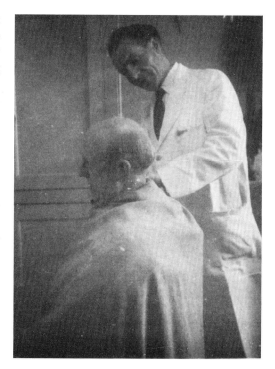

Maurice Kauffman.
Courtesy of Raymond Kauffman.

'Maurice' Salon, Selwyn Clark, Gents Hairdressers 1953-1975

In August 1953 word that Maurice Kauffman was hoping to expand his business and was willing to sell the salon he had established in the Arcade reached Selwyn Clark. Keen to operate his own business Selwyn approached Maurice, a deal was struck and arrangements were made to transfer the concern.

Selwyn recalls:

> 'I remember accompanying Maurice to a solicitor's office in Scale Lane where an agreement was prepared for the transfer of the shop to me. I still have the receipt which shows that the charge was two guineas plus ten shillings stamp duty or £2.60 in present currency. The large plate glass window of the shop was painted to above eye level presumably to make it more private and the name 'Maurice' stood out boldly edged in gold. It seemed a pity to scrape it all off so I continued to trade under the name.'

In addition to having qualified as a gent's hairdresser Selwyn had also mastered the art of shaving customers with an open or 'cut throat' razor which at the time was an accepted part of the services offered by any competent barber. However the early 1950's saw the introduction of electric shavers and improved safety razors which lead to the decline in customers wanting to be

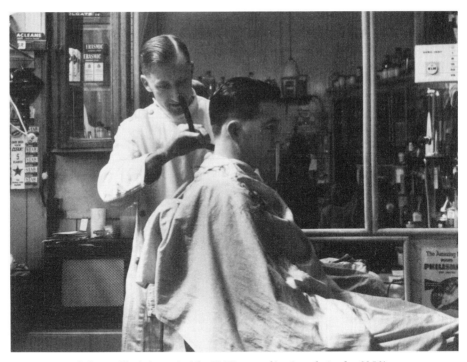

Selwyn Clark busy inside 10 Hepworth's Arcade in the 1950's.
Courtesy of Selwyn Clark.

shaved in the shop. It was perhaps partly for that reason that, shortly after taking over the business, Selwyn decided that a price increase was necessary. He recalls:

> 'The usual price for a haircut in the city at the time was one shilling and sixpence (7½ pence) and when I increased this to one shilling and ninepence (9 pence) I remember being quite concerned wondering if the customers would object to paying the extra.'

Because of its position in the city centre, in addition to the steady flow of regular customers from the many shops and offices in close proximity, the salon also attracted many strangers from very varied walks of life. Selwyn reflects that this made it a much more interesting place to work than many suburban shops at which most of the business would be provided by local residents. He recalls:

> 'Almost every working day contained conversations on a wide range of topics and meetings with unusual personalities and characters. One day a rather scruffy man came into the shop with a large mop of strange looking unruly hair and sat down waiting for attention. I kept glancing apprehensively at the tangled mass wondering what he expected me to do with it. When his turn came he sat in the chair and explained that he was wearing a theatrical wig which he had just purchased from Dinsdale's Joke Shop and asked if I could snip a bit off to make it a little more respectable. Another unusual incident

82

happened at the time of industrial unrest when all businesses were badly hit by sudden power cuts. One dark winter evening a foreign seaman came into the shop and although he could not speak a word of English he used hand movements to indicate that he wanted his long hair cutting quite short. I worked around his head with the electric clippers and had got about half way round when the whole area was plunged into darkness. I used my cycle lamp to find an old pair of hand clippers and then asked another customer to hold the lamp while I endeavoured to give him a reasonable appearance. Throughout the duration of the haircut there was no conversation because of the language barrier and the poor fellow must have wondered what on earth was going on.'

For Selwyn, who is pictured in his later years in the Arcade, being self employed, in addition to the obvious benefits, also had several disadvantages. No holiday or sick pay and often pressure of work across lunchtime which prevented him from getting regular meals and eventually his health started to suffer. He recalls.

'My opportunity for a change of profession arose when the county of Humberside was formed in the early '70's. Reorganisation in local government created several vacancies in Council departments at the Guildhall. After twenty-two memorable and enjoyable years in that little shop down the Arcade a career change that I had never envisaged came about and I finished my working days at the City Treasurers.'

Selwyn Clark in his salon in Hepworth's Arcade in the early 1970's.
Courtesy of Selwyn Clark.

Now retired Selwyn still lives in the city and often pops into the Arcade for a chat and perhaps a spot of reminiscing with George Dinsdale and Ken Furmage and from time to time pays a visit to his successor at no. 10, Geoff Matchett, at his new salon in George Street.

Geoff Matchett, Gents Hairdresser 1975-1979

After nearly two years training as a ladies' hairdresser at two different establishments in Hull Geoff Matchett attended Bradford Hairdressing College for one year qualifying in both ladies and gents hairdressing. On his return to Hull Geoff had a brief spell with Sid Fenby at his salons in Cottingham and under the ABC in Ferensway, followed by three and a half years with the Classic Salon in Jameson Street (under the old Pioneer Café). Geoff recalls that his time with Classic was very valuable to his training with the salon always busy and being called upon to execute a wide variety of haircuts. Towards the end of 1972 Geoff was approached by a friend, also a hairdresser, and asked if he would be interested in the two of them going into business together. Although Geoff admits that he had never thought of being his own boss the idea did tempt him and although that particular offer later fell through, the seeds had obviously been sown in Geoff's mind to own his own business. During the early months of 1973 an opportunity to purchase the existing hairdressing business in Hepworth's Arcade was offered in the *Hull Daily Mail* and following discussion with the owner Selwyn Clark it was agreed that Geoff would take over the business from March that year.

Geoff recalls:

'I remember being very nervous when I first went to see Selwyn even though my wife and I had managed, through working a lot of overtime, to save the seven hundred and fifty pounds being asked for the business. My fears were soon proved to be unnecessary as I found Selwyn to be a very easy-going man who seemed keen to help me. A price of £624.00 was agreed and such was the generosity of Selwyn that he said that I did not have to settle immediately but could pay him at a rate of £4.00 per week for the next three years. I recall that the final weekly wage that I received from Classic was £30.00 and that in the first week in my own shop I took a total of £91.00 which after deducting £4.00 for Selwyn, £4.00 for rent and rates and £2.00 for incidentals left me with a wage for the week of £81.00. I knew from that first week that I had made the right decision to become my own boss. Although I would like to think that it was due to my own expertise it was probably more because of the position of the salon in the centre of Hull's professional area in which worked a large number of men that I was always kept busy and I recall that in an average week I would do around 150 haircuts. Some weeks were of course busier than others and I remember well one tiring week when I set my own personal record of 204 haircuts. Because lunchtime was a particularly busy period I had an arrangement with the café opposite whereby they would save me some lunch which I would eat around 2.00 p.m when my rush had died down. One Saturday afternoon whilst enjoying my lunch at just after 2.00 o'clock I noticed a queue forming outside my shop awaiting my return. Determined to finish my lunch break I sat tight and counted as the queue started to grow. At 3.00 o'clock when I finished my lunch and made my way across the Arcade I had a line of 25 men stretching from my door and along the Arcade past Fanthorpes. Unfortunately as my shop only measured 12 feet by 6 feet I could not even fit all of the prospective customers in let alone have time to give them all haircuts before I closed at half-past five and had to insist that anyone who could get into the shop would be attended to that day but the others would have to call back on Monday. I thoroughly enjoyed my time in the Arcade and had it not been for my wish to expand the business (you cannot expand much in 72 square feet) I would probably still be there to this day.'

When Geoff left the Arcade in 1979 he moved to larger premises in Whitefriargate although, as he admits, he would have preferred a bigger shop in the Arcade. He has since moved his business again to George Street where, sixteen years on, he still cuts the hair of some customers who first came to him during his days in Hepworth's Arcade.

The Doll's House, Clothes Boutique 1979-1981

Although having been involved in the printing industry for much of her working life Mary Taylor had always fancied the idea of owning her own clothes shop and when a friend Geoff Matchett told of his intention to give up the lease on number 10 Hepworth's Arcade Mary saw her opportunity. When Geoff had taken over the shop he had bought it as an established gents hairdressers, but as he was continuing that business from new premises in nearby Whitefriargate he was keen to ensure that the shop was not taken by another barber who might gain from the goodwill he had built up over the years, so Mary's suggestion of a clothes boutique suited both parties.

The business which was christened The Doll's House from an idea by Mary's daughter Angelina who commented that the shop was so small it could not really be called anything else and in the early days sold mainly ladies high fashion. It did however later develop into a supplier of theatrical clothing ranging from evening suits and dresses to top hats and furs.

Whilst running the business Mary also continued to work on a part-time basis in the printing department of the Humberside Police Force at their Headquarters in Queens Gardens and following nearly two years in the Arcade the opportunity arose for a full-time position. Mary chose to accept the offer but remembers fondly her days in Hepworth's Arcade.

Mary recalls:

'I remember there being a wonderful friendly atmosphere between the shop owners and assistants in the Arcade. We were just like one great big family and could often be seen popping in and out of each other's shops for occasional cups of tea.'

La Femme, Ladies Underclothing and Nightwear 1981-1982

Following the decision of Mary Taylor to return full-time into the printing business Peter Tarbotten, a friend of Mary's husband John, took over the lease of no. 10.

Peter, who is probably better known locally as the owner of the Spiders Night Club in Cleveland Street, along with his friend Alan Stephenson, saw the vacant shop as the ideal premises from which to sell the ladies lingerie and nightwear which they had the opportunity of buying as clearance lines from the large mail order catalogue companies.

The venture failed to be the success that the partners had envisaged and after just over six months they made the decision to close the shop and sell the lease.

Larry's, nearly New Clothing 1982-Present Date

Prior to opening her shop Lorraine Willby (or Larry as she has been known since infancy), like many other businesses in the Arcade, started on the markets of the area where she sold manufacturers' 'seconds' clothing. She later supplemented her market income by operating a party plan side to the business and in 1982 took over the lease on no. 10 Hepworth's Arcade selling new and nearly new fashions.

Larry recalls:

> 'I have always liked sewing and making alterations to old clothes to bring them up to date fashion-wise so found more enjoyment in dealing with the fashions of yesteryear than the current ones. The fabrics were much better in those days than the ones used today and it is a pleasure being able to work with those materials to re-vamp an old garment.'

During the past thirteen years Larry has built up a reputation second to none for being able to supply a whole outfit at a fraction of the price one would expect to pay in the high street stores. In 1990 such was the extent of the reputation of Larry's shop that Yorkshire Television chose it to be one of those featured in their Posh Frocks and New Trousers programme. Larry recalls:

> 'The producers of the programme decided that it would make good viewing to take a particular ensemble from the pages of one of the fashion magazines which had cost a small fortune to put together and see how cheaply a similar look could be created from shops like my own. They sent fashion model, Annabel Giles, with a team of researchers and a camera crew to Hull and called at my own shop, Mim's (Arcade Curios) and Beasley's on North Church Side. After a certain amount of rummaging they produced an outfit of similar appearance to the one in the magazine but withouy spending anywhere near as much money.'

The shop has always proven popular with the student fraternity of Hull and the name of Larry's often receives a mention in the yearly guides to newcomers to the City as being the place to go to 'bag a bargain'. It has been said that Larry's is the place to go if you want something a little different and one recent customer would certainly confirm this after being the envy of her friends in a

86

Seventies style suit the likes of which cannot be found anywhere else in the City (well not during the past two decades anyway).

NO. 12 HEPWORTH'S ARCADE

Thomas Kenny, Coal Merchant, 1897-1933

Thomas Kenny was born in Louth, Lincolnshire in 1858. He is known to have been living in Hull by 1887 and the 1891 census lists him as residing at 401 Church Street which later became a part of Wincolmlee. His name first appears in the Hull Directories in 1895 when

Hull Daily Mail advertisement 1901.
Courtesy of the Hull Daily Mail.

he is shown as Tom Kenny, coal merchant, Frosts Villas, Northumberland Avenue an address which later proved to be his residence. By the following year he is recorded as operating from the Hull and Barnsley Coal Depot in Lockwood Street and one year later in 1897 at Cannon Street Station and no. 12 Hepworth's Arcade (see photograph taken circa 1921). In 1900 Thomas changed residence moving to no. 8 Vermont Street where he stayed until 1914 when he moved again to no. 355 Beverley Road. By this year he was credited in the directories as having four outlets with Hessle Road and Ella Street having been added to Cannon Street Station and 12 Hepworth's Arcade.

When Thomas died in 1926 the business passed to his eldest son also Thomas who had been living in Birmingham but returned to Hull to take over the company. This caused some ill-feeling between Thomas Junior and his younger brother Frederick who resented Thomas getting the business when their father died. This resentment was probably compounded by the fact that, whilst Thomas Junior was living in Birmingham, Frederick was helping his father run the company. Both Thomas Junior and Frederick moved to Bridlington when they became partners in a business in the Amusement arcade there to supplement their incomes as coal merchants. In 1927 the business employed a young lady by the name of Emily Cook who was perhaps better known by her middle name of Marjorie. Marjorie (now Marjorie Bennion) recalls:

'I was the first female assistant with the company and earned fifteen shillings (75 pence) a week. The shop in Hepworth's Arcade was only tiny with one room downstairs and a small office on the first floor. There was a cold water tap under the stairs if I needed a drink but no heating or toilet facilities so if I needed to go I had to lock up the shop and go to the Public Lavatories in the corner of the Arcade. By the time I married in 1934 the business had moved to Paragon Arcade and Mr. and Mrs. Kenny bought me a lovely bedroom suite which still has pride of place in my house here in Suffolk over sixty years later. I left the business in 1935 to start my family, but remember affectionately my days with the company in Hepworth's Arcade.'

In 1933, in addition to the office in Hepworth's Arcade and the depots at Lockwood Street (Cannon Street station) and Hessle Road (Dairycoates) the business opened a second office at no. 13 Paragon Arcade. It is a possibility that the new office could have been acquired as a replacement for the one in Hepworth's Arcade as by the following year (1934) that office had closed. Thomas Kenny and Son, coal merchants as they were still known even after the death of Thomas Senior, continued to operate from Paragon Arcade until 1953 when they were one of two coal merchants in Paragon Arcade. The following year their competitors Rafferty and Watson were listed as having two offices in Paragon Arcade having also taken over the telephone number previously assigned to Kenny's and it is therefore assumed that the Kenny brothers, who were by that time both well into their sixties, decided to retire and sold the business.

George William Dinsdale, Cycle Agents 1935-1936

See no. 10 Hepworth's Arcade.

A. Wood, Toys and Musical Instruments (The Accordion Shop) 1948-1967

Arthur Wood or 'Art' as he was better known to his friends and customers first took over the premises at no. 12 Hepworth's Arcade in 1948. He was an accomplished player of both the accordion and the harmonica and would spend his summer evenings entertaining holidaymakers on the "Yorkshireman" moored in Bridlington Harbour. He was president of the Hull Accordion and Harmonica Club and, according to other people involved in the music business in Hull at the time, was undoubtedly the man to see for any advice on or repairs to either instrument. Pictured is an advertisement taken from the *Hull Daily Mail* in December 1952.

In addition to the supply of musical instruments Art, like many of his predecessors in the Arcade, had another string to his bow and, also similar to those predecessors, his secondary occupation was probably as diverse from the first as it could possibly be — Art was a chimney sweep. In the advertisement taken from the Hull Telephone

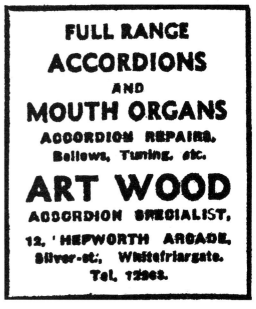

Hull Daily Mail advertisement 1952.
Courtesy of the Hull Daily Mail.

Directory of 1954 he indicates that a brush is always used, presumably a guarantee that his competitors did not offer. In 1965 Art died and although his widow Vera took over 'the Accordion Shop', as it was also known for a short while, the business closed in 1967. Following the death of Arthur, Vera later married George Dinsdale Senior and was a close member of that family until her death in the early 1980's. The sale of harmonicas in the Arcade was however kept alive as, following the closure of the Woods' shop, George senior took over the remaining stock and this instrument can still be purchased from Dinsdales to this day.

Hull Telephone Directory advertisement 1954. Courtesy of Kingston Communications (Hull) plc.

Vera Wood. Courtesy of Shirley Dinsdale.

The Provincial Coin and Stamp Company 1967-1969

When Patricia Tuxworth and Alan Johnson first opened in July 1967 this was the first business of its type in Hull and undoubtedly filled a gap and proved popular with the City's numismatists and philatelists. Although Patricia was a founder member of the Hull Numismatic Society neither she nor Alan (see also no. 20 Hepworth's Arcade) had any previous knowledge in this field but despite that lack of past experience the partners must nevertheless have built up enough steady trade to make the venture of interest to John Smith of Stonegate Coins of York, himself an established dealer, when they chose to 'sell up' in 1969 to take over the café across the Arcade (see also no. 11 Hepworth's Arcade).

Hull Collectors Centre 1969-1970

See Stonegate Coins — below.

Stonegate Coins (Coin and Stamp Dealers) 1970-1979

Stonegate coins had been established in York since 1967 and the owner John Smith was keen to expand beyond the realms of that city. Consequently when, in 1969, the existing coin and stamp dealers business in Hepworth's Arcade came onto the market he grasped the opportunity. Together with John Marshall he took over the concern and commenced in business under the name of Hull

Collectors Centre. Ian Blower was employed to manage the outlet and the same year John took onto his staff in York a young man by the name of David Baxter. In 1970 the partnership dissolved and the premises in Hepworth's Arcade took the name of their parent company in York —Stonegate Coins. Later that year when Ian Blower left to start his own business the opportunity to promote David arose and he was made manager of the Hull outlet.

Eight years later in 1978 David was made a partner in the Hull branch of the business and the following year bought out his former employer to become sole owner of the venture.

Baxter's Coin and Stamp Exchange 1979-1991

By the time David Baxter become sole proprietor of the business in 1979 he had already gained ten years experience in this field which was to prove to be of great benefit as, unlike Patricia Tuxworth and Alan Johnson who had initiated the sales of collectable coins and stamps in the city without any local rivals, David had the additional task of competing for the limited market with Ian Blower (see also Stonegate Coins) who had, since leaving the Arcade, opened up in competition in Savile Street. David continued to build the business for a further twelve years at no. 12 before moving to larger premises in the Arcade at nos. 20 and 22. The new larger shop gave him the opportunity to expand his range of merchandise and whilst extending his range of 'collectables' to cover model cars etc. he also moved into the gift market stocking a wide variety of unusual and high quality giftware. He has recently been joined in the business by his eldest son Tim which could perhaps spell the start of another 'Arcade dynasty' to follow those of the Bastows', the Kennys', the Dinsdales' and the Furmages'.

Satin 'N Lace (Haberdashery Dealers) 1991-1994

Following many years as a power station manager including a six year spell in Saudi Arabia David Martin returned to England and, along with his wife Christine commenced in business selling haberdashery on the markets around their home in Rochester, Kent. Following their move North where they settled in Beeford the couple continued the business under the banner

Baxter's Coin and Stamp Exchange circa late 1980's.
Courtesy of Hull City Council
Planning Department.

of Rose Cottage Motifs. They would often leave their home in the early hours of the morning to 'stand' a market as far afield from their home base as Cottingham, Beverley and Malton. After four years of trading from market stalls the opportunity to take over the lease of the shop at no. 12 Hepworth's Arcade arose and they made the decision to take it. From their new 'permanent' base they expanded their lines to include craft materials and later, in 1994, dolls houses and accessories. (see also The Doll's House).

The Doll's House (Dolls Houses and Accessories) 1994 - Present Date

During 1994, in addition to their usual haberdashery lines, David and Christine Martin of Satin 'N Lace (see above) began stocking small accessories for Dolls Houses with the hope of perhaps attracting collectors to their shop. The response was good and they soon found themselves being asked for other accessories not currently stocked and for the dolls houses themselves. A decision was reached that this was the direction which their business would take and in the latter part of that year the necessary arrangements were made to change the name of the business to The Doll's House. The venture is still in its infancy but the apparent growth in this sector of the collectors market combined with the limited amount of local competition would suggest a wise move by David and Christine and the growing number of customers seen studying the miniature articles in their window would seem to confirm this. The Doll's House have recently been appointd local agents for Dijon miniatures which are reputedly amongst the cream of dolls houses and their fittings.

NO. 14 HEPWORTH'S ARCADE

Reame, Wokes and Co./A. Reame and Co., Electrical Engineers 1899-1905

Albert Reame first appeared in the Hull Directories in 1896 when he is listed as an electrical engineer living at 6 Alexandra Avenue, Mayfield Street. The name of Wokes did not appear until 1899 when Reame, Wokes and Co. are shown at no. 14 Hepworth's Arcade. The same year Cooks Directory also attributes the business with premises at 53 Albert Road, Middlesbrough, but it would appear that their attempt to establish themselves in that area was unsuccessful as by 1901 that address was unlisted in the Kelly's Directory of Middlesbrough and the names of Reame and Wokes had vanished. By 1900 the business was listed in the directories as occupying, in addition to the shop in the Arcade, premises in Burlington Buildings, Charlotte Street, but by the following year that address had disappeared. It would also appear that the partnership had dissolved as no. 14 Hepworth's Arcade was listed under the name of A. Reame and Company whilst Albert's ex-partner Charles was operating from premises at 68 Brook Street under the name of Chas. Wokes and Co. The same directory gives 7 Wilton Street as being the home of Albert Reame and 8 George Street as the residence of Charles Wokes. It would appear that each of the gentlemen was experiencing a certain degree of success as by 1904 both businesses had full page advertisements in the Directories.

The same year A. Reame and Co. moved to new premises at 45 Hedon Road and although the advertisements for both companies were repeated the

Advertisement from Kelly's Directory of Hull.　　*Advertisement from Kelly's Directory of Hull.*

following year this was the final year in which A. Reame and Company were listed and by 1906 Albert also failed to be included at his home address. Meanwhile Charles Wokes, who had in 1905 changed residence to 73 Coltman Street, continued to operate his business and other than another change of home abode in 1908 to 42 Sandringham Street the entries for his company remain unaltered until 1910. In that year, although the business was included in the directories, it was no longer under the name of Chas. Wokes and would appear to have been either taken over by or amalgamated with another electrical engineering firm. The address at 68 Brook Street was retained, but from that year the business was conducted under the name of the Humber Electrical Engineering Company which included the statement 'Incorporating Chas. Wokes and Co.' in their advertisement. That firm continues to operate to this day and is currently under the control of Charles E. Shuttleworth, the grandson of William Shuttleworth who directed the merger with Chas. Wokes and Co.

Isaac Adler, Oriental Mat Dealer 1901

The name of Isaac Adler appears in the Hull Directories for one year only and even then only in one publication — Cooks Directory of Hull. The Kelly's Directory for the same year indicates the continued occupation of Albert Reame, so it is possible that the inclusion of Mr. Adler is an error by Cooks. It is however also possible that, as this was the period in which Reame, Wokes and

Co. changed to A. Reame and Co., the electrical engineering business did vacate the premises for a short while after the partnership was dissolved and that Albert Reame returned to operate under his own name by the time the Kelly's Directory was published later that year. No other reference has been uncovered for Mr. Adler and it has not even been possible to establish whether he actually dealt in mats or if that was an attempted abbreviation of materials.

Isaac Gardiner, Watchmaker 1906-1936

See no. 10 Hepworth's Arcade.

Edward Sugarman, Alteration Tailor 1946-1975

Edward Sugarman.
Courtesy of Mrs. D. Sugarman.

The name of Sugarman in connection with tailors in Hull can be traced back as far as 1905 when Israel Sugarman is listed as operating as a tailor from 26 Great Thornton Street. It was at those premises that Israel taught his sons the trade with Edward and his three brothers all qualifying for their Master Tailors Certificates.

Prior to the Second World War Edward worked from both a shop on the corner of Posterngate and King Street and a stall on the nearby open market before being called up for active service. After being demobbed and finding he was unable to resume on the market he took the opportunity of leasing the shop at no. 14 from which he performed an alteration service.

Eddie, as he was better known in the Arcade, was recognised as being a very competent craftsman who took a pride in his work and he continued to occupy the premises for nearly thirty years before retiring in 1975.

Arcade Curios, Antique Dealers 1975-Present Date

Arcade Curios was opened in 1975 by Gary Holmes and his girlfriend Miriam Benson. Prior to starting the business Gary had for many years worked for Withers Newsagency in Jameson Street as Manager before buying the business in the late 1960's or early 1970's.

From an early age Gary had always had a fascination with antiques and had himself, over the years, built up a considerable collection. Following his decision to sell the newsagency business Gary pondered for a few months but then took the decision to turn his hobby into his living and, following negotiations with Edward Sugarman, an agreement was reached that he would take over the shop at 14 Hepworth's Arcade at the beginning of 1975.

Together with Miriam (or Mim as she prefers to be known) the shop was stocked entirely from their own collection and opened for business selling an

Mim Benson inside Arcade Curios late 1970's.
Courtesy of Mim Benson.

assortment of antique furniture and bric-a-brac, militaria, clocks, postcards and various items of Victoriana.

Sadly, in 1976, Gary became seriously ill and the operating of the business became more and more the responsibility of Mim. She recalls:

> 'Gary had always dealt with the purchase and valuation of our stock as he had years of experience and following his illness I would often have to ask people to leave their pieces with me and call back the following day for our offer. I would then take the item to the hospital when I visited Gary that evening and get his opinion. The nurses at Princess Royal Hospital got quite used to me turning up with anything from an antique clock to a Victorian chamberpot.'

Mim is pictured in the shop during the 1970's.

Gary passed away in January 1977 and the running of Arcade Curios was taken over full-time by Mim. She recalls:

> 'In the early days things were far from easy as, in addition to running the business, I had two young children to bring up and although I had learned a lot from Gary over the years I did not have his experience and expertise in the world of antiques.'

Mim therefore decided that, whilst remaining in the antique trade, she would concentrate on items unusual to most antique shops — clothes. Over the next few years she reduced the stock of antique furniture replacing it with a wide array of clothing dating from the Victorian era through the twenties and

94

thirties and into the fifties. She continued to deal in old jewellery and bric-a-brac, but became well known throughout the area for her massive collection of period clothing ranging from a Victorian evening gown or top hat to a pair of 1950's winkle-pickers or more recently 1970's platform shoes. When a book on *Hull in the Fifties* was published in 1994 and a large local bookshop decided to have a window display to promote sales it was Mim whom they called on to supply the necessary apparel etc. She willingly obliged by supplying a gents suit, ladies dresses, a clock, and a television all from the 1950's.

Mim remains to this day the proud owner of Arcade Curios and has recently, following the current Seventies revival, been kept busy with customers eager to get the right look but with the original fashions.

NO. 16 HEPWORTH'S ARCADE

Mrs. Harriet Riley, Costumier 1896-1897

Regrettably no information has been uncovered on Mrs. Riley other than that she appears to have been the first tenant of nos. 16 and 18.

James Brook, Artificial Teeth Manufacturer/Drug Stores 1899

Although listed as a manufacturer of artificial teeth in the Cooks Directory of 1899 (one of five operating in the city at the time) when the Kelly's publication was printed later that year James' shop was described as being a Drug Stores. Although the business commenced occupying both no. 16 and the neighbouring premises of no. 18 by the time the 1900 directories were published it had vacated no. 16 and dropped the description of Artificial Teeth Maker completely. Neither the name nor the business were listed after 1900.

National Cash Register Co./George Bright, District Agent 1900

George Pendrill Bright is listed as living at 16 Hutt Street for seven years from 1897 but is only attributed in one year as being a tenant in the Arcade. That was in 1900 whilst district agent for the National Cash Register Company. The company had been in existence in the city since 1899 in which year they were listed at 44 Chariot Street.

National Cash Register Co./C. Millward, Agent 1901

Following the brief existence of George Bright came an equally short stay as area agent for the National Cash Register Company by C. Millward. Following their departure from the Arcade the company had offices in George Street, Jameson Street, Carr Lane and West Street before moving to Storey Street during the War. They are last listed in the city as NCR Ltd. in Tivoli House, South Street in the late 1970's.

The National Electric Alarm Clock Co. 1901-1903

Quite possibly an extension of the above mentioned company The National Electric Alarm Clock Company obviously failed to make an impression either nationally or at least in Hull as they are not listed after 1903.

Isaac Gardiner, Watchmaker 1904-1911

See no. 10 Hepworth's Arcade.

Farmer and Co., Cutlers 1913-1937

See no. 18 Hepworth's Arcade.

George William Dinsdale, Dealer in Novelties 1939-Present Date

See no. 10 Hepworth's Arcade.

NO. 18 HEPWORTH'S ARCADE

Mrs. Harriet Riley, Costumier 1896-1897

See no. 16 Hepworth's Arcade.

James Brook, Artificial Teeth Manufacturer and Drug Stores, 1899-1900

See no. 16 Hepworth's Arcade.

G. Farmer and Co., Cutlers and Fancy Goods Dealers (later known as Leather and Fancy Goods) 1901-1973

The founder of this business George farmer was born in Hougham in Lincolnshire in 1849, the son of an agricultural worker. By 1875 when he married Eva Oldale he had moved to Sheffield and was working as a wireworker. It would undoubtedly have been in Sheffield which is noted for its fine cutlery where George would have learned his trade as a cutler before moving to Hull in 1898.

The 1899 Hull Directory shows G. Farmer and Co. (Cutlers) as occupying no. 9a Mytongate, but by the following year the concern had moved next door to no. 8. A year later in 1901 the business was listed with two outlets, also having opened at no. 18 in the Arcade.

By 1903 at which time George was listed as living at 6 Wycliffe Grove, Argyle Street, the Mytongate address had disappeared leaving just one shop at 18 Hepworth's Arcade.

In 1906 George moved his family home to 16 Argyle Street but only appears to have stayed there for one year as the following year, 1907, in addition to opening a second shop at no. 4 Charles Street, he moved house again to no. 3 May Villas, May Street. The same year the business, which since its formation in 1898 had been known as G. Farmer and Co., altered its name to

George Farmer.
Courtesy of Basil King.

E. Farmer and Co. It is a reasonable assumption that George, who had been listed in the 1906 Directory not as a cutler but as a cutlery salesman, possibly, at that time, went out selling leaving his wife Eva to run the shop, hence the change of name.

By 1908 the shop in Charles Street was no longer listed and the following year (1909) the Farmer family again moved house to no. 65 De Grey Street where George was to live until his death some 19 years later.

1913 brought about expansion with the business taking over the neighbouring shop no. 16 which had previously been vacated by Isaac Gardiner, watchmaker.

George Farmer retired in 1920 at the age of 71 and five years later in 1925 he and his wife Eva celebrated their Golden Wedding

Eva Farmer.
Courtesy of Basil King.

Anniversary. He died on 17th April 1928. Of his six children only George Junior and Florence survived him the others having apparently died in infancy.

On the retirement of his father in 1920 George Junior took over the family business be it for only a very short time. George Junior had apparently previously worked and trained with his father, but unlike him had little interest in the business or the work involved and would reportedly grasp any opportunity that would take him away from the shop. Consequently the business suffered to such an extent that a decision was reached by Mr. and Mrs. Farmer that their daughter Florrie would take over the business with her husband Ernest Wurr. George Junior was, along with his wife, set up in a grocery and sweets shop in Princes Road but he seemed unable to settle into anything for long and later moved to Canada. Again unable to settle he returned to the UK and for a time ran a wood-yard in the Princes Road/Queens Road area. George Farmer Junior died in 1947 aged 68.

Ernest Wurr who was a painter and decorator by trade is first listed as being the proprietor in the 1926 Directory which also showed his home address as being 65 De Grey Street the home of Mr. and Mrs. Farmer. He remained in the business until 1934 when, reverting to his own trade, he opened a wallpaper shop on Chanterlands Avenue which he operated until the beginning of the War when the family were evacuated to Mythomroyd. After the War the couple returned to Hull and resumed the business in the wallpaper shop but later in the early 1950's left the city again moving to Ryde, Isle of Wight where they opened a boarding house. Ernest Wurr died in 1957 and his wife Florrie four years later in 1961.

Ernest and Florence Wurr.   Courtesy of Basil King.

During the time the business was being operated by George Farmer Senior and his wife Eva they took into their employ a young lady by the name of Olive Dean. In later years Olive became a close friend of the family and would join them each year for Christmas dinner. When the running of the business passed to Mr. and Mrs. Wurr she continued to work in the shop and in 1934 when Ernest and Florrie decided to move away from Hull the business was sold to Olive.

Olive took the decision to return to just one shop and prior to passing the business over Ernest Wurr rebuilt the wall which had been removed over thirty years earlier to join the two premises.

Olive was assisted in the shop by her elder sister Ada who, like the founder of the business, was very active in the local Labour Party.

In addition to the cutlery on which the business was based the two ladies crocheted armchair covers which were sold in the shop along with a selection of luggage, leatherware and fancy goods.

The sisters continued to run the shop for nearly forty years by which time Ada was in her nineties and Olive in her late eighties. Neither of the ladies ever married and they shared a house in Anlaby before passing away within seven weeks of each other in the early part of 1973.

Mrs. Muriel Wilson who was a niece of the two ladies recalls:

'I remember as a young girl calling to visit my two aunts at the shop in the Arcade. It was only a small shop and had a cast iron stove in the corner on which they would boil their kettle to make tea. Whenever one of the children in the family had a birthday we would have a little party in the room above the shop. The old part of Hull was, at one time, often flooded and I recall one occasion when this

98

happened during opening hours and my father had to go down and carry my aunties out of the Arcade.

Keith Yeomans recalls:

'The two ladies were my great aunts and when I was a youngster in the 1950's and early 1960's I was often taken to visit them at the shop in the Arcade. I recall it being like walking into a bygone age with pre-war adverts dotted around the walls.'

George William Dinsdale, Dealer in Novelties 1974-Present Date

See no. 10 Hepworth's Arcade.

NO. 20 HEPWORTH'S ARCADE

Bowden Brothers, Confectioners 1899-1929

Ada and Olive Dean.
Courtesy of Muriel Wilson,

The business of Bowden Brothers was first established in the latter part of the nineteenth century in Ashton-under-Lyne by the sons of Rev. Andrew Bowden, the Baptist Minister for the area. It is not known if all of the sons (there were four in all) played a part in the business but sources would suggest that at least three were involved. The 1891 census lists Andrew, then aged 21, as a confectioner so it is very likely that he contributed the basic knowledge to the business whereas his brothers Herbert (24). Carey (19) and Arthur (15) are all shown as accountants. It is known that Carey was very involved and it was apparently he who led the business from a local concern based at the old manorial flour mill which stood on the River Tame to become a household name throughout the north of the country as 'Bowden's Biscuit Bazaars' opened up in many of the major towns and cities in Yorkshire and Lancashire. Additional outlets were opened, mainly in Market Halls and Arcades, as the fame of Bowden's biscuits and sweets spread south with branches in the Potteries and Wales. In 1923, to extend their business as biscuit, sweets and chocolate manufacturers the firm acquired the long established company of John Hill and Sons, biscuit and cake manufacturers based in Smith Street, Ashton. Carey or Carey Megaw Bowden to give him his full title was appointed Chairman and the two businesses, although managed as separate concerns, operated side by side at the Tudno Works, Smith Street for over forty years. During this period Carey who had been keen for many years to involve himself in local council affairs stood as a Conservative candidate in 1928 and was elected as representative for the St. Michaels Ward. Later in 1933 he was elected Mayor and in 1944 at the age of 72 was made a Freeman of the Borough in

Carey Megaw Bowden.
Courtesy of Tameside Library.

recognition of his public services. In 1945 the business was sold to Mr. Hugh William Smith but Mr. Bowden retained his position as Chairman until 1954 when Mr. Smith succeeded him. Carey did however continue to attend the office up until his death on Boxing Day 1955 aged 83 and it is said that when the grand old man died so did a part of the company as it was then that they ceased to manufacture cakes and concentrated on biscuits having built up a business which supplied not only the 'Bowden's Biscuit Bazaars' but also thousands of customers at home and abroad.

Mrs. Kathleen Holgate who started working for Bowdens in 1936 aged 14 recalls:

'Mr. Bowden was the perfect English gentleman with a flair for figures. He could do an addition of four columns of figures adding pounds, shillings and pence in his head and his total was always right.'

In the late 1960's to enable the company to concentrate on manufacturing, the retail side of the business (known as Bowdens Retail), was sold to Elkes Biscuits of Uttoxeter. When that company was taken over by Adams Biscuits in 1972 the 26 shops still remaining were sold to former Elkes employee Fred Hodgson. Fred Hodgson recalls:

'When Adams took over Elkes they had no interest in the retail outlets which covered a very wide area from Newcastle in the north to Pontypool in the south and from Wrexham in the west to Grimsby in the east. I took control in 1972 but regrettably the main business of loose biscuits was rapidly being killed off by pre-packed biscuits and cut price supermarkets. I sold off the outlets independently over a nine year period with the final one to go being the branch in the Market Hall at Longton in the Potteries which closed in 1981.'

Hill's Biscuits continues to prosper in Ashton-under-Lyne once again in private ownership following a fourteen year spell from 1965 to 1979 when they became a part of John McIntosh and Sons Ltd. The name of Bowden also still has a presence in the area as following the sale of John Hill and Sons in 1965 Hugh Smith formed another company dealing with investments by the name of Bowden Holdings. This business continues to this day in nearby Cheadle and is managed by his son Tony.

The name of Bowden Brothers in Hull first appeared in the directories in 1899 as occupying nos. 20 and 22 Hepworth's Arcade an address at which they were to stay for over thirty years. During that time, in 1906, they opened a second branch in the city occupying stall nos. 17 and 18 in the New Market Hall as it was then known for eleven years before reverting to just the shops in the Arcade. In 1925 they were again credited with two branches having taken over a shop at no. 40 Hessle Road and five years later, in 1930, although maintaining the number of outlets at two, reduced the size of their premises in the Arcade by vacating no. 20. The business continued to operate from 40 Hessle Road and 22 Hepworth's Arcade until 1933 and it is known that at least one branch survived in the City until 1936 but after that date the name of Bowden appears to have vanished from the streets of Hull. It remains something of a mystery why the firm which by all accounts appeared to be prospering at the time should choose to end its presence in a city that just three years earlier was supporting two outlets and it is indeed difficult to even speculate what could have prompted such a sudden and abrupt termination of trading in Hull by the company.

Myton Cycle Depot, Cycle Agents 1930

Cycling in the 1920's and 1930's was very popular not only as a form of transport but also as a pastime, so it is not surprising that the directory for 1930 lists a total of 80 cycle makers, agents and repairers in the City. The Myton Cycle Depot first appeared in the Hull Directories in 1928 as cycle accessory dealers at premises at no. 10 Mytongate, but it is noted that the same address is also attributed to a Percy Cheals who is described as a cycle maker, dealer and repairer. By the following year the address of 10 Mytongate had been taken over by The Wholesale Supply Co. who coincidentally were also cycle dealers and had previously operated from the neighbouring premises at nos. 11 and 12. Mr. Cheals was operating from his home address of 123 Mersey Street and the Myton Cycle Depot was not listed. When the 1930 directories were published the name of Myton Cycle Depot had been resurrected at new premises at no. 20 Hepworth's Arcade although Percy Cheals was still listed at his residence. It is therefore not possible to establish whether that gentleman was behind this concern or if he merely shared the property in Mytongate with them. Regardless of the ownership of the venture the Myton Cycle Depot was listed in the Arcade for one year only after which time they failed to be included in the directories and it would therefore appear that the venture was a casualty of the slump that spelled the end for many businesses in the decade before the Second World War.

Arts and Crafts, (C. and M. Stocks) Handicrafts Supplies 1950-1964

See no. 7 Hepworth's Arcade.

Arts and Crafts, (P. Tuxworth and A. Johnson/Brenda Rankin) Handicraft Supplies 1965-1970

Following the sudden death of Christopher Stocks (see no. 7 Hepworth's Arcade) the shop at nos. 20 and 22 was closed for some time although the stock from his business remained on the premises. Following discussions with the

101

Council and the descendants of Mr. Stocks, Patricia Tuxworth and Alan Johnson (see also nos. 9/11 and 12 Hepworth's Arcade) plunged into a business about which they had little practical knowledge and took over the handicrafts shop.

Whether it was from their own efforts or possibly through the trade that Christopher Stocks had built up over the years is unsure, but regardless of the reason Pat and Alan successfully operated the business for a period of five years.

In 1970, having sold off their interest in the coin and stamp shop at no. 12 the previous year to take over the running of the café at nos. 9 and 11, the partners obviously decided to concentrate their efforts and finances on that business and consequently signed both the lease and the business over to Patricia's sister Brenda Rankin. Brenda kept the concern for only a very brief period before closing later the same year after agreeing terms with Brian Tozer and Alan Mayes for the lease on the premises.

East Coast Ceramic Company, Hand Made Ceramics Etc. 1970-1973

Whilst studying ceramics and hand painted textiles at Hull College of Art Brian Tozer met Alan Mayes, a student in sculpture. In later years, together with Brian's wife Sally, they formed the East Coast Ceramic Company and commenced in business from premises in Princes Avenue where they produced a wide range of hand crafted goods.

When they took over the lease of nos. 20 and 22 Hepworth's Arcade in late 1970 it was the original intention of the partnership to transfer the whole operation there including the potters' wheels and kilns. Regrettably due to restrictions in the lease this was not possible and Brian and Alan continued to produce from their base in Princes Avenue and Sally took charge of sales in the shop.

The range of goods being sold extended from hand-painted ceramics and pottery to a wide range of crocheted articles, leatherware, candles and hand-made jewellery. Brian later admitted that the very concept of the business was probably 'before its time' as, in the early 1970's, the public did not fully appreciate the appeal or individuality of hand-crafted goods as they have in later years and consequently the venture struggled to survive.

Towards the end of their lease in 1973 they were approached by Peter Young who owned the premises on the corner of Prince Street and King Street near the Hull open market. Peter operated a business from the building which was formerly a turf accountants selling hand-made goods including ceramics and Brian and Sally became 'Potter in Residence' in the workshops on the first floor. Although the upper floor, which was once the workshop, has since been converted into a café, the ground floor remains to this day an outlet for pottery and decorative ceramics and still operates under the original title of Studio 10 and a half.

In later years Brian and Sally became involved in various 'Action in the Community' projects based at Humberside (later Spring Street) Theatre and ran summer workshops in pottery and other crafts. They have since moved to Pickering where they continue to manufacture and sell hand crafted goods

under the banner of Rock Cottage Crafts named after their home in the town.
Brian Tozer recalls:

> 'I remember whilst we were tenants the Council undertook a phase
> of modernisation in the Arcade including the replacement of the
> original Victorian toilets. Three of those were beautifully decorated
> both inside and out with a blue handpainted design on a white
> background and were destined for the scrapheap before I rescued
> and restored them. Two, I believe, were sent abroad by their buyers
> but the third I recall being bought by a gentleman who was
> converting an old school house in Market Weighton into living
> accommodation. To the best of my knowledge it is probably still
> there — Edwin would be pleased.'

Sally adds:

> 'The atmosphere in the Arcade at the time was very much of a
> well-knit community. Many of the proprietors or their employees
> had children, (we had three girls at the time) and they all played
> together, with respective parents taking turns in supervision. There
> was always a tacit understanding of communal co-operation.'

Handicrafts of Hull Ltd., Handicraft Supplies 1973-1987

Supercast Ltd. was founded in 1966 and occupied premises in Blanket Row,
Queen Street, Hull from where they manufactured moulds for garden
ornaments etc.

Handicrafts of Hull.
Courtesy of Hull City Council Planning Department.

103

*Rosa Barker with Womble
in Hepworth's Arcade.*

Following expansion into larger premises in the same street the company decided to branch out into the retail trade and negotiated the purchase of the business owned by Ann Shimmels at 17 Hepworth's Arcade. Shortly after that deal was completed the shops at nos. 20 and 22 Hepworth's Arcade became available and, following discussions with the Arcade landlords — Hull City Council, it was agreed that the company would move the concern to those premises.

As the retail operation was to be controlled independently from the parent company it was decided to name the venture Handicrafts of Hull. Under the management of Rosa Barker the shop sold, in addition to the moulds manufactured by Supercast, a wide array of handicraft materials. Rosa recalls:

> 'Over the years we supplied felt for displays at Hull Museums, helped theatre companies such as Remould and Truck with stage dressing and, as students enjoyed a discount, I feel we also contributed to many City and Guilds achievements.'

Rosa is pictured with a three feet high Womble which she made as the prize in a competition to raise funds for the children's ward at Hull Royal Infirmary. A six feet version of the same creature, also made by Rosa, stood for many years in the children's waiting area at the hospital. At the beginning of 1987, following nearly fifteen years of trading, Handicrafts of Hull closed for business for the final time. The parent company Supercast moved from its base in Blanket Row in 1980 taking new premises in Hawthorn Avenue and to this day continues in the manufacture of moulds not only for the home trade but also for export to many countries throughout the world.

Baxters Coins and Stamp Exchange and Gift Shop 1990-Present

See no. 12 Hepworth's Arcade.

NO. 22 HEPWORTH'S ARCADE

R. Cheffings Bird, Jeweller 1896-1897

Reuben Cheffings Bird was born in Spilsby in Lincolnshire in 1850 and was by trade a jeweller. In 1889 he is listed in the electoral registers for Hull as living at number 7 North Church Side which was just a few doors from his place of employment — William Taylor's Jewellers at 50 Market Place.

It is known that in 1891 at which time he was residing at Purbeck House, 227

Boulevard, with his wife Emily and one servant, he was manager of Mr. Taylor's establishment and it could safely be assumed, judging by his improved residential address coupled with the fact that he was in a financial position to employ a servant, that he was significantly successful in that position.

In 1896 Reuben left the employ of Mr. Taylor and started in business himself taking over the previously unoccupied shop at no. 22 Hepworth's Arcade. His new premises were not far from Mr. Taylor's shop which stood on the corner of North Church Side and Market Place and it is possible that Reuben had this fact in mind when he took the shop perhaps with the hope of luring some of the customers he had established over the years he spent with Mr. Taylor to his own business. If indeed that was his intention the 'Christmas at the Shops' article published in the *Hull Daily Mail* in December that year would certainly have done his cause no harm and read as follows:

> 'Mr. R. Cheff Bird has just opened a jewellers and fancy shop in Hepworth's Arcade, Mr. Bird, as many readers of the *Mail* know, was for 14 or 15 years Manager at the shop, 50 Market Place, and his many friends will doubtless note his removal and will easily find him in his new place of business. He is prepared to supply athletic clubs, football clubs and angling clubs with medals, cups or any other description trophy or prize at his well known low prices. Mr. Bird has a nice stock of fancy goods and all are fresh and new. There are watches, chains, gem rings, marble clocks, brooches, gold and silver ornaments, all kinds of plate, wedding rings and many articles suitable for gifts this season. As an old optician it may be mentioned that Mr. Bird supplies glasses and spectacles suited to all sights. Clubs and societies supplied with his well known care and attention.'

For the purpose of his business Reuben's full name was often shortened to R. Cheff. Bird, but the *Hull Daily Mail* definitely did not do him any favours in the advert he placed on 4th February the following year pictured and it is very likely that the instructions for this were taken verbally and misheard as he is inadvertently shown as Jeff Bird.

By the time of publication of the Cooks Directory later that year Mr. Bird had moved his business from the Arcade and taken new premises at 50 Market Place. That address was one which was, at the time, shared by six different businesses and was probably therefore a large shop that had at some

HAVE YOU BEEN THROUGH THE NEW ARCADE, MARKET-PLACE ?

IF SO; HAVE YOU NOTICED

JEFF BIRD'S

NEW WATCHMAKING AND JEWELLERY ESTABLISHMENT ?

If not, go at once and see the Grand Display of Presentation Prizes, Medals, &c., for the Norton Cycle Club. Hull and District Rugby Union Football Clubs, Hull Bicycle Club, Hull Commercial School, Humber Total Abstinence Cycling Club, Fenner's Cricket Club, Universal Angling Association, Londesboro' Quadrille Assembly, George and Dragon Recreation Club.

REPAIRS, RE-GILDING, &c., a Speciality

CLOSE AT ONE ON THURSDAYS.

Hull Daily Mail advertisement 1897.
Courtesy of the Hull Daily Mail.

stage been split into several separate units. It is however noted that the only alteration from the Kelly's Directory earlier that year was the absence of Mr. Taylor's establishment so it would appear very likely that Reuben had taken over his ex-employer's shop. Reuben remained at those premises for a period of three years during which time he was also attributed with the address of no. 1 North Church Side although, as no. 50 Market Place was on the corner of the two streets, it is likely that the two addresses were one and the same building or alternatively were perhaps joined to make one larger shop. In 1900 Mr. Bird was on the move again, this time to more extensive premises further south down Market Place at no. 44. The new property was a three storey building situated immediately north of where the new extension to the King William Public House now stands and the shop, onto which the name R. C. BIRD, CITY JEWELLER was painted in large letters, can often be seen in the background of the many photographs and illustrations of the King William Statue from around the turn of the century.

On Monday 9th December 1901 Reuben attended his business as usual but was, later that day, taken home ill. He died the following day of heart failure aged only 51.

His widow Emily continued in the business for a further two years trading under her own name, but by 1904 had obviously sold the concern as no. 44 Market Place, although still listed as a jewellers, was attributed to a Mr. Alfred Moss.

Bowden Brothers 1899-1933

See no. 20 Hepworth's Arcade.

Arts and Crafts (C. and M. Stocks) 1950-1964

See no. 7 Hepworth's Arcade.

Arts and Crafts (P. Tuxworth and A. Johnson/B. Rankin) 1965-1970

See no. 20 Hepworth's Arcade.

East Coast Ceramic Company 1970-1973

See no. 20 Hepworth's Arcade.

Handicrafts of Hull 1973-1987

See no. 20 Hepworth's Arcade.

Baxters Coin and Stamp Exchange and Gift Shop 1990-Present

See no. 12 Hepworth's Arcade

NO. 24 HEPWORTH'S ARCADE

Although the address of no. 24 Hepworth's Arcade is the newest addition to those in the Arcade the premises themselves are not new but are actually the greater part of the ground floor of no. 61 Market Place. In 1994 the tenants of that property Eddison, Jackson and Dufton decided that they no longer required the ground floor part of their premises although they wished to maintain their occupation of the upper floors and the cellar. Arrangements were therefore made to convert part of the ground floor into an independent shop unit. As the premises at no. 61 already had two doorways with one facing Market Place and one leading into the Arcade the transformation was not a difficult one and following a brief period a separate shop was formed with Eddison Jackson and Dufton retaining the Market Place entrance and window space and, by means of a corridor created at the rear of the new shop, access to the cellar beneath the property.

Kingston Stationers 1994-Present Date

Although the name of Kingston Stationers did not appear on the streets of Hull until the early 1980's the business to which it refers can be traced back to the last century. Under the name of W. R. Goddard and Co. (later Goddard and Lancaster, Goddard and Son and Goddard, Walker and Brown) the business occupied premises in Silver Street from as early as 1838 operating as printers, stationers and lithographers. In later years, having changed their name to Goddard and Crawley the concern occupied the premises directly to the east of the Silver Street entrance to the Arcade at no. 7 Silver Street in addition to operating from an address in Ropery Street. In the late 1970's a decision was made to concentrate on the printing side of the business and that the stationers outlet in Silver Street would be sold. Because the name of Goddard and Crawley would be retained by the printing operation the new owner Pat Tuxworth (see also nos. 9 and 11, 20 and 22 and 12 Hepworth's Arcade) renamed the shop Kingston Stationers. The business was later moved to the newly built shops in North Church Side and in 1992 was sold again to the current owner. Two years later, following the alterations to the ground floor of no. 61 Market Place creating no. 24 Hepworth's Arcade, Kingston stationers moved to their present address. Although now operating from smaller premises the business continues to provide a much needed service to the many solicitors, accountants and other professional offices that occupy the 'Old Town' of Hull.

61 MARKET PLACE

Although the ground floor premises at no. 61 Market Place are relatively small, because of the extensive additional space on the first, second and third floors this shop is one of the largest properties in the Arcade. As explained previously the ground floor area has recently been separated from the rest of no. 61 to form a self-contained shop but the front door and window along with the cellar beneath the property still form part of no. 61. It has been noted that, prior to the building of the Arcade, Joseph Hepworth's shop at nos. 60 and 61 Market Place also had a cellar and it is therefore very likely that the current cellar was formed from that part of Mr. Hepworth's premises. The upper floors of the property span the Arcade and also a part of no. 60 Market Place and the first floor is, like the ones at numbers 8 and 9 Silver Street, at a slightly higher level than those in the rest of the Arcade.

Mrs. Kate Stanton, Boot Warehouse 1895-1924

Thomas Stanton who was born in Leeds around 1846 commenced in business in Stockton-on-Tees in 1868 in a small way from premises at 8 Bishop Street. By the following year he had taken over the neighbouring premises of no. 9 and two years later, still at the same address advertised under the name of the Royal Star Boot Company.

The 1881 census would suggest that after just thirteen years the business was a prospering one as listed as residing with Thomas and his wife Kate at their home at 127 High Street, Stockton were their three children, four shoeshop assistants (including Kate's two brothers Michael and Daniel), five servants and a nursemaid. This would imply that not only was their house, which incidentally was only a few doors from their shop at 139 High Street, considerably large but also that the family was a wealthy one being in a position to afford a total of six servants.

In the twenty years following his first venture into business and leading up to his death in 1888, Thomas had expanded the once small affair into one of the principal boot and shoe retailers in the North East of England having established branches in Newcastle, Sunderland, Middlesbrough, West Hartlepool and Darlington.

Following the death of her husband the reins of the family firm fell to his wife Kate who was born in Liverpool around 1853. She was presumably assisted by her two brothers.

By 1897 Kate had not only managed to maintain the business empire founded by her late husband but had overseen further expansion to include shops in South Shields, Liverpool, Bradford, Dewsbury and Hull. The branch in Newcastle which had become the firm's headquarters was a four-storey building in Clayton Street in the city and one publication in the latter part of the last century estimated the total stock held between the various branches as being in excess of half a million boots and shoes. A sketch of the premises in Clayton Street was used by the company on their bill heading.

The company advertised widely and the name of Stantons and Stantonia Footwear became, according to one publication, synonymous with all that is good and profitable in the boot and shoe business.

Following the turn of the century the business became known as Kate Stanton and Son and although it is known that Mrs. Stanton had two sons —Thomas and John — it has not been possible to verify which of these joined

K. Stanton Billheading.
Courtesy of Newcastle upon Tyne Library.

her in the family firm. It has, however, almost certainly been established that only one of the boys came into the business so it is possible that the other either died young or opted for a career elsewhere.

By the 1920's the advertising undertaken by the firm had reached far greater proportions as, in addition to advertising regularly in the press and other publications, they also undertook to have the words 'STANTONIA FOOTWEAR' emblazoned across the roof of the South Stand of Middlesbrough F.C.'s Ayresome Park. Part of that advertisement can be seen on the photograph taken from a match programme in 1929.

The name of Stanton's footwear first appeared in the streets of Hull in 1895 when Kate took over the newly completed shop at the North Eastern end of Hepworth's Arcade — 61 Market Place.

A *Hull Daily Mail* advert announcing the opening day of 2nd August enquired:

Advertisement from Heavysides Almanac.
Courtesy of Stockton on Tees Library.

'Ask your friends in Bradford, Liverpool, Newcastle, Sunderland, South Shields, Hartlepool, Middlesbrough, Stockton and Darlington who Mrs. Stanton is'

and responded to its own question with

'They will tell you she is the great boot provider of the North.'

Within two months Mrs. Stanton again advertised in the *Hull Daily Mail* expressing her grateful thanks to the people of Hull for their liberal support since opening which would suggest that the latest addition to her growing chain of branches had made a prosperous start in the city.

A later advert for the business taken from the 27th February 1896 edition of the *Hull Daily Mail* would suggest that advertising played a great part in the success of the company and that great efforts were made to ensure that the Stanton's adverts stood out from the rest. It could be suggested that this approach was a successful one as by 1906 a second branch at 300 Hessle Road had opened.

An 1897 publication entitled *Kingston upon Hull Illustrated* quoted the following rhyme which was presumably used by the company to further encourage potential customers:

The south stand of Ayresome Park, Middlesbrough showing Stantonia advertisement.
Courtesy of Middlesbrough Football Club and Pat Webster.

'The Town is ringing with the news
'Stantons' are best for boots and shoes.'

The article also included an illustration of the premises on Market Place but it could be suggested that the artist perhaps tried to enhance the appearance of Stanton's shop and has included no. 60 Market Place as being part of their premises. That address was, at the time, occupied by Jacksons Hatters.

Little changed in the fortunes of the company locally until 1924 when the Market Place shop closed but the Hessle Road branch continued to trade for another half century before closing its doors for the final time in the mid 1970's.

As a company it is known that the firm passed through three generations of the Stanton family from Kate to her son and in turn to his two sons who eventually sold off the business in the 1950's to move into the property market.

Mrs. Mary Marrington who was manageress of the ladies' department of the Newcastle branch for fifteen years between 1945 and 1960 recalls:

'There were two brothers running the company at the time. The elder boy we did not see much of but Mr. Arthur who visited regularly was, I recall, the most charming man one could wish to meet, a gentleman to his

---

TIME AND TIDE WAIT FOR NO MAN,
NOR DO STANTON'S ALLOW THEIRS TO LAG.

THEIR BIG HALF-YEARLY
CLEARANCE SALE OF BOOTS AND SHOES
IS NOW IN PROGRESS,
AND ALL SURPLUS STOCK HAS BEEN MARKED DOWN, AND THOUSANDS OF PURCHASERS ARE TAKING ADVANTAGE OF THE MARVELLOUS BARGAINS OFFERED.

GO WITH THE TIDE
TO
STANTON'S GREAT BOOT SALE·
ARCADE CORNER, MARKET-PLACE, HULL.

BRANCHES—
STOCKTON, MIDDLESBROUGH, DARLINGTON, WEST HARTLEPOOL, NEW-CASTLE, SUNDERLAND, BRADFORD, SOUTH SHIELDS, LIVERPOOL, &c., &c.

Advertisement from the Hull Daily Mail 1896.
Courtesy of the Hull Daily Mail.

fingertips. One day he called whilst I was having lunch and rather than disturb my break he joined me for coffee and explained that he and his brother had sold the business to a company called Easifit, but that they were keeping the building in Clayton Street as they were going into the property market. He also told me that day how long Stantons had been in shoes and that his grandmother had started out selling odd pairs of shoes from a barrow in Stockton market. Apparently Easifit had always wanted a shop in the centre of Newcastle and that was one of the main reasons that they had chosen to buy the Stantons chain of branches.'

It is understood that, despite their takeover of the company, Easifit continued to trade under

Illustration of Stanton's premises in Market Place circa 1897.

the long established name of Stantons for some time after the acquisition.

The last known record of a branch shop outside of Hull using the name of Stantons was one listed at 2 Queen Street, Darlington in 1970.

Harry Dibb, Toy Dealer (Kiddieland) 1929-1948

See no. 60 Market Place

Thos. E. Kettlewell and Son, Shipbrokers 1952-1982

Thomas Edward Kettlewell gained his experience in shipping whilst working in his home town of Goole for the Goole Steam Shipping Company. Fed up with being overlooked for promotion Thomas took the brave move to start up in business alone and opened his first office in Goole in 1919.

Although not a young man, being into his late forties when he first ventured into business alone, Tom proved to be successful and in 1928 by which time he had been joined in the Company by his son Thomas Clayton Kettlewell, he opened a second office in Hull under the management of Eric Peasegood.

The Hull office which was based in Exchange Buildings, Bowlalley Lane, prospered in the business of ship's Agencies, Freight Forwarding and Chartering. During the Second World War the Company were the Humber Agents of British Iron and Steel Corporation and handled immense quantities of steel earmarked for the War effort. The Company was also involved in the

111

Thomas E. Kettlewell.
Courtesy of T. A. Kettlewell.

manufacture of some of the sections built for the Mulberry Harbour towed to Normandy following the invasion.

After the War it was felt that more space was needed if expansion was to continue and the decision was taken to move to premises at 61 Market Place on the corner of Hepworth's Arcade which offered a ground floor reception area and three spacious upper floors. The interior of the building was still badly affected by War damage and with all types of building materials at a premium and subject to Licence, it was necessary to make do with what could be secured and much of the office was patched up with hardboard. Whilst the Company was at 61 Market Place those premises became the head office of the Holderness Steamship Company. That business was an associated Company managed by Kettlewell's and operated a dozen coasters of about 1200 tonnes cargo capacity around the coast of the United Kingdom to the near Continent and into the Baltic up to the mid 1960's.

The photograph kindly supplied by Kettlewell's shows the offices and the Arcade in the early 1950's. Note the lack of parking restrictions in those days.

By 1974, Thomas Anthony Willmott Kettlewell, the grandson of the founder, had taken over responsibility of the Hull operation and in that year was appointed Consul for the Netherlands at Hull.

The Company spent thirty years at the offices in Market Place, but in 1982 moved again having purchased premises at 41 High Street which they fully refurbished and restored the remaining fragment of the Crowle Mansion which now forms the office entrance from the Courtyard.

Thomas Anthony Kettlewell, or Tony as he is known probably to avoid confusion with his father or grandfather, still heads the business interests in the City and is in fact the first of the Kettlewell family to work exclusively from the Hull branch. He is now assisted by his son Steve.

The original office in Goole still thrives under the management of Tony's brother Jeremy John Kettlewell and the Company's longstanding reputation in the steel trade is being furthered by successful developments headed by Tony's second son, Richard.

Times and business change, but Kettlewell have moved into fresh fields and have developed a significant warehousing and national distribution business

112

specialising in food, paper and palletised products from two sites they have developed at Ossett, West Yorkshire, adjacent to the M1 Motorway. With two members of the fourth generation now active in the business there is every hope for many further years trading in Hull to outshine the thirty good years they spent in the offices at the Market Place end of Hepworth's Arcade.

Tom Jackson and Dufton Ltd./Eddison, Jackson and Dufton/Eddisons Commercial, Estate Agents, 1982-Present Date

The company of Eddison, Jackson and Dufton was not, as might be expected, a business formed by three individuals, but actually three individual businesses which later amalgamated to form one large company. For the

Market Place entrance to Hepworth's Arcade circa 1950's.
Courtesy of T. A. Kettlewell.

purpose of this project it is therefore necessary to trace the history of the company not only to the date of its formation in 1987 but much further back to when each of the three separate businesses were founded.

The firm of Eddisons was formed in Huddersfield in 1852 by William Eddison and from the early days the majority of the company's business was that of auctioneers. Following the death of Mr. Eddison in 1874, Thomas Taylor, a senior partner in the business, took control and changed the name to that of Eddison and Taylor. In 1896, by which time the concern had expanded adding Valuers, Estate Agents and Fire Loss Assessors to its business description, a further partner John Booth had his name added to the title and the company became known as Eddison, Taylor and Booth. In later years the business came under the ownership of the Leeds Permanent Building Society and, until the merger with Messrs. Jackson and Dufton, traded under the name of Eddisons.

Tom Jackson commenced in business around the turn of the century at Arnold, Nr. Skirlaugh, as an auctioneer and valuer dealing predominantly in agricultural commodities and properties in the surrounding rural area. Some years later he was joined by his son also named Tom (but preferring the name of Bob) who, following a brief spell with his father left to join the R.A.F. He returned to the family business in 1950 and was made a partner, with the company name changing to Tom Jackson and Son. In 1959, three years after the death of Tom Jackson Senior, Bob was joined by Jim Richardson who later, in 1963, also became a partner. By this time the firm had expanded from the early days in rural Holderness and had established themselves as general auctioneers and estate agents with new offices at Craven House, 688 Holderness Road. The practice prospered and following the recruitment in 1969 of John Dennis who was made a partner after just three years with the firm, further expansion took place in 1976 when the company acquired the old established practice of Arthur Toby and Son in Hornsea.

James Dufton was born in Handsworth, near Sheffield in the early 1850's and some years later came to Hull as District Superintendent Inspector of the Sceptre Life Assurance Company. The 1891 census lists James at 34 Granville Street with his wife Mary and two daughters. The Sceptre Life Assurance Company was, by all accounts, a friendly society which it is understood was in later years taken over by the Eagle Star Insurance Group. James apparently originally worked as a collector for the company but later also started collecting rents on properties and later still developed his own business as an estate agent. Following a change of family residence to number 44 Granville Street from which address James was, in 1896, first listed in the directories as an estate agent, he opened his own offices in Bank Chambers, no. 11 Scale Lane. By 1901 in which year, in addition to the title of estate agent, he was also listed as being an insurance and mortgage broker, James again changed family residence moving to no. 12 St. Georges Road which could suggest that the venture was prospering. In later years James' eldest daughter Jessie married William Arthur Yell. Without a son of his own but keen that the business that he had founded and developed should not only stay within his own family but also maintain the family name, James put a proposition to his son-in-law. He proposed that, subject to William agreeing to change his name to Dufton, he would take him into the company and eventually make him a partner. William accepted, became William Arthur Dufton and helped to develop the property management side of the business. The consequent growth of the company necessitated removal to larger premises and the property of no. 2 Manor Street was acquired. During the early 1920's the business became known as J. and W. A. Dufton and following the death of the founder in the latter part of that decade William continued alone until 1931 when he was joined by his son James Ronald Dufton. By 1936 the company was known as J. and W. A. Dufton and Son and although the career of young James was interrupted by the Second World War he later returned to the family business. Whilst serving his country James held a commission in the Royal Artillery until he was invalided out of the Army due to a leg wound. The company remained at the office at 2 Manor Street for a period of nearly half a century although during that time found the need to establish additional premises at 169 Ferensway. In the early 1970's both Malcolm Dufton, the great grandson of the founder, and Jeremy Holmes joined the firm later to become directors and both gentlemen are, to this day, still involved with the concern. Following further expansion into premises at 12 Manor Street and 15a Manor Street the firm, under the title of the Dufton Partnership, relocated to no. 173 Ferensway whilst maintaining the shop premises at no. 169.

In 1980 the companies of Tom Jackson and Son and the Dufton Partnership merged to become Jackson and Dufton Ltd. and two years later moved their head office to no. 61 Market Place on the corner of Hepworth's Arcade.

Following the purchase of the company in 1987 by Property (Leeds) Ltd., a subsidiary of the Leeds Permanent Building Society, Messrs. Jackson and Dufton were amalgamated with the firm of Eddisons already owned by that company. Under the new name of Eddison, Jackson and Dufton the business offered wide expertise in all aspects of property surveys, valuation and management in addition to many years experience in auctioneering and agricultural transactions.

Since the merger the concern has again been divided into individual operations with the commercial side of the business under the name of Eddisons Commercial operating from the Market Place premises and the residential sector being catered for by the numerous branch offices under the name of Jackson and Dufton. Jeremy Holmes is currently based at the Market Place office and Malcolm Dufton at the branch in Beverley, although apparently spending much of his time in the West Riding overseeing the company's interests in that area.

NO. 60 MARKET PLACE

No. 60 Market Place is probably the most unusual of all of the shops in Hepworth's Arcade because it actually occupies two completely separate buildings. The photograph on page 35 clearly shows that the side of the shop to the north is part of the Hepworth's Arcade construction, whereas the southern section is actually part of the neighbouring building which was built over one hundred years earlier (see also B. Cooke and Son, 21 Hepworth's Arcade). The wall to the south of the premises forms part of the old Spread Eagle Entry and was originally the exterior wall to the Spread Eagle Tavern or Dram Shop. Evidence of two old doorways which at some stage have been bricked up can vaguely be seen in it. Above the shop on the first, second and third floors, the property is split with the northern portion being part of the upper floors to no. 61 and the southern section forming part of the neighbouring property of nos. 58/9.

Jacksons Ltd., Hatters 1896-1910

The origins of this company date back to 1862 when Isaac Jackson, originally of Staffordshire, left the employ of Jones and Sons, drapers in Sheffield and moved to Leeds. He formed a partnership with a Mr. Lomas under the name of Lomas and Jackson and commenced trading from Brittania Street in the City producing hats and caps. Following eighteen years in business, the partnership was dissolved and Isaac together with his son Samuel who had joined his father in the firm some five years earlier began operating under the name of Isaac Jackson and Son.

Following the death of Isaac in 1881 Samuel's brother Egerton Jackson joined the family firm which continued to grow and later changed its name to

Samuel Robinson Jackson.

Jacksons Ltd. Both Samuel and his brother were keen cricketers, with Samuel being captain of Leeds Cricket Club for thirteen years and having played for the County on two occasions. He also held the distinction of receiving the first ball ever bowled at Headingly Cricket Ground.

In addition to continuing their trade as wholesalers supplying a great number of outfitters throughout the country, Jacksons Ltd. also expanded into the retail market themselves. During a five year period spanning the late 1880's and the early 1890's the business established no fewer than 128 retail branches in England, Scotland and Ireland. It is possible that they later discovered their growth was perhaps a little premature to be successful as by the turn of the century that number had been reduced to around thirty.

The company became well known for supplying hats at one price — three shillings and ninepence (19 pence) and later when the business had expanded into selling boots which were also sold at one price — ten shillings and sixpence (52½ pence), became more so because of their advertising jingle.

'Jackson's boots and hats are fine
ten and six and three and nine.'

Such apparently was the success of this approach that all branches were reported in 1893 as doing a thriving trade with the public.

Jackson Ltd. hatters first appeared in the Hull Directories in 1895 with premises at 13 Waterworks Street, but by the following year had added the previously unoccupied shop at 60 Market Place on the corner of Hepworth's Arcade. It is possible that the lease of their second shop in Hull may have been acquired through a personal association with the Hepworth family whose business was very near to that of Jacksons in Leeds and it is also feasible that the Jackson brothers may have moved in the same social circles as either Joseph Hepworth or his son Norris.

The company continued to operate both outlets until 1908 when the shop in Waterworks Street moved several doors to no. 18 and in 1905 had received a tribute in the *Hull Daily Mail* from which the following extract is taken:

'Hats at one price — three shillings and ninepence — have made the name of Jacksons Ltd., well known in Hull. They have premises at 13 Waterworks Street and 60 Market Place ... These hats are to be

116

had in several shades besides the popular black, in a variety of shapes whether hard or soft .... Some stylish caps are also shown at one shilling and one shilling and sixpence. Last year the firm went into the boot business and have found it a very successful addition. These boots are all sold at one price ten shillings and sixpence in box calf, glacé kid and Krupp leather. They are also to be obtained in brown....'

Any possibility of a close trading relationship with Hepworth's is probably strengthened by the fact that in 1911 when Hepworth's moved their outlet from 8 Silver Street to no. 59 Whitefriargate, Jacksons also moved out of the Arcade to take over the neighbouring shop to Hepworth's at no. 57.

By 1914 the business in Hull must have been flourishing as, in addition to keeping their outlet in Whitefriargate, the company saw the need to expand their Waterworks Street shop into no. 20 next door.

Although both branches were maintained for over twenty years by 1936 the Whitefriargate shop had closed and although nos. 18 and 20 Waterworks Street were still listed in 1939 the company fails to be included in any of the local telephone directories either during or following the Second World War. It is a distinct possibility that the shop may have been demolished following the bomb damage sustained by many of the buildings in the area during the War and that following the end of the hostilities the company chose not to re-open in Hull.

It has been established that by the mid 1930's the firm was no longer under the control of the Jackson family although Samuel's son Edmund Horner Jackson was, at the time, a district manager with the company.

In 1936 Edmund left the business founded by his grandfather and ventured into business alone. The split with Jacksons Ltd. was by all

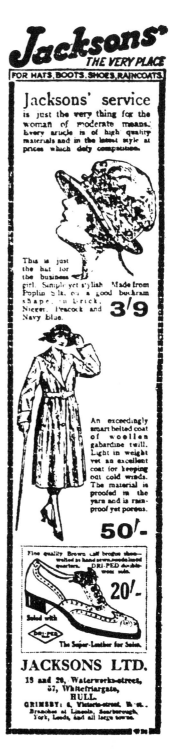

Hull Daily Mail advertisement 1922.
Courtesy of the Hull Daily Mail.

117

accounts a very amicable one with the company allowing him to take control of the outlets in Vicar Lane, Leeds and in York from which he operated under the name of Edmund Jackson Ltd. and dealt in a variety of gents apparel including both hats and boots.

Following the Second World War, by which time he had been joined in the business by his son Edmund Peter Jackson, Edmund Senior purchased Wm. Greensmiths Ltd., a long established gentlemen's outfitters in Harrogate and proceeded to run that business in tandem with his outlets in Leeds and York.

When Edmund Horner Jackson died in 1954 his son Edmund Peter took control of the business and three years later Jacksons Ltd., who were by that time dealing mainly in footwear, changed their name to the Saxone Shoe Company who are now part of the British Shoe Corporation.

In the mid 1970's Edmund Peter was joined in the family firm by his own son Edmund Paul Jackson.

The business continues to operate to this day under the banners of Greensmiths in Harrogate and Edmund Jackson Ltd. in York under the watchful eye of Edmund Paul Jackson (or Paul as he prefers to be known), the fifth generation of the Jacksons to take the reins of the family firm.

Harry Dibb with his daughter Mary.
Courtesy of Mary Hodges.

Emanuel Jacobs, Milliner 1911

Little evidence is available on Mr. Jacobs other than he occupied the premises for one year only in 1911. It is possible that Emanuel, who may even have been an ex-employee of Jacksons Hatters, saw the opportunity to capitalise on their departure by opening a similar business at the premises they had recently vacated. If that was the idea it can safely be assumed that it was not a successful one as by the following year the property is not listed in the directories and Mr. Jacobs also fails to be included in that or any of the successive publications.

Harry Dibb, Toy Dealer (Kiddieland) 1913-1926

The name of Harry Dibb, toy dealer first appeared in the Hull Directories in 1910 with premises at 143 Holderness Road. By 1913 he had expanded the business to two branches having taken over the empty shop at the south-eastern end of Hepworth's Arcade — no. 60 Market Place.

118

Harry who is pictured with his daughter Mary at their home in 1922 maintained the two shops until 1926 when he moved his Holderness Road branch from no. 143 to no. 203. He was at the time residing at East Thurston, Sutton Ings, which later became 849 Holderness High Road and was a large semi-detached house which would suggest that the business was prospering. By 1929 the Holderness Road branch had closed and the outlet on Market Place had transferred across the Arcade to No. 61 Market Place. The new shop was considerably larger than the one vacated and had additional space on the first, second and third floors which also spanned the Arcade.

With the new premises came a new name and 'Kiddieland' as the shop was christened soon became known throughout the region as the first place to call for all types of children's toys ranging from imported German and Czechoslovakian dolls with china heads to rocking horses and small cycles. In 1933 Harry changed residence moving to a larger house further along Holderness High Road which he named 'Eastfield' and the following year it has been noted that he was advertising in the local newspapers for a maid which would also suggest that the business was a successful one.

Marjorie Bolton (formerly Marjorie Merrylees) recalls:

> 'I started working for Mr. Dibb when I left school at the age of 15 in 1935. My cousin was a friend of Miss Worsnop the shop manageress and it was through that contact that I got the job. Christmas was a particularly busy time and I remember that Mr. Dibb would take over one of the vacant shops in the Arcade for the season and use it for selling cheaper toys. We had to work very late in the days leading up to Christmas and on Christmas Eve when we were open extra late Mr. Dibb would auction toys off to clear them. On several occasions when no other form of transport was available I got the job of walking dolls prams from Market Place to houses in the Avenues area. It was a long walk but I quite enjoyed it as it gave me a break from the shop.'

Ethel Worsnop who is mentioned in the recollections of Marjorie Bolton had been employed by Harry Dibb since leaving school and had worked her way up to become the shop manageress. Ethel apparently had a gift for repairing dolls and the 'Dolls Hospital' part of the business became well known throughout both Hull and the East Riding.

Mary Hodges (formerly Mary Dibb — Harry's daughter) recalls:

> 'As a child I often visited my father at the shop but was not allowed to play with the toys in stock although I do remember getting a rather nice fairy bike one Christmas. In later years I would help out during the busier times and recall that on one occasion when both my father and Miss Worsnop were unwell I was left to run the shop.
>
> Because of the shortage of new toys caused by both the recession and the War and probably because of the lack of money around in the 1930's people were more inclined to get their children's dolls repaired and Miss Worsnop became very proficient in replacing missing limbs and repairing loose heads.

In addition to the three upper floors the shop also had a cellar which would regularly flood when we had a high tide and was often knee deep in water and because of that problem could only be used to store the large wooden toys and old packing cases. In addition to toys the shop did a good trade in 'Bass Bags' which were made in very pliable straw and were sold as shopping bags. The doorway on Market Place had a mosaic floor with Kiddieland spelt out in the tiles.'

The shop was kept busy proving very popular with both visiting seamen and the farmworkers from Lincolnshire who made frequent shopping trips to the city via the Humber Ferry and the Christmas trade no doubt strengthened by late-thinking fathers who staggered from the many public houses in the area a little worse for wear and realising that Christmas was almost upon them.

Betty Tulloch (formerly Betty Drake) recalls:

'I worked at Kiddieland for four years from when I first left school in 1939. We were open until 6.00 p.m Monday to Friday and 9.00 p.m on Saturdays and had a large showroom on the first floor. Christmas was always a hectic period and it was seldom before midnight on Christmas Eve that we managed to serve the final customer and make our way home. After leaving Kiddieland I worked for a while for Harry Dibb's brother William, also a toy dealer, who had a shop on Cottingham Road.'

Harry Dibb, ably assisted by Ethel Worsnop, continued to operate the shop until the late 1940's when Harry retired and sold the business. The lease on the premises had expired so the new owners moved to nos. 15 and 17 in the Arcade taking with them not only the vast stock of toys and games but also Ethel who, with her years of knowledge of toy sales and repairs, was undoubtedly a valuable asset and continued in her position as manageress. (see also Arcade Stores, 15 Hepworth's Arcade).

Sadly, in 1951, just a few years after retiring from the business that became his life for nearly forty years, Harry Dibb was killed in a road accident. His shop in Market Place is fondly remembered by many generations of people in Hull some of whom recall being taken there as children and returning in later years with their own children.

Florence Ashton, Newsagent 1926-1946

See no. 10 Hepworth's Arcade.

Lawrence and Lazenby, Newsagents 1946-1950

When the names of Lawrence and Lazenby were first attributed to no. 60 Market Place in 1946 they already operated an existing newsagency at no. 58 King Edward Street. In the years that followed other branches were added and within two years of taking over from Florence Ashton the partnership operated no less than seven newsagency shops throughout the city. By 1949 that number had been reduced to four and the following year the whole business was sold to Tom Spencer.

T. Spencer (Hull) Ltd., Newsagents 1950-1961

It has not been possible to obtain much information on this company other than that it took over the interests of Lawrence and Lazenby in 1950 and that by the following year had added an additional outlet in Hessle. By the mid 1950's the number of branches had been reduced to just the shop on Market Place and that on King Edward Street. It is believed, although unconfirmed, that the owner Tom Spencer died and that following the death of her husband the business was sold by his widow. Further investigations uncover that a Tom Spencer, aged 78, died in Whitby in late 1960 although it has not been possible to establish, beyond doubt, that this was the same man.

R. and S. Sangwin Ltd., Newsagents/Arcade Newsagency 1961-1975

The name of Roy Sangwin first became known in the Hull area during the 1950's not as a newsagent but as a haulage contractor. With a national election looming which threatened to change the face of the transport business throughout the country, Roy began looking for alternative interests into which he could invest and opened a sweet shop in South Street in July 1959. Roy explains:

> 'There was a general election pending and the Labour Party had indicated that if they were voted into power it was their intention to nationalise the haulage industry. Obviously that would have had a severe effect on my own business so my wife and I looked around for alternative business oportunities and were offered a vacant shop in South Street which we opened as a sweet shop under the title of Shirley's named after my wife.'

The venture was obviously a success to such an extent that less than two years later in May 1961 Roy and Shirley successfully negotiated the purchase of T. Spencer (Hull) Ltd. which at the time operated shops at both 58 King Edward Street and 60 Market Place. The couple changed the name of the business to R. and S. Sangwin Ltd. and gave the outlet in Market Place the title of Arcade Newsagency. Following further expansion in May 1964 when the business also opened a branch in Hessle Square which coincidentally had in previous years been occupied by Thomas Branton's daughter Olive (see Brantons — no. 13 Hepworth's Arcade), the couple continued to operate all four outlets for a further three years before selling South Street in 1967. In 1971 the Hessle branch was sold and four years later the remaining business of R. and S. Sangwin Ltd. was bought by Phillip and May Rackham. Roy later retired to Cornwall from where he happily recollects on his days as a newsagent in Hull.

Arcade News (Phillip and May Rackham) 1975-1991

When, in 1975, Roy Sangwin decided to sell his remaining two shops Phillip Rackham and his wife May showed immediate interest. The couple operated a newsagency business on Holderness Road but, following the purchase of R. and S. Sangwin Ltd., gave up that concern to concentrate on the two outlets in the City centre. Phillip recalls:

> 'When we took over the shop on the corner of Hepworth's Arcade we also acquired the services of the resident cat Sammy. Apparently a

121

couple of years earlier Roy had experienced a problem with mice and when the cat owned by the Employment Office in Market Place had kittens he was offered one. Sammy stayed with us until his death in 1988 when he was about 15 years old and was probably one of my longest-serving employees.'

Phillip and May sold the shop in King Edward Street in 1988 separating the ownership of the two branches for the first time since the mid 1940's, but continued to operate Arcade News for a total of sixteen years before selling up in 1991.

Arcade News, (Peter Lee Spencer) 1991-Present Date

Following an early career with local manufacturers Reckitt and Colman Peter Spencer, together with his wife Jacqueline, moved into the newsagency business taking over the existing concern of East Park News on Holderness Road in 1981. Following nearly ten years at those premises the couple heard that the long-established newsagents at 60 Market Place was to be sold and following successful negotiations with the owner Phillip Rackham and the sale of their previous outlet the couple took over Arcade News in December 1991. Now in their fifth year of occupation Peter confesses that he prefers the hustle and bustle of a City centre newsagency and enjoys working in Hull's 'Old Town'.

NO. 21 HEPWORTH'S ARCADE

The address of no. 21 Hepworth's Arcade has only ever been allocated to two different businesses and not only were those listings over ninety years apart

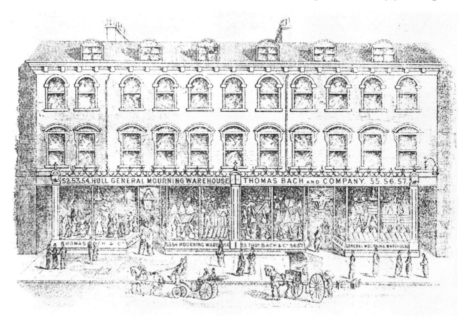

Illustration of the premises of Thomas Bach and Co. in Market Place.

122

but they also did not refer to the same premises. For the purpose of explaining this unusual situation in further detail the section covering no. 21 Hepworth's Arcade has been sub-divided into two separate headings 'Old' and 'New'.

NO. 21 HEPWORTH'S ARCADE (Old)
Thomas Bach and Co., Furriers 1899

Although Thomas Bach and Company were only attributed in the directories as having premises in Hepworth's Arcade for one year they were, for over forty years, one of the largest companies of general drapers, mourning warehousemen, milliners, costumiers and furriers in the City, occupying extensive premises in nearby Market Place. An advertisement taken from

51, 52, 53, 54, 55, 56 & 57, MARKET PLACE, HULL.

MOURNING
IS OUR
SPECIALITY.

COMPLETE

MOURNING OUTFITS
MADE TO ORDER

*By our own Experienced Staff on the Premises
at a few hours' notice.*

REASONABLE ESTIMATES GIVEN FOR

Household Mourning.

Grey is the prevailing colour this Season, in numberless shades. Black Grenadines will also be worn as the weather gets milder.

THOMAS BACH & CO.

Advertisement from the Hull Examiner 1890.

Atkinson's Directory of Hull in 1888 proclaims that the company offered the largest stock of mourning mantles, jackets, costumes and millinery in Yorkshire and that complete mourning outfits for either families or servants could be made to order at a few hours notice.

It was reported in an 1890 publication that the Company premises at 51-57 Market Place, Hull had no fewer than 22 different departments and that upwards of 150 hands were employed, and went on to add that, of those, fifty took all of their meals on the premises. The census of 1891 further verifies that at least twenty of the staff also lived on the premises.

Mr. Thomas Bach, the founder and sole proprietor of the business, resided in his later years at Ardmore House, Cottingham Road and continued to operate the concern until he passed away at the age of 72 in 1897. Although following his death the business continued to operate, it can be assumed that the new proprietor perhaps did not have the flair or expertise of Mr. Bach as by 1908 the business which had occupied seven shops whilst under the control of the founder had been reduced to only five and by 1911 had disappeared from the directories completely. The fact that a business with such extensive premises not twenty yards from the Arcade entrance should choose also to occupy what would be a comparatively small shop within it would seem a little unusual, although it is possible that the company might have thought their presence in the Arcade would perhaps help create an increase in sales at their main outlet. What, however, is even more puzzling is the shop credited to the Company — no. 21. As this section verifies that shop has only once, in 1899 whilst in the occupation of Bach and Co., been listed in the directories and none of the early plans that have been uncovered give any reference to a shop with such a number. It can, therefore, perhaps be assumed that the reference to no. 21 was a publisher's error and that either the number quoted was incorrect or that Bach and Company never actually occupied the Arcade. The latter is, however, unlikely as the entry not only appears in the Street section of the directory but is repeated in both the Alphabetical and Trades sections. The advertisement shown is taken from an 1890 edition of the *Hull Examiner* and further verifies the trade description attributed to Bach and Co. in the Hull Directories — Funeral and Mourning Warehousemen.

NO. 21 HEPWORTH'S ARCADE (New)

When a decision was taken to build a covered walkway between Hepworth's Arcade and the Market Hall which also entailed creating an extension at the rear of the Café it was necessary for the Arcade owners — Hull City Council to acquire a section of land owned by B. Cooke and Son and situated behind their premises on Market Place. Following negotiations with that company an agreement was reached whereby, in consideration of giving up the piece of land needed, the Hull City Council would build a new shop facing onto the Arcade for the company. The new shop which was built on land that had previously formed part of the Spread Eagle Entry (see plan on page 42) is situated immediately to the east of nos. 17 and 19 Hepworth's Arcade (see plan on page 16). Although the premises are the newest of all of those in the Arcade their only occupant, B. Cooke and Son, can lay claim to being the longest established of all of the current local tenants.

No. 21 Hepworth's Arcade.   Photograph by Graham Hardy.

B. Cooke and Son Ltd., Nautical Instruments Manufacturers, 1994-Present Date

Barnard Cooke was born in Allerthorpe, near York in 1812 the third son of a shoemaker. Both Barnard and his eldest brother Thomas chose not to follow in their father's footsteps but elected for careers in the study and manufacture of optical instruments. It is unlikely that their father, as a shoemaker, would have been able to provide the necessary finance to set his sons on the path for such a career and although little is known of Barnard's early working history it has been established that Thomas supported himself by working as a part-time tutor whilst devoting as much time as he could spare to a study of optical and mechanical

Barnard Cooke.
Courtesy of Pamela Gardam.

125

problems associated with the construction of telescopes. It is therefore feasible that Barnard, who was five years younger, followed a similar early career and possibly even gained some of his early training from his elder brother.

Thomas began in business in York in 1837 as a manufacturer of reflecting and refracting telescopes and it has been established that Barnard, who was listed in the 1841 and 1851 census returns as an optician, worked with his brother before moving to Hull some years later to start a business of his own. The first record of Barnard Cooke in Hull was in the 1863 Directory in which he is listed as an optician operating from 56 Savile Street, whilst residing at 23 Storey Street. By the time of publication of the 1867 Directory the business was listed as Barnard Cooke and Son and had moved to no. 55a Savile Street. It has been verified that Barnard had two sons and one daughter. Charles Henry Cooke, the elder of the two sons, is known to have been involved in the business and as the company has always been known as Barnard or B. Cooke and Son in the singular it is very likely that it was Charles to which the title refers. Sadly Charles died in 1868 aged only 24 and, although his younger brother Thomas Edwin joined the family business for a short while, he did not apparently have the same interest or dedication as his father or brother. By 1872 the business was on the move again taking new premises at no. 44 Savile Street above which Barnard lived and were unusually described as opticians and sewing machine agents. Barnard's daughter Fanny married Phillip Crook who was later appointed both Sheriff and Lord Mayor of Hull and became one of the most prominent residents of the City, but around 1880 Thomas, unable to settle into the family business, left England to start a new life in Australia. By 1882 the business, still operating from 44 Savile Street, was described not only as opticians but also as chronometer and clock makers. It is quite feasible that this would be a natural progression for an optician as it is well known that watchmakers and jewellers at the time also made and sold spectacles since they had both the equipment and the technical know-how required so it is equally possible that the same ruling in reverse should apply to opticians. That entry which also confirmed that Barnard was still residing at the same address as his business was the final one to include Mr. Cooke personally and it is known that he sold the concern shortly afterwards and returned to York. He died in 1887 aged 74.

It has not been possible to establish by whom the business was purchased but by 1885, although the concern was still listed as opticians, the title of chronometer and clock makers had been replaced by that of mathematical instrument makers. By 1900 the business had relocated to 35 Paragon Street and continued to operate from that address, which they later titled 'The Kingston Observatory' for twenty-seven years. During that time, in 1918, the company was sold again to the London firm of Henry Hughes and Son who installed an employee from their branch in the capital, Mr. Stacey Dickenson, as manager. It has been noted in the 1922 Directory that the name of B. Cooke and Son, to which the full title had been abbreviated, was unlisted and the premises at 35 Paragon Street were attributed to Henry Hughes and Son Ltd. operating under their own name. This may have been an error by the publishers but it is also conceivable that the owners may have thought it was time to introduce their own name to the people of Hull. Regardless of the reason for the omission, by 1925 the address was again listed as being in the occupation of B. Cooke and Son who were given the somewhat grand description of opticians, nautical instrument and compass makers and adjusters and wireless dealers. The following year Stacey Dickenson bought out the interests of B. Cooke and Son from his previous employer and four years later approached and secured the services of a Benjamin Saferty who had been apprenticed to that company in London. He persuaded young Ben to join him in Hull and later the same year moved the business to new premises at Monument House, Alfred Gelder Street.

The following year the firm was listed for the first time as being a limited company and was described simply as nautical instrument makers. By 1933 B. Cooke and Son Ltd. had moved again and occupied no. 1 Market Place on the corner of the junction with Scale Lane, and although that building sustained substantial damage during the Second World War the company stayed at the address for twenty-five years. During that period further premises at 48 Upper Union Street were added and Ben Saferty who had obviously progressed with the growth of the business was appointed onto the board of directors. During a meeting in 1988 with Pamela Gardam, the great, great-granddaughter of

B. Cooke and Son. The Kingston Observatory, 1 Market Place, Hull.
Courtesy of Sam Allon Ltd.

Barnard Cooke who was conducting some family history research, he recollected on his early days with the business and his early morning trips to the docks to try to promote sales on visiting ships and his meeting with seamen who later became famous ships owners including Aristotle Onassis during his days as a mere crewman. He remained active in the business until March 1991 when he retired after 61 years with the company. He died later the following year aged 79. Stacey Dickenson who had joined the company five years earlier passed away in 1980 aged 83.

Following their quarter of a century at no. 1 Market Place the company moved for the sixth and final time to the property currently occupied at 58/59 Market Place. As with all of the premises occupied by the business over the last eighty plus years the title of 'The Kingston Observatory' has accompanied them and from their present home the company continues to manufacture and sell nautical instruments that have made the name of B. Cooke and Son of Hull known to mariners throughout the world for over seventy years. Current manager of B. Cooke and Son Ltd., Mike Plaxton, reflects:

> 'Many of the instruments that we supply here in Market Place such as compasses, barometers and sextants have not changed in design in over a century. Although all seabound vessels now have sophist-icated radar and other modern-day technology they still carry a basic magnetic compass as back-up. One big change is that, whereas several years ago every officer on a ship would have and carry his own sextant, each vessel now only has one, again as back-up.'

As the design of the instruments has not altered in over one hundred years neither, in many cases, has the method of manufacture and to this day B. Cooke and Son employ a number of craftsmen who skilfully hand-make instruments to order. Although in recent years the decline in the ship building industry in the United Kingdom has resulted in a reduction in the home trade for the company Mike happily reports a noticeable increase in the firm's substantial export market. Together with the sale of nautical charts and other scientific equipment it would appear that this company who are incidentally still under the control of descendants of Stacey Dickenson with his daughters, Patricia MacPherson and Dean Yonge currently being the major shareholders, appear to have their future 'well charted'.

NO. 19 HEPWORTH'S ARCADE

When, in 1899, no. 19 Hepworth's Arcade was first listed in the Hull Directories, the premises to which the entry referred were those immediately to the east of no. 17. From the evidence available it would appear that although those premises were perhaps at one time considered to be potentially a separate shop they have never, as such, been so and have, throughout the existence of the Arcade, formed an extension to the shop at no. 17. Although no evidence of a dividing wall at ground floor level has been discovered it should be noted that on the first floor the property is divided by a wall around the point where the shops would be separated. It should also be recognised that the columns in the Arcade, in most cases, are situated between the individual shops and that in the

Numbers 17 and 19 Hepworth's Arcade.
Photograph by Graham Hardy.

case of numbers 17 and 19 an additional column is situated between what could have been originally intended as two separate shops. Following the departure of Millard Bros. from the Arcade in the 1930's the address of no. 19 Hepworth's Arcade has not been used.

Marks and Spencer, Smallware dealers 1899-1931

See no. 15 Hepworth's Arcade.

Millard Bros. Bazaar Proprs. 1933

See no. 15 Hepworth's Arcade.

NO. 17 HEPWORTH'S ARCADE

As briefly explained under 19 Hepworth's Arcade the premises of no. 17 have, since the opening of the Arcade, been joined to that property. They have also, on a number of occasions, been connected to the other neighbouring property of no. 15. Indeed, from the evidence available, it would appear that, apart from a twenty-five year period following the Second World War and the last three years the shops at numbers 15, 17 and 19 have always been connected to form the largest of all of the shops in the Arcade.

Mrs. E. B. Smith. Fancy Repository 1896-1898

Mrs. Eliza Boston Smith first appeared in the Hull Directories in 1889 in which year she was credited with a Fancy Repository at 21 Savile Street. By 1892, in addition to those premises, she was listed as a toy dealer at 68 Hessle Road. Both establishments were maintained until 1895 but by the following year appear to have been closed and replaced with the previously unoccupied shop at no. 17 Hepworth's Arcade.

Eliza continued to trade in the Arcade for three years during which time, in 1897, she was also credited for one year with premises at 72 Wright Street which was possibly another shop but might have been her residential address.

In her final year of tenancy in the Arcade (1898) the electoral register records her full name as Elizabeth Boston Pinchon which suggests that she had remarried and that the previous references to Eliza were actually an abbreviation of her full Christian name. The residential address given in the register was 171 Beverley Road which, the following year, the directories attributed to a William Henry Pinchon, master mariner who, it can safely be assumed, was her new husband.

Marks and Spencer, Smallware Dealers 1899-1931

See no. 15 Hepworth's Arcade.

Millward Bros. Bazaar Proprs. 1933

See no. 15 Hepworth's Arcade.

Arcade Stores, Toy Shop 1948-1954

See no. 15 Hepworth's Arcade.

Selby Leedham and Co., Handicraft Supplies, 1954-1973

See no. 7 Hepworth's Arcade.

Supercast Ltd., 1973

See no. 20 Hepworth's Arcade (under Handicrafts of Hull).

N. T. Leslie, Antiquarian Bookseller 1973

See no. 4 Hepworth's Arcade.

Kaye Books, Antiquarian Booksellers 1973-1992

See no. 15 Hepworth's Arcade.

Beasley's, Casual Clothing 1993-Present Date

Christopher and Fran Beasley commenced in business together in 1978 on a stall on Hull Open Market from which they sold a wide variety of goods from sweets and cigarettes to bankrupt stock which ranged from fruit juices to washing powder. They later changed lines completely and began selling Army Surplus clothing which, proving popular with the student fraternity, led them to take their stall to the Student Union markets held at Hull, Bradford, Leeds and Manchester Universities.

The trade in Army Surplus clothing proved to be successful and in 1982 the couple progressed to taking occupation of a unit in the newly opened Kings Market in South Church Side in Hull. From that base they expanded into American Second-hand and Retro clothing which also proved popular with the youngsters of the City to such an extent that within three years they had outgrown their premises in the Kings Market and sought a larger outlet for their merchandise.

In 1985 Beasley's, as the business was known, took over the vacant shop at 15 South Church Side not far from their previous premises in Kings Market and overlooking their original stall on the open market. For a period of eight years they continued to build their reputation before taking the decision that further expansion was needed and making moves to secure the lease on the recently renovated shop at no. 17 Hepworth's Arcade.

When, in early 1993, the couple took occupation of their new premises, they decided that, whilst the outlet on South Church Side would continue with the Army Surplus, American Second-hand and Retro clothing, the shop in Hepworth's Arcade would concentrate on new casual clothing.

Now into their third year of occupation Beasley's have quickly built a reputation locally for stocking a wide range of casual clothing and footwear at prices which have once again made them very popular with the youngsters of the City.

NO. 15 HEPWORTH'S ARCADE

Marks and Spencer, Smallware Dealers, 1899-1931

The history of the business which is undoubtedly the most eminent and successful of all of the past tenants of the Arcade has previously been covered to great extent and with much attention to detail in various publications and by the media. It is therefore not the intention of this book to try to emulate what has already been achieved very successfully but to condense the facts provided by those sources to give a brief outline of the early days of this world-famous company whilst attempting to bring to light a few of the lesser known facts about their presence in the city of Hull.

Michael Marks was born in June 1859 in Slonim in the Russian province of Grodno. He was the youngest child of Mordecai Marks, a tailor and his wife Rebecca. His mother died in childbirth and he was raised by an elder sister.

Following the assassination of Tsar Alexander II in 1881 came a new wave of violent anti-semitism in Russia forcing some two million jews from their homeland to Western Europe and the U.S.A. As one of the 130,000 Jewish refugees who settled in England Michael arrived in this country with no money and knowing nothing of the language.

No exact date has been established for Michael beginning his new life and indeed there is some speculation as to where in this country he first stepped onto English soil with suggestion that, amongst other ports, Hull was a firm possibility. However, what little evidence exists, suggests that it was more likely Hartlepool in County Durham, where he landed and that his early trading was more probably on the streets in the area surrounding Stockton-on-Tees than in villages in the Yorkshire Dales. This theory is conceivably strengthened by the fact that he is said to have met Hannah Cohen, who later became his wife, in Stockton.

By 1882 Michael had found his way to Leeds apparently searching for the firm of Barran clothing manufacturers the founder of which John Barran was well known even in Eastern Europe for his generosity in employing refugees. He worked the villages around Leeds as an itinerant pedlar selling door-to-

Michael Marks.
Courtesy of Marks and Spencer plc.

door and on street corners and around that time met Isaac Dewhirst, a wholesaler who sold supplies to travelling pedlars. Isaac befriended him and in 1884 agreed to lend him £5.00 which Michael used to buy stock from Dewhirst's warehouse. He took a stall on the city's Kirkgate market and, as he spoke little English, erected a sign stating — Don't ask the price, It's a penny. That phrase was later to become synonymous with the names of Marks and Spencer and was featured in the chain of penny bazaars that they built up throughout the country. The goods being sold were simple items —nails, screws, pins, needles, buttons, soap, cups, handkerchiefs, sponges, baking tins etc. but regardless of this the formula proved successful.

By 1894, just ten years after his humble beginning on the market in Leeds, Michael had established stalls on several markets, opened his first shop at 20 Cheetham Hill Road, Manchester (above which he lived) and had formed the firm base of what is now conceivably the most famous retail organisation in the world. It was at this time that he invited Tom Spencer to join him in the business.

Tom Spencer was born in Skipton, Yorkshire in 1851 and was, until the time of Michael Mark's offer, employed as a cashier with Isaac Dewhirst from whom Michael had borrowed his initial capital. In September 1894 Tom

Tom Spencer.
Courtesy of Marks and Spencer plc.

invested £300.00 in the business and Marks and Spencer was born. Over the next few months drawings from the company reduced Michael's existing investment of 453 pounds 15 shillings and 11 pence to the same amount giving the two partners an equal stake in the business. Two black one penny notebooks, reputedly taken from stock, marked Mr. Marks and Mr. Spencer, still survive and show details of the trading fortunes of the business from September 1894 to January 1898. During that period their initial capital of 753 pounds, 15 shillings and eleven pence had increased to 5000 pounds. This was a nett figure after substantial personal drawings of 2000 pounds each had been deducted.

Their hard work and business acumen ensured that the business thrived and by 1903 when Tom Spencer retired they had a total of 40 outlets in both Market Halls and what were then the newest form of shopping centres — Arcades. Michael Marks had previously moved his stalls into covered markets following the death of a sales assistant who contracted pneumonia whilst working on an open market. By the time of Michael Marks' early and untimely death in 1907 a further 20 branches had been added.

Following the death of his father, Michael's son Simon, who was born in 1888 during the early years of the business, took control and it is to his genius that must be attributed the growth of the modern concern we know today.

Pedlar's Certificate.

No. **3215**

In pursuance of "THE PEDLARS' ACT, 1871," I Certify that _Ephraim Sieff Walker Street_ Hull, in the County of York, aged _26_ years, is hereby authorised to act as a Pedlar within the Hull Police District, for a year from the date of this Certificate.

Certified this _8th_ day of _February_ 1886

Signed _Chas Jones_

Chief Constable.

This Certificate will expire on the ___ day of _February_ 1887

Pedlar's Certificate granted to Ephraim Sieff.
Courtesy of Marks and Spencer plc.

An interesting point to those of us from Hull, although only a very minor one in the history of the company, is that the wife of Simon Marks —Miriam Sieff and her brother Israel who later married Simon's sister Rebecca and later still went on to become a driving force in the future of Marks and Spencer, were the children of Ephraim Sieff who, like Michael Marks, was a Russian refugee. Ephraim Sieff landed in Hull in 1886 and was, whilst living in Walker Street in the city, granted a street pedlar's license. This was signed by Charles Jones who was at the time Assistant Chief Constable of Hull.

The history of Marks and Spencer in Hull began in 1899 when they opened three shops at 15, 17 and 19 Hepworth's Arcade and were described in the Cooks Directory for that year as being smallware dealers.

Little is known about the early days of the company in Hull other than that in 1906, in which year the penny bazaar in Liverpool topped the 'league tables' of yearly takings with 9857 pounds, Hull came seventh with 4513 pounds. By 1910 when Brixton topped the 'table' with 9367 pounds, Hull had moved up to fourth with 7015 pounds. A later comparison on figures to indicate the profitability of shops as a percentage of turnover showed Hull to be 'top of the table' for four consecutive years from 1907 reaching their peak in 1910 with a profitability figure of 17.4 per cent compared with Brixton's 13.1 per cent.

The early bazaars employed few staff and these were usually recruited locally on local terms but both Michael and Tom were aware that all staff needed supervision and would, it appears, make unannounced visits to their various branches. It has been recalled that Tom Spencer and his wife once called into the bazaar in Hull and found one assistant busy 'doing' another assistant's hair. The young ladies were obviously unaware of who he was and when Mr. Spencer asked to be served one of them responded "Ark at 'im.' Spencer promptly sacked the lot and took over with his wife until new staff could be recruited. No date has been given to that story but considering Tom Spencer died in 1905, it must have occurred whilst the bazaar was in Hepworth's Arcade.

The number of lines being sold by the company at this time had expanded dramatically and even in those days many of the products were manufactured bearing the names of Marks and Spencer printed on them. (The trade name of St. Michael was not registered until 1928). Amongst the new lines were books of sheet music which proved very popular in days when many homes had their own piano. Copies of two of these show amongst their listings of branch establishments the shops in Hepworth's Arcade.

As the photograph taken around 1906 shows, the shop in the Arcade was unlike a conventional shop with a front door through which customers would pass but favoured an open plan 'market stall' effect. This style was used in the Penny Bazaars throughout the country as it was the policy of the company that shoppers should be encouraged to browse as they would on an open market and be under no obligation to buy. This practice was almost unknown at the time other than on open markets and in market halls and Marks and Spencer erected 'Free Admission' signs at many of their outlets to invite the public to come in and browse.

Edna Anderson (formerly Edna Whittingham) who worked for the company at the Hepworth's Arcade branch for five years from 1922 recalls:

'When I was 14 years old a friend I knew from school who worked at Marks and Spencer called on me one lunchtime and said that a lot of the girls had walked out and asked if I could help out. Although my parents clearly didn't like the idea I jumped at the chance and took the job earning ten shillings (50 pence) a week. There were about twelve girls working there at the time plus a manageress and we

FROM

Marks & Spencer's

ORIGINAL

PENNY BAZAAR

CHIEF OFFICES AND WAREHOUSE:—

18, ROBERT STREET, CHEETHAM, MANCHESTER.

BRANCH ESTABLISHMENTS:—

Upper Arcade, Bristol	26, Berry Street, Liverpool
8, Abingdon Street, Blackpool	63, Stretford Road, Manchester
29, Snow Hill, Birmingham	60, Oldham Street, Manchester
92, Winchcoomb Street, Cheltenham	New Arcade, Sunderland
Hepworth's Arcade, Hull	19, Market Place, S. Shields
Makinson's Arcade, Wigan	

MARKET HALLS.	MARKET HALLS.	MARKET HALLS.	MARKET HALLS.
Ashton	Cardiff	Newcastle	Scarboro'
Bolton	Glossop	Rotherham	Wigan
Birkenhead	Huddersfield	Slalybridge	Wolverhampton
Bath	Hartlepool	Sheffield	Warrington
Birmingham	Leeds	Southport	Wakefield
Castleford	Middlesboro'	St. Helens	

LONDON BRANCHES:—

20, London Road, Southwark;

25, New Cut, Lambeth.

Sample of books of sheet music sold by Marks and Spencer.
Courtesy of Marks and Spencer plc.

Sample of books of sheet music sold by Marks and Spencer.
Courtesy of Marks and Spencer plc.

opened from 9.00 o'clock in the morning until 6.00 o'clock Monday to Thursday, 7.00 o'clock on Fridays and 9.00 o'clock on Saturdays. The week before Christmas we worked until midnight every day. When the shop closed for the evening it was sealed off from the Arcade for security purposes by large roller shutters.

I remember that the stock would arrive in large wooden crates and we had to crowbar them open in the Arcade before carrying the contents to the storeroom upstairs. The manageress was a fierce lady who seemed to enjoy making us miserable. One day on which I had worn my best clothes for work with the intention of going straight out when the shop closed (probably to the Grand or the Alexandra) I had just put my coat on to go when she told me to go and scrub the stockroom before I left. I explained that I was wearing my best clothes and asked if I could leave it until the following day but she insisted. I refused and was promptly sacked. My father was furious and wrote a letter to the head office in London who sent instruction to the manageress that I was to be reinstated immediately.'

Whilst in Hepworth's Arcade the Penny Bazaar was a popular atraction which proved to be beneficial not only to Marks and Spencer but also to the other businesses around it, and several ex-tenants have commented that the day Marks and Spencer left was the day the Arcade started to die. It is likely that, although the fact that a shop like Marks and Spencer moving from the Arcade could have had some effect on business or the number of people passing through the Arcade, this would only have been one contributory factor to any down-turn in trade. The 1930's also saw the depression which had an adverse effect on businesses throughout the country and it was also around that time that the centre of shopping for Hull started to move away from the Old Town with shopping areas in the newer part of the city centre towards the railway station becoming more popular.

136

Marks and Spencer Penny Bazaar, Hepworth's Arcade circa 1906.
Courtesy of Marks and Spencer plc.

Marks and Spencer left the Arcade in 1931 and opened at new premises at 42 and 43 Whitefriargate a site which the company still occupies although the branch has now expanded to also include nos. 40 and 41. As a business they continue to grow and now have around 700 stores worldwide with an annual turnover in excess of 6.8 billion pounds.

Despite their massive growth in just over a century Marks and Spencer have always been noted for their caring attitude towards their staff and it is very likely that this can be traced back to the founder Michael Marks. It is reported that in the early days of the business Mr. Marks would share his food with his salesgirls, give them Christmas presents and, whilst the business was being operated from market stalls, arrange for wooden platforms for them to stand on so that their feet would not get cold.

When Alec Taylor retired as the manager of the Hull branch in February 1983 he apparently wrote to Lord Sieff (Marcus Sieff, son of Israel Sieff and grandson of Michael Marks who was Company Chairman from 1972 to 1984) and is quoted as saying:

> 'Thank you very much indeed for taking the trouble to talk to me on the telephone today and wish me good luck in my years of retirement... There is no real substitute for the very top man talking to you... The highlight of the year was when you or your uncle or your father telephoned the store and probed the health of the takings, the health of the staff and the health of the business in general... It is a subject on which I feel very intensely and which I hold to be the real secret of success of our Family Business.'

It would appear that the theory of Michael Marks and that of the business empire of which he was founder is one of 'Look after your staff and they will look after you' a concept which, the very growth of the company to its present size would indicate, has proved to be very successful.

Millard Bros., Bazaar Proprietors 1933

The name of Millard Bros. first appeared in the Hull Directories in 1899 when they were listed as pawnbrokers operating from premises at 178 Beverley Road. By the following year they had added a second outlet to the business at 204 Beverley Road. The advertisement shown is taken from the *Hull Topic* just prior to the turn of the century and boasts that the stock is composed almost entirely of Genuine Second-hand Articles.

By 1901 the brothers had added furniture dealers to their list of activities and were actually named as Thomas William and Joseph Henry Millard but by that time had vacated the premises at 178 Beverley Road. The same directory also lists Joseph alone as a pawnbroker at 28 Sculcoates Lane.

In 1904 having also expanded the branch in Sculcoates Lane to include the neighbouring shop of no. 26 the brothers opened their first City centre branch at no. 1 West Street, but later that year Thomas left Hull and England to start a new life in America leaving Joseph to continue with the business. By the following year the name of Millard Bros. had vanished and Joseph was listed alone. He had vacated the shops in Sculcoates Lane and was shown as a pawnbroker and furniture dealer at 204 Beverley Road and 1 West Street.

The branch at 204 Beverley Road was maintained for a further four years during which time the shop in West Street had been replaced by one just around the corner at 65 King Edward Street and Joseph had changed his home address from 3 St. Leonards Road to 222 Victoria Avenue which would suggest that the business was prospering.

By the time the 1909 directory was issued although the Beverley Road branch maintained the description of pawnbroker and furniture dealer the one

MILLARD BROS.,
PAWNBROKERS,
178 BEVERLEY ROAD.

———

Our Stock is composed almost entirely of GENUINE SECOND-HAND ARTICLES, which we are either selling on commission for private clients, forfeited pledges, or purchased outright for cash.

EXCEPTIONAL BARGAINS in all classes of goods, of which our customers get the fullest advantage.

Advertisement from the Hull Topic circa late 1890's.

in the City centre was listed under the name of Joseph Henry Millard, Jeweller. It is highly likely that although Joseph had commenced in business as a pawnbroker loaning money against goods, because the valuables owned by many of his customers would have only extended to their furniture and jewellery, he soon acquired some expertise in those commodities and it is probably for that reason that his business diversified in such a way.

It would appear that by 1910 Joseph had ceased dealing in furniture as his listing in the directory for the year shows just one outlet at 65 King Edward Street at which he is described as a pawnbroker and jeweller. Two years later in 1912 the title of pawnbroker had also been dropped and the entry of Joseph Millard, jeweller continued until 1921 although in the final year the business address had been changed to no. 67 King Edward Street. By 1925 the title of Millard Bros. had been resurrected although this was not an indication of the return of Thomas William from America but the formation of a partnership by Joseph's two sons Joseph Junior and Thomas. The brothers were listed at 54 Brook Street at which they were described as antique dealers whilst the jewellers business previously conducted under the name of their father also became known as Millard Bros. and relocated to premises at nos. 3 and 4 Paragon Arcade previously vacated by Jacob Friedenthal (see no. 1 Hepworth's Arcade).

It would appear Joseph Senior was indeed a shrewd businessman and that his investments were proving successful as by the late 1920's he had changed his home abode again and was living at 345 Beverley Road. Just a few years later in 1930 he once again moved the family home having purchased a large detached

Joseph Junior, Thomas Percival and Joseph Senior Millard at Riverside, Hessle.
Courtesy of Rosemary Glusick.

residence at Cliff Road, Hessle by the name of Riverside. The house which is still in the ownership of the family was so called because of its close proximity to and uninterrupted view of the River Humber and Joseph no doubt considered it to be the perfect place to which he could retire. That decision was no doubt prompted by the popular belief at the time in the advantages to one's health that could be gained by living in the country which, at the time, was exactly where Hessle was conceived to be.

No change is noted in the listings of the business until 1929 when the antique side of the concern opened an additional outlet at 4 North Street which, by the following year, had replaced that in Brook Street. By 1933 that too had vanished, the premises probably being a casualty of the massive programme of demolition which took place in the area prior to the development of Ferensway in the early 1930's. In that year, in addition to their listing as jewellers at 3 and 4 Paragon Arcade, Millard Bros. also boasted two additional entries in the Directories being shown as Bazaar Proprietors at nos. 15, 17 and 19 Hepworth's Arcade and as Ironmongers at no. 18 Paragon Arcade.

It is known that, in later years, although all of the different businesses owned by the Millard family were known collectively under the banner of Millard Bros. each was operated independently by a different member of the family and it is therefore very feasible that it was in that year that Joseph Junior and Thomas who had no doubt worked together whilst dealing in antiques chose to go their separate ways. As it has been established that the ironmongery concern was under the control of Thomas it can safely be assumed that Joseph Junior was responsible for the venture in Hepworth's Arcade and that Joseph Senior continued to operate the jewellers side of the business.

The opening of the bazaar at nos. 15, 17 and 19 Hepworth's Arcade followed the departure from those premises of Marks and Spencer who had successfully operated a Penny Bazaar from the Arcade for over thirty years and it is highly probable that this was an attempt by Millard Bros., to perhaps capitalise on the succeess achieved by that company. However it would appear that their bid to gain from the reputation built up by Marks and Spencer was an unsuccessful one as by 1935 the bazaar had closed and the premises remained empty for a period of thirteen years. The name of Millard Bros. can vaguely be made out in the photograph of the Arcade taken in 1935 shown on page 78.

The ironmongery business at no. 18 Paragon Arcade which, the same year, became part of the Millard Bros. chain had been in operation from those and other premises for over thirty years by an Arthur Bruce Hodgson, and it is therefore likely that the family bought out Mr. Hodgson's interest in the business and installed Thomas to supervise the venture.

By 1937 Joseph had again established another branch to the family business having opened Paragon Sales and Exchange at no. 42 Carr Lane. This concern which was described in the directories as a general dealers was, it is understood, primarily a secondhand shop although it has also been verified that Joseph Junior, who was a keen philatelist, also used the premises for buying and selling collectable stamps whilst also dealing in a wide variety of goods including leatherware and luggage.

Although all three branches of the business were included in the Kelly's

140

Directory to Hull in 1939 the local telephone directories published in the years that followed did not include the jewellers at nos. 3 and 4 Paragon Arcade and listed the ironmongery business at no. 7 Paragon Street under the name of T. Millard. Whilst the information obtained from that source is of course inconclusive because only telephone subscribers were included it is known that Joseph Senior died in 1942 aged 75 and therefore possible that, following his death, the jewellery side of the business was either sold or ceased trading. The new address credited to the ironmongery side of the business is also perhaps a little misleading as no. 7 Paragon Street was actually the shop at the northern end of Paragon Arcade which adjoined no. 18 within the Arcade. Those premises had for many years been connected to form one large shop although it would appear that Thomas had perhaps either moved the entrance which previously led from within the Arcade to one leading from the main street or merely preferred the address of the business to be on Paragon Street.

The company letterhead would indicate that the brothers perhaps attempted to give the impression that their business was somewhat larger that it truly was and indeed boasted more branches than were actually in operation. Whilst 42 Carr Lane and 3-4 Paragon Arcade are confirmed by various directories as being in the occupation of the business and are therefore undisputed as indeed was 7 Paragon Street, number 194 Hallgate, Cottingham was actually the home residence of Thomas, no. 18 Paragon Arcade was, as previously mentioned, adjoined to no. 7 Paragon Street, and as Paragon Arcade only contains 18 shops number 22 has never existed. As Thomas did not move to Cottingham until 1940 it does however confirm that the jewellers business was still in existence in that year and further confirms the likelihood that it continued to operate until the death of Joseph Senior.

Joseph Junior who remained a bachelor throughout his life continued to live, with his mother, at Riverside in Hessle and in 1948 was joined by Thomas who returned to the family home with his daughter Rosemary following the untimely death of his wife. The brothers continued to operate their separate sections of the business and were apparently a regular and impressive sight when they walked each morning, with bowler hats and briefcases, to the nearby Hessle Railway Station to commute into Hull.

By 1949 T. Millard, Ironmonger had become T. P. Millard and Co. and

MILLARD BROS.
HULL.

DEPARTMENTS—
IRONMONGERY
HARDWARE
DOMESTIC WOODWARE
SPORTS GOODS
TRAVEL REQUISITES
JEWELERY
FANCY GOODS
FOREIGN STAMPS

HEAD OFFICE—
7 PARAGON STREET.
—
BRANCHES :
3-4, 18-22
PARAGON ARCADE.
42 CARR LANE.
194 HALLGATE,
COTTINGHAM.

Millard Bros. letterheading.
Courtesy of Rosemary Glusick.

four years later in 1954 was listed at no. 53 Paragon Street. The new address once again however did not indicate a move of premises by the business but was the result of the renumbering of the street that year. During that time the name of Millard Bros. did reappear on the streets of Hull for a brief period and was attributed to premises at 22 Carr Lane and listed as being dealers in foreign stamps, leatherware and fancy goods. Those premises formed part of the Grosvenor Hotel Building which was demolished in 1956 and with the structure disappeared for the final time the name of Millard Bros.

In 1957 the ironmongers shop on the corner of Paragon Arcade which has been in operation under various names for over fifty years closed its doors for the final time but the closure did not spell retirement for Thomas nor the disappearance of the name of T. P. Millard and Co. from the local telephone directories. That entry continued to be included for a further sixteen years from the address at Riverside, Cliff Road, Hessle from where Thomas successfully expanded what had begun as a hobby into the final diversification of the family business — that of quail breeding. From a number of outbuildings at the rear of the property which is now shadowed by the Humnber Bridge he skilfully reared the tiny birds for use in the catering industry and just prior to his death was sending an average of fifty oven ready birds to Smithfields Market and was reportedly one of the largest privately operated breeders in the country. Joseph Junior continued to operate the Paragon Sales and Exchange Shop in Carr Lane and for a brief period in the mid 1960's also had premises operating under his own name at no. 7 Midland Street from where he dealt in his lifetime hobby of stamp collections. It is believed that he continued to work until his death in 1969 aged 67. Thomas, or Thomas Percy Millard to give him his full title passed away in August 1973 aged 68.

Throughout the past one hundred years the shops in Hepworth's Arcade have been home to numerous businessmen and women who have diversified in many different ways from their normal trade or profession but none, it would appear, to the extent of the business of Millard Brothers. Throughout their near eighty years of existence the Millards progressed through the titles of pawnbrokers, furniture dealers, jewellers, antique dealers, bazaar proprietors, ironmongers, leatherware and fancy goods dealers and stamp dealers before finally retiring to the unusual profession of quail breeders and one can only admire the obvious abilities of the different members of this family in being capable of turning their hands to such different and diverse ways of earning a living.

Arcade stores 1948-1955

In 1948, a Mr. and Mrs. Robert E. Holmes purchased the business of Kiddieland from Harry Dibb. Prior to purchasing the concern the couple operated from a stall on the open market in Hull. When they first took over Mr. Dibb's toy business the lease on the shop at 61 Market Place which 'Kiddieland' had occupied for nearly twenty years had expired and it was necessary to find alternative premises for the venture. The joint shops at nos. 15 and 17 Hepworth's Arcade, which had been empty since being vacated by Millard Bros. in the 1930's, were suitable being situated not far from the original Kiddieland premises but were perhaps a little larger than required. It is possibly for that reason that Mr. and Mrs. Holmes chose not only to use the shops for their own venture but also to sub-let parts of them to other traders creating a mini indoor market, presumably hence the name of Arcade Stores.

It would appear that the idea was a successful one for a short period at least and was still listed in the 1954 directory but by 1955 the shops had obviously been divided, with no. 17 being occupied by Selby Leedham and Co. and no. 15 attributed to Mr. and Mrs. Holmes under their own names and operating as Wholesale and Retail Toy Specialists.

D. and E. Holmes, Wholesale and Retail Toy Specialists 1955-1963

Following the closure of the indoor market they had created in the late 1940's and the replacement of the dividing wall between nos. 15 and 17, Mr. and Mrs. Holmes continued to operate the toy business from no. 15. The venture continued into the early 1960's although in the latter years it is known that Mrs. Holmes was operating it alone. In 1964 following a period of ill health she sold the business to Arthur Fanthorpe and, it is understood, retired to Canada to live with her son who had moved there some years earlier.

A. Fanthorpe Ltd., Toy Dealers 1963-1966

When Mrs. Holmes announced her intention to retire and sell the business Arthur Fanthorpe showed immediate interest although it was not the temptation of a long established toy business that attracted him but the premises themselves. Arthur was obviously restricted from expanding his business due to the lack of space at his own premises at nos. 6 and 8 and saw the larger premises of no. 15 as the ideal opportunity to develop by moving into domestic appliances such as washing machines and refrigerators. However, although Mrs. Holmes was indeed keen to sell the lease, she also needed to dispose of the remaining stock and insisted that the two assets were sold as one package. Consequently Arthur Fanthorpe became the new owner of the toy shop and recruited the assistance of his wife Laura to run the shop. Mrs. Laura Fanthorpe recalls:

> 'I remember distinctly that some of the toys which we acquired from Mrs. Holmes as part of the deal were very very old and had been packed away in cases in the storeroom upstairs presumably because they were of no interest to the children of the 1960's. I think that if we still had them today they would probably be worth a small fortune.'

It is very possible that the stock to which Mrs. Fanthorpe refers had probably also been part and parcel of the business when it was originally purchased from Harry Dibb in the late 1940's and could therefore have dated back as far as the early part of the century. Old toys in those days were of very little value, unlike more recent years when they have become highly collectable items worth many times their original selling price.

A. Fanthorpe Ltd. maintained the shop for a period of three years but never actually succeeded in altering the premises to an outlet for domestic appliances as originally planned. In 1966 following discussions with Norman Leslie arrangements were made for the two businesses to 'exchange' shops with Norman taking over no. 15 and Fanthorpes extending into the premises vacated by him at no. 4. (See also A. Fanthorpe — no. 6 Hepworth's Arcade).

N. T. Leslie, Antiquarian Bookseller, 1966-1973

See no. 4 Hepworth's Arcade.

Kaye Books, Antiquarian Booksellers, 1973-1992

Although Barry Kaye actually took over the business at nos. 15 and 17 from Norman Leslie in 1973 he did not immediately change the name of the shop and continued to trade under the well established name of N. T. Leslie for a further nine years. In 1982 he changed the name to Kaye Books and operated under that title for a period of ten years before closing in 1991. The following extract is taken from the *Hull Daily Mail* and explains the imminent closure of Kaye Books:

> 'A chapter of Hull's history comes to an end next month with the closure of the city's oldest secondhand bookshop. Kaye (Books) Ltd. in Hepworth's Arcade has been selling old books, prints and maps for more than 45 years under various trading names. Partner Alan Turner said he was very sad to see the doors shut. 'I've been here for 18 years and during that time I've become very attached to the place' he said. 'You get to meet a huge variety of people who bring in old books that have been left to them — many are family

Kaye Books, Hepworth's Arcade circa 1980's.
Courtesy of Hull City Council Planning Department.

heirlooms.' Mr. Turner added 'The attraction of old books is that you're handling part of history. When you pick up a book that has been signed by someone like Kipling it really gets you thinking."

Since the departure from the Arcade of Kaye Books, Barry Kaye continues to offer the catalogue and mail order service initiated whilst in the Arcade from his home in York. The business whilst in occupation of nos. 15 and 17 is pictured below.

Whispers, The Gift Boxed Lingerie Shop, 1992-Present Date

Like many other tenants of the Arcade both past and present Graham Hardy commenced in business selling ladies' lingerie from a stall on Hull Open Market. Under the title of Teaser Lingerie he attempted to concentrate on the gift market and to attract trade from his competitors in that field sold all garments packaged in gift boxes creating a 'ready wrapped' present for his customers to give. Graham expected the majority of his customers to be gentlemen but contrary to what he had envisaged the larger percentage were ladies and once he became established it was necessary to expand the venture to two stalls. During that period he was joined on the market by his girlfriend, later to become his wife, Debbie and between them the couple also built up the party plan side of the business helping to promote the name of Teaser Lingerie to a wider audience. The stalls on Hull Open market are pictured below.

It was always the ambition of the couple to acquire a more permanent outlet for their merchandise and when the refurbishment of no. 15 Hepworth's Arcade was completed in 1992 they successfully tendered for the lease and, following a hasty fitting out of the shop with the intention of catching the Christmas trade, opened for business on 30th November that year. Graham and Debbie decided that the name of Teaser Lingerie was unsuitable for their

Teaser Lingerie stall on Hull Open Market.
Photograph by Graham Hardy.

retail premises which they named Whispers, The Gift Boxed Lingerie Shop, maintaining their previous title for the party plan side of the business.

Although the early days were difficult ones for the shop the business soon became established and now, in its third year, boasts a string of regular customers from as far afield as Lincolnshire, Nottingham and London as well as proving a regular shopping place for the many foreign seamen who visit the port of Hull.

NO. 13 HEPWORTH'S ARCADE

Mrs. Amelia Coombes, Milliner 1896-1897

Mrs. Coombes first appears in the Hull Directory as a milliner in 1885 residing with her husband George at 22 Cave Street, Stepney. George was, at the time, assistant schoolmaster at Courtney Street School. Following that entry Amelia is not listed again until she opened the shop in Hepworth's Arcade eleven years later in 1896 and it is possible that she took time off from her profession to raise a family. It is also however feasible that, as by 1889 George had become Master at the Fountain Road, Clifton Board School, the couple no longer needed the extra income earned by Amelia. This theory is probably strengthened by the fact that the Coombes had by that year also changed address moving to the more well-to-do area of St. Johns Wood taking residence at no. 11 Alexandra Road. In 1896 by which time George was Master at the Charterhouse Board School Amelia took the previously unoccupied premises at 13 Hepworth's Arcade but only stayed for about one year before presumably selling out to H. Pedley. Neither Amelia nor George are listed in any directories after 1897.

H. Pedley, Milliner, 1897

It has not been possible to establish any other information on H. Pedley even to the extent of whether this tenant was male or female. It is likely that the business was purchased from the previous tenant Amelia Coombes but failed to succeed as it was only included in the directories for one year, with the name of H. Pedley not being listed either prior to or following 1897.

Sutton and Walsh, Printers, Stationers and Ordnance Map Depot, 1898-1900

The census taken in 1891 lists Joseph Lightfoot Sutton, a stationer's assistant, aged 25, born in Howden as living at 12 Camden Terrace, Beverley Road. The same census also lists an Alfred Walsh, a printer's compositer, aged 22, born in Hull as living at 33 Canon Street. Joseph is first listed in the Hull Directories in 1895 when he is listed as a shop assistant, an entry which was repeated in 1897 but it was not until 1899 when Sutton and Walsh are first recorded at premises at no. 13 Hepworth's Arcade that either gentleman was attributed with owning a business, so it can be safely assumed that this was the first venture into self employmemt by both parties.

The earliest reference to the company that has been uncovered is in an 1898 advertisement in the *Hull Daily Mail* in which the gentlemen declare themselves as being successors to M. C. Peck and Son. That company was an old established printers, stationers and bookbinders who had, for over fifty years until 1897, operated from premises at no. 10 Market Place, practically opposite the Arcade entrance. It is possible that Messrs. Sutton and Walsh, who were known to have previously been in the same trade, may have perhaps worked for that company prior to its closure and made an agreement to utilise the name in advertisements to attract the goodwill that had no doubt been built up in the half century previous. The advertisement also featured the Royal Crest to indicate that the company had been appointed by Her Majesty's Government as the sole agents for the area for the

Hull Daily Mail advertisement 1898.
Courtesy of the Hull Daily Mail.

sale of Ordnance Survey Maps. Later the same year the business was featured in the 'Christmas at the Shops' article in the *Hull Daily Mail* which reported that the business made a strong feature of Private Christmas Cards which were printed by themselves on the premises. A further advertisement the same month establishes that these would probably only have been of interest to the wealthier residents of the City because of their cost — one shilling and sixpence (7½ pence) per dozen. It is noted that in both advertisements the company announce their address as Market Place Arcade which may suggest that even though the Arcade had been open for around three years the title of Hepworth's Arcade was possibly not easily recognisable and that the partners wanted to be in no doubt that prospective customers would know where to find them.

Just three years after first advertising in the local press and only two after their first listing in the directories the partnership of Joseph Sutton and Alfred Walsh was dissolved. It is not clear as to what caused the two gentlemen to go their separate ways although the fact that the next tenant of no. 13 appeared to have taken over the business would suggest that it was probably not due to lack of trade. Whatever the reason, by the time the 1901 Cook's Directory was issued both Joseph and Alfred were listed separately from their home addresses. Joseph was residing at 96 Sharp Street and describing himself as a stationer and Alfred at 8 Walton Villas, Brunswick Avenue and was listed as a printer and stationer. When the Kelly's East Riding and Hull Directory was published later the same year Joseph Sutton was no longer listed and failed to be so in all future directories. Alfred or Alfred Bernard Walsh, to give him his full title, soon established a business on his own and by 1906 was shown as operating from premises at 75 Lowgate and 4 Hannover Square under the title of A. B. Walsh Ltd. Although the listing of two addresses probably added to the prestige of the concern studies of maps of the area around that time show that the two addresses were probably one and the same building built in an L shape around the corner which formed the junction of the two streets. Part of that building now houses the Economic Development and Property Department of Hull City

Council. By 1912 the printers had moved to the neighbouring premises of 77 Lowgate (also now occupied by Hull City Council) which was at the time also premises for Jones and Company, a firm of Hull printers established at that address some years earlier. Although it is possible that the two concerns may have shared equipment it is unlikely that they had amalgamated as each was listed separately and they were attributed with different telephone numbers. By 1912 Alfred was residing at 74 Park Street which would imply that the business was prospering and little changed for A. B. Walsh Ltd. over the next 27 years with the exception of entitling the premises in Lowgate 'Caxton Buildings' presumably after William Caxton an early pioneer in the printing industry. The 1940 Hull Telephone Directory lists, alongside the entry for the business at their premises in Lowgate, a G. H. Walsh of 24 Eastella Drive. This would suggest that Alfred, who if still living would be 71 years old and therefore likely retired, had probably passed the business onto a son or nephew. A. B. Walsh Ltd. continued to be listed from the address in Lowgate until 1965 and although it has not been clearly established it has been suggested that they were neither taken over nor bought out, but merely ceased trading.

Arcade Press (Charles H. Jones) Printers, Stationers and Ordnance Map Depot, 1901-1905

Because of the similarity in the types of business conducted by the two parties it is very likely that Charles Jones took over the existing business of Sutton and Walsh after that partnership was dissolved in 1901 and continued the venture started by the two men under the new name of Arcade Press. It has also been established from a *Hull Daily Mail* advertisement feature that Mr. Jones had continued with the printing and supply of personalised Christmas cards for which he was apparently willing to accept orders up until the 24th December, and the fact that Arcade Press was the new local supplier of Ordnance Survey Maps would strengthen the theory further. There is a distinct possibility that some of the copies of those maps which local historians now study in depth during their research (the author of this book included) may have, at one time, been found on the shelves of this shop whilst under the ownership of Mr. Jones or his predecessors.

At the time he took up tenancy in the Arcade, Charles lived at 4 Charlotte Terrace, Clarendon Street, but later in 1904 moved to 71 Charles Street from where he also dealt in stationery and fancy goods. The final home address given for Mr. Jones was in 1905 at 33 May Street and it was in that year that Arcade Press were last listed in the Arcade. The following year the business was shown as occupying premises in Blue Bell Yard which had been vacated five years earlier by a firm known as Elsom and Co. who were also printers, but by 1907 both Arcade Press and Charles H. Jones had disappeared from the directories.

Following the departure of Arcade Press from no. 13 in 1906 the premises are unlisted in the Hull directories for a period of 48 years. As it has not been established beyond doubt if a subscription had to be paid to the publishers for inclusion in the directories it is feasible that the shop was from time to time occupied but each tenant opted not to be included in the directories. It is

148

equally possible that the no. 13 may have discouraged prospective tenants of a superstitious nature. It can be verified that the property was empty in 1935 from the photograph on page 78 and it is very likely that, considering the economic climate prior to and during the War, remained empty until after the hostilies ceased in 1945.

R. A. P. Rented Radios, 1951-1961

The first listing locally of R. A. P. Rented Radios was in the Hull Telephone Directory of 1951 which showed them at the premises

Hull Daily Mail advertisement 1952.
Courtesy of the Hull Daily Mail.

13 Hepworth's Arcade. After a ten year tenancy on which it has regrettably not been possible to obtain any information other than that the manager's name was Eric and he lived in Hornsea (many thanks to George Dinsdale) the business moved to new premises at 66 King Edward Street. Although listed at that address for two years — 1961 and 1962 — the business was not included in the 1963 Telephone Directory.

Brantons Ltd., Jewellers, 1967-Present Date

Thomas Capes Branton, the eldest of seven children was born in 1872 in the room above his grandfather's butcher shop in Hannover Square, Hull.

The unusual middle name given to both him and his father Thomas Senior originated from two generations previous. Thomas Senior's grandmother was Hannah Branton and was a spinster at the time of the birth of her son also Thomas. One year later she belatedly married Thomas Capes of Skeffling and for convenience forgot the name of Branton as regards her son who became known as Thomas Capes. It was apparently the practice of the Church of England at the time to require proof of baptism prior to conducting wedding ceremonies and when, in later years, young Thomas decided to marry Mary Ann Wells the vicar of the Holy Trinity Church insisted that they be married under the names of Thomas Branton and Mary Ann Wells. Immediately after the ceremony the young couple re-assumed the name of Capes. Following similar refusal by the Church to recognise the surname of Capes when the couple baptised their first two children the baptism of the third child was deliberately registered Thomas Capes Branton. This child was the father of the gentleman to which this section refers and the

Thomas Capes Branton.
Courtesy of Partricia Jorna.

149

relevance of these explanatory notes will hopefully become clear later in this article.

Thomas junior suffered from infantile paralysis or polio at birth and for this reason was apparently Christened twice. It was evidently a superstition at the time that a second baptism helped to cure any infant unfortunate enough to be born with such a handicap. It could be suggested that this remedy was to an extent successful because although Thomas apparently had one leg shorter than the other he proved in his growing years to be a keen sportsman enjoying success in both cycling and bowling. It is, however, more likely that his disability made young Thomas more determined than his able-bodied competitors to succeed. As a young man he was awarded a medal for cycling 100 miles inside 12 hours despite the fact that one of the pedals on his cycle was fixed to accommodate his shorter leg. Thomas also enjoyed cricket and was a competent batsman and during his younger days was allowed to use his younger brother Arthur as his runner. As he grew older this was no longer permitted and he consequently turned his attention to the game of bowls in which he went on to win countless trophies. Thomas also enjoyed watching sport and for many years was a season passholder for both of Hull's rugby clubs.

In later life Thomas became a prominent member of the Masonic circle in Hull and during that time held every position in the De La Pole Lodge with the exception of Grand Master, a capacity which he once evidently commented that he had deliberately avoided because he could not really afford it.

The first record of Thomas in Hull was in the 1891 census which listed him as a watchmaker's apprentice aged 18 residing with his parents, four brothers and two sisters at no. 1 Zion Terrace, Bean Street. It has been suggested that Thomas may have been taken on as an apprentice through a family connection on his paternal grandfather's side and it is noted that there was at the time a watchmaker/jeweller by the name of Capes operating from premises in Bridge Street, Hull. This theory is quite possibly an accurate one as in those days it was the normal practice to pay tradesmen in return for teaching their trade to apprentices and it is unlikely that Thomas senior who was a cooper, with a wife and six other children to support, would have been in a financial position to afford such training for his son.

The earliest record of Thomas junior having established a business of his own is in the advertisement which appeared in the *Hull Critic* during July 1894 and announces him as Thomas Branton, Watch and Clock Maker at 119 Witham (now occupied by Kingston Studios).

Advertisement from the Hull Critic 1894.

In 1896 he married Bridget Emily Kaye daughter of Thomas Swain Kaye sawmaker and tool merchant whose firm was, for many years, well known in Hull. The same year he moved his business into the City centre taking premises at 57 Carr Lane which can vaguely be seen on the sketch by F. S. Smith in 1897.

Illustration of Carr Lane circa 1885 by F. S. Smith showing Branton's shop at no. 57.
Courtesy of Hutton Press and Hull City Museums and Art Galleries.

Thomas apparently lived over his business for a short while before moving his family to a new residence at 30 Perry Street. In 1900 Thomas changed his home address to 26 Wright Street and the following year not only transferred his business along Carr Lane to no. 44 but also opened a second branch at 52 Hessle Road. Although at the time both business premises and houses were generally rented Thomas actually purchased the shop on Carr Lane and retained its ownership until his death. Those premises are still standing despite major developments around them over the last 95 years and have recently been renovated by their current owners. A copy of the Registry of Deeds relating to the ownership of that property still survives and confirms the right of the owner to use both the passageway at the rear of the premises leading into South Street and the lavatory and water-closet situated in the property adjoining on the west jointly with the owners of that property.

In a 1901 advertisement which included an illustration of the premises Thomas proudly boasted keeping the largest staff of watch, clock and jewellery repairers in Hull. The illustration from that advert later formed part of the bill heading used by the business.

Whether it was due to the prosperity from a successful business or for some other reason is uncertain but that year Thomas again changed his home address moving around the corner to no. 19 Percy Street. He was at this time not only listed as a watchmaker and jeweller but also as an optician. It was apparently quite common in those days for jewellers and watchmakers to take on the work now carried out by opticians as they not only had the complex equipment but also the technical know-how to manufacture spectacles.

Four years later in 1905 Thomas was on the move again, this time to the fashionable new houses on St. Georges Road. Although his new address would have been very beneficial for travelling to his shop on Hessle Road it was not a convenience that was to be of benefit for long as by the following year that shop

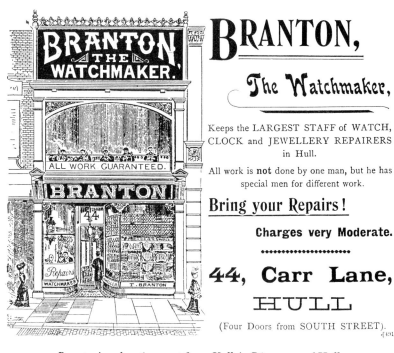

Branton's advertisement from Kelly's Directory of Hull.

had closed. Thomas kept just the one shop at 44 Carr Lane until 1908 when he again opened a second outlet this time at 39 Charles Street although that appeared to have an ephemeral existence and was only listed for the one year. The same year Thomas moved home again, choosing Hessle for the new family residence. He rented a shop in Prestongate above which there were four good living rooms into which he moved with his wife, two sons and one daughter. Around this time Thomas was given the contract for maintaining and often supplying the clocks, watches, spectacles and sunglasses to Tranby Croft and he was particularly proud of the 'By Appointment' Board given to him by King Edward VII who visited there. His success in business did not apparently detract him from his bowls and other pleasures of life. On Saturdays whilst Thomas enjoyed his rugby and also during his frequent periods of ill-health Bridget took charge of the business. The couple also enjoyed regular musical evenings at which Thomas would, by all accounts, regularly win wagers to play any musical instrument offered providing he was given two weeks in which to learn and practice.

The change in residence to Hessle had apparently been made on the advice of the family doctor who felt that the country air would be greatly beneficial to Mr. Branton's failing health.

It would appear that this advice, if at all successful, came too late as, after a lengthy illness, Thomas Capes Branton passed away on 6th November 1912 and was laid to rest at Hessle cemetery. He left a widow, two sons and a daughter.

His widow Bridget, left with three children to support and well aware that the value of the goodwill attached to her late husband's business should not be allowed to lapse even for one day, made the bold decision to sell the business. A deal was struck with a Mr. Shapero a former friend and fellow mason of Thomas and the transaction actually agreed and confirmed with a handshake in one of the funeral cars on their return from the burial service.

Following the sale of the business Bridget retained the shop in Prestongate and started a draper's business under the name of B. E. Branton. This business, which in later years moved to premises in Hessle Square, passed from Bridget to her daughter Olive and was still operating until the mid 1960's. She also bought a house in Beverley Road, Hessle and moved her family. The shop was quiet and she could not sleep without the ticking, striking and chiming of the clocks and later explained that she could not bear the silence of the place where Thomas and all of his clocks had died. The house in Hessle in later years passed to Thomas Branton's eldest son Thomas Kenneth Branton and was, until just prior to his death earlier this year, still occupied by him.

It has not been possible to establish any information about the Mr. Shapero to whom Bridget Branton sold the business not even to the extent of confirming his Christian name. It is however noted that, around the time that the business was sold, the Hull directories listed three pawnbrokers by the name of Shapero and it is likely that one of either David, Myers or Phillip, who were possibly brothers, was the gentleman who took over Brantons.

In 1914, two years after the death of Thomas, the business was listed in the directories for the first time as Brantons Ltd. and it continued to operate under that name from 44 Carr Lane for a further 15 years until 1929 before the name mysteriously disappeared from the Hull directories. It remained absent for a period of seven years before re-appearing at premises at 3 Anlaby Road in 1937. Further studies of the directories show that in 1930 when Brantons first failed to be listed, the address of no. 44 Carr Lane is attributed to The Tru Fit Optical Company, Opticians. That company was still listed at the same address in 1933, but by 1936 had moved to no. 5 Midland Street and the shop in Carr Lane had been taken over by a newsagent. It is very feasible, although unproven, that Mr. Shapero had chosen to concentrate on the optician's side of the business and felt that a name that more notably attached itself to that profession was needed. Meanwhile the premises at 3 Anlaby Road at which the name of Brantons was resurrected in 1937 were occupied by Harry Anstey Watchmaker (later also known as Anstey and Anderson) and it is equally conceivable that Mr. Shapero either also owned that business throughout the period or purchased it around 1937 and reinstated the well-established name of Branton the Jeweller.

When, in 1954, the business of Brantons was sold for a second time to the current proprietors it was still under the ownership of a Mr. Shapero but, considering the 44 years that had elapsed since it was first purchased from Thomas's widow Bridget, it is very probable that this gentleman was more than likely a son or other descendant of the Mr. Shapero who was a friend of Thomas Branton.

The decision to purchase the business by the current owners, the Furmage family, came about in unusual circumstances. At the time Brantons Ltd. employed a jeweller and watchmaker by the name of Sidney Clarke. On hearing of Mr. Shapero's decision to sell the business Sidney, concerned about his own future, approached Bob and Ken Furmage the owners of Gardiners Jewellers in Hepworth's Arcade with the suggestion that they should go into partnership with him and purchase the business of Brantons from Mr. Shepero. Following negotiations between the two parties a deal was struck, but prior to this being finalised Sidney Clarke withdrew his interest. Regardless of that the deal went ahead and shortly after Bob Furmage and his son Ken became the new owners of Brantons Ltd.

In the mid 1960's a decision was made by Hull City Council to widen the section of Ferensway south of Anlaby Road. This entailed the compulsory purchase and subsequent demolition of several properties including the premises occupied by Brantons. Around the same time Bob Furmage heard of the vacant shop at 13 Hepworth's Arcade and the fact that Brantons would soon be needing new premises coupled with his own desire to re-establish his business in the Arcade where he had begun his working life resulted in his decision to take the empty shop.

Brantons opened at no. 13 in 1967, but continued to trade from the premises on Anlaby Road until just prior to their demolition in 1969.

The business remains to this day at no. 13 Hepworth's Arcade although ownership of the concern has now passed to the next generation of the Furmage family in the form of Ken's two sons Rob and Anthony and his daughter Janet, with Anthony taking charge of the Brantons side of the business. (See also Isaac Gardiner — 10 Hepworth's Arcade).

The jeweller's scales which belonged to Thomas Capes Branton in 1895

John Hiam.
Courtesy of Kathleen Hiam.

shortly after he established his first shop at 119 Witham, were discovered by the author in a local antique shop whilst searching for material for this book. They have since been purchased by Anthony Furmage and will soon be displayed in the Brantons shop in Hepworth's Arcade.

NO. 11 HEPWORTH'S ARCADE

Mrs. Fanny Hiam, Confectioner (later Hiam's Refreshment Rooms and Hiam's Café), 1896-1969

John Hiam came to Hull in the early 1880's from a farming community in Cambridgeshire and first appeared in the Hull directories in 1888 when he is listed as a dairyman residing at 13 Park Road. Four years later in 1892, although John himself is

154

not listed, his wife Fanny is shown as being a confectioner trading from no. 7 in the newly built Paragon Arcade (now occupied by Segals Jewellers). By 1895, in which year the couple changed their home address to 3 Lawrence Villas, Newland Avenue, Fanny had also moved the confectioners to the larger premises of no. 5 (now occupied by G's Sweater Shop). The following year the business was transferred across the city to the previously unoccupied shop at no. 11 Hepworth's Arcade and by 1899, by which time it had been expanded into the neighbouring shop of no. 9, was described in the directories as being a confectioners and refreshment rooms. John and Fanny, who were by that time both involved in the running of the business, moved house again in 1900 to 180 Newland Avenue which would be a fair measure that their venture was prospering. In their café or 'Hiam's Refreshment Rooms' as it was correctly titled they were ably assisted by five sisters, Sallie, Nellie, Emmie, Eva and Lily Spencer. Sallie had trained in the business in Bradford from where the family originated and became the Café manageress. When Fanny Hiam died in 1903 aged 64 her husband John continued in the business but at the age of 70 obviously felt the need for some younger assistance and recruited the help of his daughter Emily. Emily had previously been employed for twenty years at Brombys Newsagents on Monument Bridge and when she came into the business insisted on playing a background roll rather than taking charge

over Sallie who was by that time very ill. Following the death of his wife, John (and daughter Emily) moved house once more to no. 4 Auckland Avenue, Cottingham Road, but in 1917 he too died, aged 84. To assist his sister in the running of the family business Emily's brother Thomas, a surveyor, living at the time in Andover moved to Hull. He took a house across the road from his sister at no. 5 Auckland Avenue and between them the pair continued in the business taking care to achieve the high standards that had been set by their parents. Apparently each morning Thomas would inspect the waitresses to ensure a neat and tidy appearance. In later years Thomas's wife Bessie was proprietor of Gwenap in Princes Avenue which was, at the time, a very popular ladies fashion shop in one of the more prestigious areas of the city. Around 1920

Emily Hiam.
Courtesy of Pat Smith.

Thomas Hiam.
Courtesy of Kathleen Hiam.

the Hiams took into their employ a new cook by the name of Alice Sutton. Alice had, since leaving school aged 14 in 1918, worked at nearby Marks and Spencer but saw the vacancy at the café as an opportunity for a change in career. She was presumably reasonably successful in her new position as in later years, after leaving the Arcade and following a spell with Fields Restaurant and Café, Alice became the first cook employed at Jackson's prestigious new restaurant in Paragon Street. In 1927 the daughter of Eva Spencer who had by that time married and was known as Eva Simpson came into the business. Her name was Ena and she was destined to spend the whole of her working life at the café which she joined at the age of 14 and ended up owning for over twenty years before retiring after 42 years in 1969. Here follows some brief extracts from the diary of Ena Simpson (later Lumley) which she aptly entitled 'FROM WASHER UP TO PROPRIETORESS'.

"The business was built up on very good pure food, well cooked and served by happy, very loyal people. All of my aunties stayed with the business until they married or in the cases of Sallie and Nellie when they died at an early age. When Miss Hiam joined the business she stayed and did all the kitchen work rather than go over Sallie who by that time was very poorly, but kept being away ill and coming back for over two years. That was the background to my loyalty to a person who had been so wonderful to my family and whom my Dad wanted to repay by sending his eldest child, and from a child of three I can remember my mother taking me to see Miss Hiam and being told 'You will work here someday'. I can remember how lovely the Arcade used to look with hanging baskets all the way down the unusual roof and a small orchestra on the balcony. Miss Hiam told me one day that my mother had ordered a ham sandwich from Da. Hiam as she called him. 'Will you cut the bread thin Da?' she asked, 'Aye and the ham and all my lass', was his sharp reply. He was a jovial man with a lovely long white beard, rosy face and twinkling eyes. I can only vaguely remember him.

I started work at Hiams when I was 14 and was very excited when my mother bought me a uniform of 6 dainty white nippy aprons, 3 white headbands slotted with black velvet, a black dress, black shoes, black wall stockings and 3 overalls including a black one to wear to tend to two great big fire ovens which I had to clean out and light. It was a very small kitchen and I had to work 1 week scrubbing floors and taking out trays, 1 week baking the pastries and 1 week as waitress. My first day seemed endless and one of the staff suggested that I put the clock on one hour whilst Miss Hiam was having her tea but forgot to tell me that she had her own watch

Eva Spencer (later Eva Simpson).
Courtesy of Pat Smith.

and so by the time she emerged we had got all cleared up and were ready for home. 'Who put the clock on?' she cried and after a silence during which I could feel myself going more and more red and feeling more and more guilty I owned up and was told I would be getting my cards on Saturday. When I went for them I was given a talk on J. R. Ferens and that his success was that he was never a clock watcher. Needless to say I was told 'You will be told lots of times you will get your cards but I hope you will learn some day not to be led by others.'

I am afraid that I was a raw lass and that giggling was one of my greatest failures. Many a time I

Ena Simpson (later Lumley).
Courtesy of Pat Smith.

Emily Hiam.
Courtesy of Kathleen Hiam.

was sent into the Arcade until I stopped laughing only to come back and be as bad as ever. I was often reminded that my mother was a wonderful waitress and a great asset to the business and I was told later on by Miss Hiam, 'I want you in the shop — you can sell more than anyone. You make people think that they are hungry even if they are not.' I was badly teased at first. One morning when Miss Hiam and the manageress were not there the older girls got me on the red flat table and came over me with all the sharp carving knives. I was terrified but they thought it a great joke. Another day, a Saturday afternoon, I was told that I had to wash the Arcade and put plenty of paper down. I started and after a while came in with tears streaming down my face. The Arcade was crowded and I had been kicked and pushed. Miss Hiam was furious with the girls.

After I had been there a few weeks I noticed a great bowl of chips thrown away every night so I plucked up the courage and asked if I could take them home. Mother would be out at night class, Dad in his billiards room at the bottom of the garden and the rest of the family in bed. I used to get out the chip pan and we all had Ena's chip treat as they used to call it. It was a rule that for anything that was spoilt we had to pay a few coppers out of our own pockets. One such day the manageress came for the shortbreads but I said that they were not done. In half an hour she came again and I told her that they were not hard yet. I did not know that they did not go hard until they were taken out. My goodness they were hard as Douglas, Doris and Jean (my brother and sisters) found out when I took them home.

After a year of really hard work Miss Hiam asked me if I would go and live with her as she was lonely and wanted company and at the age of 15 I had to make a great decision. I was happy at home where I had good parents, two sisters and a brother. I was promised only waitress work, a little more money and my keep which was worth a great deal. I decided to go and my mother made me lovely new clothes to take. I soon made a new life and was taken to Newland Chapel where I made a lot of new friends.

I soon began to know a lot of the customers and became interested in them and their children. On many occasions during meal times I would get up and make a half bottle and feed a baby so that a young mother could have a meal in peace. Years later people would say 'You used to give my daughter her bottle and now she is bringing her children in.' I remember one customer who had been married for twelve years with no family who came in every week for an apple pie. One week she came in with a lovely baby and told that she had no idea that she was pregnant but blamed it all on our famous apple pies. She was the happiest mother I have ever seen and needless to say she ordered a large dinner plate pie nearly every week. I really loved my work, the pay was poor but we were well fed. I can remember how I enjoyed beef pie and veg and used to ask for second first course instead of a pudding. Many times after lunch when I was still looking a little pathetic and hungry I was given a pudding as well. Even during the War we always had good food.

The Arcade was always crowded and Marks and Spencer's Penny Bazaar was a great attraction. In later years there was Dinsdale's Joke Shop and although we were often pestered by stink bombs I think that it brought in a lot of trade. A very special feature of our trade was one shilling teas for maid's afternoon out which used to be on a Wednesday. Fish and Chips, Tea, Bread and Cake for one shilling and various other choices. We used to get quite a lot of girls in and would often hear all sorts of stories about their mistresses. Some of our great busy days were Martinmas Tuesday when we used to have crowds of country lads who only got paid once a year. My wages at the time were nine shillings a week but I would get sixpence extra for every ten shilling order, so I would recommend double dinners, double pudding and a large plate of cakes and tea. They never refused any so I had a lot of sixpences. Another busy day was August Tuesday and I remember one day I had made a lot of minced beef pies and for a special treat I had made a date pie for the staff to have with a cup of tea when the rush was over. When I came to serve the pie it could not be found and I can only assume that it had been served up with veg and gravy but no one complained or even left any. Hull Fair Saturday was another busy day which I almost used to dread. We were always so busy and never had time to have a meal ourselves. In later years when the business was left to me I think that, because of my past experience, I knew how to treat staff and consequently got the best from them because I tried to treat them how I would like to be treated. I had always been told what to do whereas I would always ask my staff and would welcome their suggestions and ideas. During the War years getting good staff was very difficult as all the useful ones had been called up to do more important work. It was at this time that Olive came. She was rather slow but would do anything for me. After the other staff had gone home I would get a nice tea for Olive and myself after which we would scrub right through every room. Olive's mother once told me that I made Olive very happy by letting her know that I needed her and that she was helping me. That was great for me as I don't know what I would have done without her."

Hiam's café continued to prosper and was, by all accounts, the first stopping point for many of the passengers who arrived in Hull from Lincolnshire on the ferry which operated regularly to and from the pier in Nelson Street. The café can be vaguely seen at the bottom of the Arcade in the photograph taken around 1935 shown on page 64. In 1931 a young lady named Ada Richardson joined the staff at 'Hiam's Jubilee Tea Rooms' as they were then known. Ada, now Mrs. Ada Drake, recalls:

'I was only 14 when I joined Hiams and stayed until I married in 1941. The café was run at the time by Miss Hiam and her brother Thomas assisted by Ena Simpson who was Miss Hiam's companion and lived with her in Auckland Avenue. I remember that each night, before we closed, we had to put tin cans under the legs of the tables and chairs to stop the rats which used to come up from the cellar from climbing up them. I had a friend who worked at the Kiddieland toyshop at the end of the Arcade and although it is now over fifty years since we both worked there we still keep in touch.'

During the War many of the shops in the Arcade were empty but the café continued to thrive often finding itself busier than it had been previously due to the adverse effect the hostilities were having on their competitors. Miss Y, who worked as cook/waitress between 1939 and 1945, recalls:

'The cooking at Hiams was done on an old fashioned black iron coal range which caused us to be very busy as we could carry on when both Lyons and the Kardoma in Whitefriargate, who used electric and gas, were forced to close due to not being able to use their facilities. I remember that during air raids we all had to go into the cellar which was underneath the toilets in the corner of the Arcade and that, for most of us, that seemed worse than the air raid itself because it used to start to fill up with water and there were always lots of rats scurrying around.'

Edith Gilgeous who, as a girl of 14, started work at Hiams in 1940 recalls:

'I worked six days a week from early morning until 7.00 o'clock in the evening (eight o'clock on Saturdays) for the princely sum of seven shillings and sixpence a week ($37\frac{1}{2}$ pence) but soon found that good service to customers was sometimes rewarded with a tip. This was normally about twopence or threepence but I remember once getting half-a-crown ($12\frac{1}{2}$ pence) from a man in a uniform which was the equivalent of two days wages for me. I recollect that, in those days, the stairs to the upstairs were directly in front of you as you walked through the door and there was a tiny kitchen in the left hand corner. It was rather like a traditional English café, very old fashioned, and served buttered teacakes and muffins, and cakes were always presented to the customers on a cake stand. As the youngest I always got the task of taking the meals to the customers upstairs and remember both Miss Hiam and Miss Simpson being very strict with us all.'

Both Thomas and Emily died during the War years, Thomas in 1940 aged 79 and Emily 1943 aged 76. It can be assumed that with Emily surviving her brother, sole ownership of the business came to her as when she passed away three years later she bequeathed that the café should be left to her employee and companion for sixteen years Ena Simpson.

Ena, who married in 1946 and became Ena Lumley operated the café for a further 26 years until, in 1969, because of failing health, she decided to retire. She is pictured taking a stroll down the Arcade in which she had spent the whole of her working life on her final day as

Ena Lumley takes a stroll down Hepworth's Arcade, on her final day as proprietor of Hiam's Café.
Courtesy of Pat Smith.

proprietor of Hiam's Café, Friday 4th July 1969. Ena passed away in 1987 aged 74.

Hiam's Café (Patricia Tuxworth and Alan Johnson), 1969-1974

When Ena Lumley decided to retire Pat Tuxworth and Alan Johnson who were at the time operating both the coins and stamps shop at no. 12 in the Arcade and the arts and crafts outlet at nos. 20 and 22 saw the opportunity to diversify further still and purchased the business from Mrs. Lumley. Whilst retaining the existing staff they attempted to bring the café into the 1970's and began a phase of modernisation which included replacing the staircase which ran up the middle of the two shops. The existing staircase which was probably the original one was apparently very narrow and it was the intention of the partners eventually to refurbish the upper floor of no. 11, which had in recent years only been used as a storeroom, to create an additional seating area. The intended refurbishment was, however, never completed as, after five years in the business Pat and Alan sold out to Jim Kane in 1974. Their departure from the café also spelled the end of the name of Hiam's Café which had been known throughout the city and probably in a good part of Northern Lincolnshire for nearly eighty years.

The Coffee Cup, Café, 1974-Present Date

Following an extensive career in the London Hotel and Catering industry Jim Kane settled into a position of Lecturer in Food Studies at the Hull College

161

of Further Education in Queens Gardens. Whilst in that position the opportunity to purchase the long established business of Hiam's Café in Hepworth's Arcade arose and Jim decided it was a worthwhile investment. Following his take-over of the business he began a programme of changes which began immediately with altering the name of the business from Hiam's Café to The Coffee Cup and continued some years later by extending the premises into a vacant area beneath the caretaker's flat. The newly acquired space which led off the shop at no. 9 in a westerly direction behind the existing Arcade lavatories was used to accommodate a new kitchen thus allowing extra space within the original premises for additional seating. Around the same time the Arcade caretaker Edwin passed away and with Hull City Council deciding that he would not be replaced Jim successfully negotiated the take-over of the part of the caretaker's flat above his own premises. Further expansion which included the conversion of the open area to the rear of the flat into part of the upper floor and the addition of further toilet facilities followed and by the mid 1980's the upper floor of nos. 9 and 11 was opened as an additional seating area. In the late 1980's plans for a link through between the Arcade and the Market Hall were made and, as these included the area used at the time as the Café kitchen, it was necessary for an extension to be built on the rear of the premises to accommodate a new kitchen area. The staircase which led up the centre of the two shops was moved to run along the eastern wall of no. 11.

Jim and his staff continue to this day to operate The Coffee Cup enjoying a brisk trade from not only the great number of people employed in the area but also the many shoppers and tourists attracted to the 'Old Town' area of Hull.

NO. 9 HEPWORTH'S ARCADE

No. 9 Hepworth's Arcade was the only shop in the original structure not to have an upper floor. The reason for this was that the Caretaker's Flat which was situated over the Public Toilets in the corner of the Arcade extended eastwards with the sitting room/kitchen being over no. 9.

Hy. Savage, House Furnisher, 1897

Henry Savage started in business in Hull in 1895 in which year the directories list him as a wringing machine and perambulator dealer at 5 Brunswick Arcade, Beverley Road. By the following year one of Henry's neighbours in Brunswick Arcade was a young Hungarian immigrant who had taken the premises in an attempt to establish a dyeing and cleaning business in the city and was, it can be safely assumed, experiencing a certain degree of success — his name was Frederick Zerny. Two years later Henry expanded his horizons and began dealing in house furnishings from the previously unoccupied shop at no. 9 Hepworth's Arcade whilst maintaining his business and premises in Brunswick Arcade. The prosperity of the new side to Mr. Savage's business must be viewed with some doubt as by the time the 1899 directories were published he had reverted to his original premises, had ceased trading in both furniture and perambulators and was described as a domestic machinery dealer. Although that was the final mention in the directories of Hy. Savage, a man by the name of Henry William Savage was also listed in the directories between 1896 and 1900 at 139 Holderness Road, an address which coincidentally was occupied some 12 years later by Abraham Altham Ltd. (see no. 5 Hepworth's Arcade). As no trade is attributed to Henry William Savage it has not been possible to establish beyond doubt that this was the same man or whether the premises on Holderness Road were occupied by another business or were indeed, at the time, a residential property.

Mrs. Fanny Hiam, Confectioner (later Hiam's Refreshment Rooms), 1899-1969

See no. 11 Hepworth's Arcade.

Hiam's Café (Patricia Tuxworth and Alan Johnson), 1969-1974

See no. 11 Hepworth's Arcade.

The Coffee Cup, Café 1974-Present Date

See no. 11 Hepworth's Arcade.

THE DWELLINGHOUSE, HEPWORTH'S ARCADE

The dwellinghouse as the accommodation was described in the electoral registers was actually the caretaker's flat which was situated above both the shop at no. 9 and the public lavatories in the corner of the Arcade. It led out onto the balcony facing the Arcade and a rear yard at first floor level facing Ye Old Blue Bell Public House.

For ninety years this flat was home to the individuals or couples who were responsible for the cleaning, maintenance and presumably security of the Arcade.

Although, as the plan shows, the flat was only small and obviously poor by modern standards it is highly likely that, in the early days of the Arcade, this was regarded as a rather desirable abode and much superior to those occupied by many of the residents in the Old Town at the time.

Although long since disconnected, a bell to summon the Caretaker during the times when the gates were closed was situated at the Silver Street end of the Arcade and to this day the bell push is still visible to the left of no. 9 Silver Street.

Regrettably, although evidence has been uncovered on at least eight different individuals or couples holding the position of Arcade Caretaker, it has only been possible to establish any further information on three of those parties.

The succession of Arcade Caretakers is as follows:

Fergus O'Connor Brown 1900—1901

John Thompson 1903—1909

Fred Howsman 1911—1913

Fred and Maria Beckett, 1914-1926

Prior to becoming the Arcade Caretaker Fred Beckett was a Constable in the East Riding Police Force based in the Driffield area. He had joined the Force in 1882 but shortly after his retirement in 1912 came to Hull with his wife Maria and took over the vacant position of Arcade Caretaker.

Fred grew aspidistra plants which, by all accounts, gave a colourful display

163

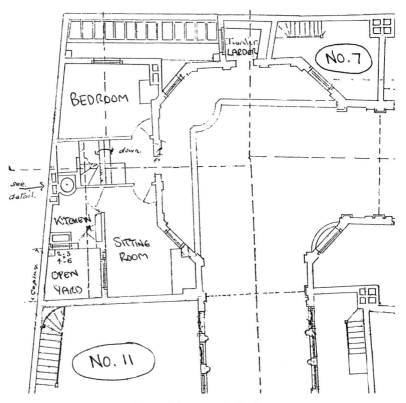

Plan of the caretaker's flat.
Courtesy of Gelder and Kitchen.

from the balcony in the corner of the Arcade outside his flat. He also bred canaries and apparently, at times, suspended the caged birds from the centre of the dome in the roof of the Arcade. He retired from the position in 1926.

William and Ellen Weddell, 1926-1935

Harry and Grace Fish, 1935-1937

Harry Fish was reportedly a keen motorcyclist and was, for a period, Secretary of the Hull Motorcycling Club. Together with his wife Grace he undertook the position of Arcade Caretaker for only a brief spell and reportedly was noted for his punctuality in both opening the Arcade gates at 7.00 a.m prompt and locking them again at 10.00 p.m. The couple kept a dog called Simmy which would guard the Arcade during closing hours and was apparently named after Mrs. Wallace Simpson who was making national headlines at the time. When the couple retired from the position in 1937 and moved to a house in Cottingham Avenue off Osborne Street they were unable to take Simmy with them and consequently gave the pet as a wedding present to the Arcade Postman Charlie Linford. Charlie recalls:

> 'Simmy could be quite ferocious to what he saw as an intruder into the Arcade and as I was often the first person to pass through in a morning I was greeted by his baring of teeth, growling and barking.

I soon realised it was wise to come prepared and began taking him a small tit-bit each morning. We soon became good friends and I was glad to give Simmy a home when Harry and Grace were unable to.'

William and Eva Ironside, 1939-1940
and finally
Alice and Edwin Jackson, 1941-1984

Alice Jackson first took over the position of Caretaker during the Second World War and although it has not been possible to verify the exact date it is likely that the year was either 1940 or 1941. It has been suggested that Alice was keen on a bet on the horses apparently with little success and that following a string of losses ended up losing her house in Great Thornton Street. Following the loss of her home and having discovered that the job of Arcade Caretaker had accommodation provided, she success-fully applied for the position and moved into the flat with her son Edwin.

Fred Beckett.
Courtesy of Lillian Robson.

Much to the annoyance of the local banks Alice apparently kept chickens in the small open area at the rear of the flat and was, by all accounts, a formidable character who normally dressed completely in black except for her old straw hat. Many people who have reflected their memories of the Arcade as a child have told of this 'wicked witch' type character and recall keeping a tight hold on their parent's hands whenever they had to pass her. Alice died in early 1957 aged 76 and the electoral registers published later that year list Edwin alone in 'the dwellinghouse', so it is likely that it was from that year he also took over the position of Caretaker. Edwin, like his mother, was of small build and was by some people cruelly referred to as the 'Arcade Gnome'. Whilst his mother was Caretaker Edwin worked for Ranks Flour Mill and when Alice passed away, was offered the position on a part-time basis. As refusal would no doubt also have resulted in the loss of his home Edwin took the job and went on to become the longest serving of all the Arcade Caretakers. Although Edwin never married he did build up a wide circle of friends amongst both the traders and customers in the Arcade and the numerous other Caretakers who were resident in the various banks and other buildings in the old town around that time. He grew particularly close to the Dinsdale family (see no. 10 Hepworth's Arcade) who would take him out on his days off including regular trips with George Senior to the main race meetings. He built up a strong friendship with George Junior, in later years acting as babysitter for George's two daughters.

Edwin, who could perhaps be described as having a bark worse than his bite, was always game for a laugh and gladly agreed to pose for Ken Furmage (see

Edwin Jackson.
Courtesy of Ken Furmage.

no. 10 Hepworth's Arcade — Gardiners) for the photograph which Ken later entered into a local photography exhibition under the title of 'The Floating Vote'.

Although long past normal retirement age Edwin continued in the position until February 1984 when he passed away aged 82. His death spelt the end of not only over forty years of occupation by the Jackson family but also nearly ninety years of Arcade Caretakers, as following the death of Edwin the Hull City Council took the decision that the position would be terminated.

Since 1984 the gates on the Arcade have been replaced to increase security and both the maintenance and cleaning are handled by outside staff. The Caretaker's flat has been divided with part, including the external area to the rear, being converted to an extra seating area for the café. What was once Edwin's bedroom is now used for storage and the small room off the balcony which he used as a pantry now forms part of the upper floor to no. 7.

NO. 7 HEPWORTH'S ARCADE

Abraham Altham Ltd., Tea Merchants, 1897-1913

See no. 5 Hepworth's Arcade.

A. Welsh, Milliner, 1915-1916

Although the business of A. Welsh, Milliner was only listed in the directories as being in Hepworth's Arcade for two years it is very possible that it was still in occupation during 1917 and 1918 when no directories were published. It is reported that although the business was listed under the name of Albert Welsh it was actually operated by his wife and that Albert was employed by a Gentlemen's Outfitter elsewhere in the City.

In 1915 Albert is shown as residing at 69 Queens Road and although the following year's directory did not list his home address it did credit him, in addition to owning the millinery business in the Arcade, as being a confectioner with premises at 18 Newland Avenue. By the time the 1919 directory was issued no. 7 Hepworth's Arcade was attributed to Miss Marion Walsh and both the premises on Newland Avenue and Mr. Welsh were unlisted.

The name of Albert Welsh remained absent from the directories for a period of seventeen years until 1933 when he re-appeared and was described as a gent's outfitter living at 6 Sutherland Avenue. By 1935 the business had been established in premises at nos. 66 and 68 Jameson Street and, although Albert died around 1950 aged only 57 and the ownership of the concern changed hands, the business of A. Welsh Ltd., prospered and continued to trade from those premises for nearly 40 years more until 1989.

Miss Marion Walsh (or possibly Mary Ann Walsh) Catholic Repository, 1919-1933

A repository is, according to the dictionary, a storage place but it is very likely that, considering this one was situated in retail premises, it also served another purpose possibly as a shop for religious books and other material. Miss Marion Walsh first appeared in the Hull directories in 1914 when she was listed as residing at 77 Coltman Street, an address which she kept throughout her tenancy in the Arcade and up to her final mention in the directories in 1939. Following its departure from no. 7 the Catholic Repository was listed as being at 81 Charles Street where it reportedly stayed until the mid 1970's. Although listed clearly in the Hull Directories as Marion Walsh the name attributed to the premises in several electoral registers was Mary Ann Walsh. It should therefore be noted that the 1891 census lists a Mary A. Walsh aged 41 and originating from Ireland as one of the Sisters at the Convent of the Sisters of Mercy on Anlaby Road. It has not been established beyond doubt that this was the same lady but, because of the similarity of names coupled with the fact that the Sisters of Mercy were an order of Roman Catholic nuns, it must be a theory worthy of consideration.

Arts and Crafts (C. Stocks), 1948-1949

Christopher Stocks first opened for business in the Arcade shortly after the Second World War selling art and handicraft meterials from no. 7 Hepworth's Arcade. Although he never had any lessons Chris apparently had a natural talent for art and painted a number of pictures which he proudly hung around the walls of his shop. It is a reasonable assumption that the business was successful as by 1950 he had vacated that shop and moved to the larger premises of nos. 20 and 22 in the Arcade where he expanded his range of merchandise to include rafia for basket making and model making plaster and casts. He continued to trade from his new address assisted by his wife Marjorie for nearly fifteen years until his sudden death in the mid 1960's.

The Leather Shop / Northern Leather Supplies / Selby Leedham and Co., Leather Specialists / Wholesale and Retail Fashion Jewellery, 1951-1969

Despite its three different trading names this business was owned by one man — Geoffrey Selby Leedham and operated by himself and his wife Irene.

Whilst serving in the Police Force in Eastbourne, Geoffrey Leedham met his wife to be Irene Foster who originated from Hull. Although the couple married in the south coast resort it was in Hull that they decided to settle and Geoffrey arranged for a transfer to the Hull City Police Force whom he joined in May 1936.

After over twelve years of service in Hull he left the force and together with

Irene and Geoffrey Leedham.
Courtesy of Angela Wright.

Irene opened a fishmonger's shop on Spring Bank West. That venture however was shortlived as Irene found it difficult to get used to both the smell and the mess of freshly gutted fish.

In 1951 the couple took over the premises of no. 7 Hepworth's Arcade recently vacated by Christopher Stocks and commenced business selling hand-crafted goods. Although the venture originally traded under the name of The Leather Shop a great proportion of the business was the manufacture and sale of basketware and lampshades. Irene was particularly talented in all types of sewing and needlework and was, for many years, wardrobe mistress for the Hull Amateur Operatic Society. Using those skills she made covers for the wire lampshade frames her husband produced and in addition to many individual private orders a steady trade was built up supplying some of the larger stores in the City including both Carmichaels of George Street and Hammonds.

In the late 1950's, wishing to expand beyond the confines of the small shop at no. 7, the couple also took over the lease of no. 17 and expanded into the manufacture of hand-crafted jewellery. A photograph of the interior of no. 17 in which the wide array of lampshade frames are clearly visible is shown. Their daughter Angela recalls:

> 'Whilst I was still at school I was often called upon to help out on a Saturday and was given the task of cementing the stones into small brooches and was paid the princely sum of sixpence in old money (2½ pence) for every dozen I completed.'

Geoffrey installed a small welding machine on the upper floor of no. 17 which enabled him to produce at a greater rate the lampshade frames that were in great demand from not only the public but also the many craft shops that had sprung up across the City during the recent years. The couple also supplied

Interior of Selby Leedham and Co. 17 Hepworth's Arcade.
Courtesy of Angela Wright.

kits enabling handicraft enthusiasts to create their own jewellery. In March 1969 the Leedhams surrendered their lease on no. 7 and seven months later retired from the Arcade completely having sold the business and the lease on no. 17 to former employee Anne Shimmels. For a short while after leaving the Arcade Geoffrey continued to work on a part-time basis manufacturing lampshades from his home in Willerby before illness forced his complete retirement. Following a trafic accident at his home Geoffrey died in November 1987 aged 77. His wife Irene passed away just eleven weeks later in February 1988 aged 79. Anne Shimmels continued to operate the concern for a further four years still trading under the name of the founder before selling the business to Supercast Ltd., in 1973.

Top Pictures (P. J. Leslie), 1969-1977

Peter Leslie was the youngest son of Norman Leslie who ran an antiquarian book shop in the Arcade (see no. 4 Hepworth's Arcade) and when he left school his first employment was with his father's friend Arthur Fanthorpe (see no. 6 Hepworth's Arcade). It was through Arthur that young Peter was introduced to Harry Screaton who had a plumbing business on Princes Dock Side and took him on as an apprentice. Peter served his apprenticeship and became qualified as a plumber, but shortly after marrying felt he needed a change in occupation and for a short time worked for his father's business making picture frames. During that period the shop at no. 7 in the Arcade became vacant and Peter took the decision to take over the lease and set himself up in business selling, framing and restoring old paintings and photographs. The venture

169

Peter Leslie.
Courtesy of Peter Leslie.

which he named Top Pictures proved to be a success to the extent that a few years later he opened a second shop in his home town of Hornsea which his father, who by that time had retired from his bookshop, ran for him. After nearly eight years in the Arcade Peter made the decision to move south to St. Mary's Church, near Babbacombe in Devon where he opened a similar shop. He has since returned to Hull and reverted to his trade as a plumber but fondly recalls his days in Hepworth's Arcade.

Top Pictures (Gavin Gray), 1977-Present Day

Following Peter Leslie's decision to sell the business and move to Devon Gavin Gray took over. Prior to taking over Top Pictures Gavin had had a chequered working history which included shipping clerk, market trader, discotheque manager, English teacher and cleaner spread between England, Germany and Spain. He was later accepted for a graphic design course at the Medway College of Design and, after cramming a four year course into just two and a half years, armed with his new qualifications, took a post with a London design agency before returning to Spain to work for the first design agency in the country in Malaga.

By the mid-seventies he had again returned to England and following a short spell with a local design agency to quote his own words Gavin 'sort of dropped out'. He explains:

> 'I went to live in a railway coach at Cowden and lived the Bohemian life keeping about thirty odd animals of various types and working on the farms in the area to make a living. I did a bit of painting and some carpentry and was just considering the possibility of taking off to Wales when someone told me that the shop in Hepworth's

Gavin Gray in his workshop.
Photo courtesy of Gavin Gray.

170

Arcade was up for sale. I decided to put my remaining money into that instead.'

Gavin (pictured in his workshop) spent the first four years of his new venture scouring the country for the stock he needed and making the contacts to enable him to supply special requests by customers. Although often a customer would require a single print for a special place in their home from time to time Gavin received orders on a much larger scale. He recalls:

'I was once commissioned to supply 100 landscape prints of all parts of the country to decorate the bulkheads of two barges moored off the Falklands to be used as personnel accommodation after the war, the idea apparently being to make the men feel at home. I like to think that they served their purpose but I understand that one of the barges eventually sank and the other was towed off to New York where it became a prison. It's to be hoped that the inmates appreciate a glimpse of old England.'

In addition to supplying paintings and prints to satisfy customers' individual needs Gavin continued the picture framing service originated by his predecessor at Top Pictures and although the necessary tools and materials were acquired with the business the practical knowledge was not and Gavin had to teach himself the skill. He admits that his earlier experience in graphic design and carpentry were of assistance but also that it took him some time to master the art. Gavin now provides a quality framing service for both individual clients and for such major concerns as British Gas and United Towing as well as holding a large stock of antique frames.

Reflecting on his time in the Arcade Gavin confesses that he had originally only intended to stay for around five years but now, some eighteen years after he took over Top Pictures, admits to having developed a great love for old things which have become the specialist field of the business and it is possibly for that reason that he has chosen to stay for some thirteen years longer than originally planned.

NO. 5 HEPWORTH'S ARCADE

Abraham Altham Ltd., Tea Dealers, 1895-1913

Abraham Altham, the founder after whom the business was named, was born in Haggate near Burnley, Lancashire in 1841. As his name suggests Abraham was born into a devoutly religious family, his father, who was the local schoolmaster, also being a preacher in the Baptist Chapels of the neighbourhood. With both of his parents dying when he was relatively young Abraham was raised by his grandfather who was a grocer and farmer at nearby Holt Hill and along with his upbringing obviously came an insight into the grocery trade which was to play a major part in his life. After leaving school Abraham did not enter straight into the grocery trade, but served an apprenticeship as a hewer of stone at Catlow Quarries near Nelson. At the close of his apprenticeship in 1864, at the age of 23, he purchased a wholesale grocery business in Bridge Street, Burnley and later, after moving premises to Manchester Road in the town, went into partnership with a firm known as

Abraham Altham.
Courtesy of Burnley Central Library.

Holgate and Co. In 1872 that partnership was dissolved and Abraham expanded into the wholesale tea business with premises in Ormerod Street in the town, and one year later opened the first of what was soon to become an extensive chain of retail tea shops. Expansion continued at a heady pace with additional branches in Burnley, Darwen, Bury and Farnworth being opened the same year. Over the next two decades the growth of the business continued until there was a total of 64 branches including Leeds (which alone had seven shops), Bradford, Halifax, Hull and York. The entrepreneurial skills of this devout Baptist were, to say the least, brilliantly effective. To attract additional business to his stores he would offer what he called presents which would vary in value depending on the quantity of tea purchased. These 'presents' were normally useful articles designed to appeal to the frugal housewives of the North. Those buying a quarter pound of tea were entitled to a pint mug, a plate or a sardine opener whereas larger purchases brought teapots, frying pans, buckets, door mats and even bedsteads. Altham issued thousands of leaflets proclaiming the quality of his teas and the presents that went with them. Special offers came out weekly and sales soared. What was presumably rather unique in Victorian England was that Altham even had his own advertising jingle which went to the tune of Auld Lang Syne.

'Its fame is known on every hand
Where'er the traveller roams,
'Tis used and loved throughout the land
In many a thousand homes.
When gathering round the evening meal
With friends and family,
What adds more to the joys we feel
Than drinking Altham's Tea.'

He also commissioned a picture of five philanthropists, including the Earl of Shaftesbury and Florence Nightingale taking five o'clock tea together. Thousands were printed and exchanged for tea labels.

After two years in the tea business Altham made a decision that was eventually to have a long-lasting effect on the direction in which the business he had founded would take. He decided to treat his customers to a day's outing to the seaside and chose Burnley Fair, an eagerly awaited local holiday, for the trip. The *Burnley Advertiser* of 25th July 1874 reported:

172

'On Thursday, the 9th inst. Mr. Altham, tea merchant of Market Place, Burnley gave his customers in Burnley and the surrounding district a grand trip to Blackpool. A special train started from Nelson at around six o'clock, calling at Brierfield, Burnley and Rosegrove arriving at Blackpool at eight o'clock. The excursionists, headed by the Brierfield Brass Band, marched to the Temperance Hall where there was plenty of hot tea to which the company did ample justice. In the afternoon the excursionists were again supplied with tea.'

Hull Daily Mail advertisement, 1896.
Courtesy of the Hull Daily Mail.

Mr. Altham told his guests that the aim of the trip was to strengthen the confidence which should always exist between buyer and seller but although rail trips were a popular feature of English life in the 1870's and employers frequently entertained their workforce in this way to take one's customers was unusual, if not unique.

Following the original venture Mr. Altham's enthusiasm for running such trips grew rapidly year by year. In 1875 some 7000 customers went on excursions from Leeds, Halifax, Burnley, Blackburn, Bury, Darwen and Farnworth, the towns in which his tea business was becoming a household name. For the 1876 trip from Burnley to Blackpool the shopper had to produce the labels from 13 half-pound packets of tea.

Until 1877 Altham had merely used the trips as a means of increasing his tea sales but that year he also became a full scale travel agent. During May of that year Altham's stores in Lancashire and Yorkshire sold tickets for a Midland Railway's excursion from various points in the area to Birmingham.

Within a few weeks Altham was running his own trips. During the weeks leading up to Burnley Fair Altham addressed himself to Sunday School Committees and others offering good discounts for anyone guaranteeing the sale of one hundred adult tickets for the trips he was running to Blackpool, Southport and Liverpool. He also announced that arrangements had been made with Thomas Cook and Son for a trip to London and one to Scotland. Around 15,000 people went on the trips he organised and 'The Prince of Tea Merchants' as he was known to the popular press was rapidly becoming 'The Prince of Travel Agents', second only in probability to Thomas Cook and Son itself.

Had Altham not died in 1885 at the age of 44 there is no telling what the restless devotion to business of this strict teetotaller and Baptist would have achieved. Inside 13 years he had built up a chain of stores selling more than eight tons of tea a week to an estimated 250,000 drinkers and had grafted onto it the fastest growing travel agency in the country. Throughout that same period, although obviously spending much of his time ensuring the growth of his businesses, Altham, who was reportedly a keen Liberal, found time to stand as a councillor. He was elected in the St. Andrews Ward, Burnley in 1876 being successfully re-elected in 1878 and again in 1881. He was made a Justice of the Peace in May 1881 and the following year made an Alderman of the Borough. He remained actively involved in the Baptist movement and was a generous benefactor to numerous charities having reportedly given a total of five thousand pounds towards the building of a new hospital in Burnley.

When Altham died he left two daughters and three sons. The eldest of the sons, John, became a clergyman and the other two, Peter and Jesse followed him into the family business and were also founders and principal shareholders of the first cotton mill in Burnley to be powered by electricity. Part of that building is now the head office of Althams Travel Services.

The tea and travel businesses, which became a limited company in 1894 under the name of Althams Ltd. continued to flourish and by 1915 by which time they had over eighty branches, the yearly tea sales reached 680 tons.

During the inter-war period Althams operated two self-contained travel bureaux and in addition 52 shops sold railway tickets. These years also saw holiday destinations expand with trips to the Continent and Cruises becoming very popular, with cruises around Scandinavia or to the Mediterranean costing as little as one pound a day. Eighty per cent of the business still, however, came from the sale of railway tickets.

Following the Second World War air travel began to contribute substantially to the company's turnover and by 1946, following the formation of the International Air Transport Association (AITA), when two Althams offices were licensed to sell tickets, the travel side of the business had started to take over from the tea shops as the prime business of the firm. In 1950 Althams, along with other leading travel companies, formed the Association of British Travel Agents (ABTA) which in its early days had just 106 members, but now boasts over two thousand.

At the beginning of the 1960's the package holiday boom had arrived making destinations like Spain, Italy and the Balearic Isles as popular with British tourists as Blackpool, Morecambe and Southport had been with the previous generation. The profits generated for the business by this new market helped the progression of the company as a major Travel Agent in addition to offsetting the decline in success of the Tea Shops which by that time, unable to compete with the ever-growing number of supermarkets selling cheaper pre-packed goods, had moved into selling china, glassware and fancy goods.

By the mid 1960's the tea stores, obviously losing their battle with the supermarkets, one by one were closed. Those in smaller towns, many of which occupied prime sites brought in substantial capital and the branches in the larger towns were converted to full travel agencies. The final closure took place in 1968 and two years later the company changed its name to Althams Travel Services.

Althams Travel Services continue to operate to this day with the great grandson of Abraham Altham, Peter Kay, being the current company chairman. They have a total of 31 branches and recently came third in a national survey organised by the *Sunday Observer* to find the country's most appreciated Travel Agent.

The name of Abraham Altham, tea merchant, first appeared in the Hull directories for 1876 when he is listed at no. 7 Silver Street, the immediate adjoining property to the east of the Arcade at the Silver Street end. That property was, in fact, the subject of an agreement between its owners — the Charterhouse and Joseph Hepworth during the building of the Arcade in which the name of Altham appears. The next available directory — 1882 shows that in addition to the Silver Street branch the business had opened two more outlets at 82 Walker Street and 166 Waterloo Street. It also lists the head office in Burnley and one shop in Freeman Street, Grimsby. In 1894 by which year the construction of the Arcade had commenced a further shop in Hull at 7 Holderness Arcade, Witham, was opened and the following year the premises in Silver Street were substituted for one of the 'new' shops in the Arcade — no. 5. By 1896 when Hepworth's Arcade first appeared in the directories the business, which by that time was listed as Abraham Altham Ltd., had only two branches in Hull — no. 5 Hepworth's Arcade and 82 Walker Street. This is surprising as, around this time, the company was expanding and opening new branches throughout the North of England. The following year Althams also took over

Althams' Price List.

the previously unoccupied shop at no. 7 in the Arcade. No further change in the trading activities of the company in this area was noted until 1906 when a branch was opened at 65 Market Place, Beverley and later in 1909 when another at 17 Jameson Street, Hull was added. By 1913 the Beverley outlet had closed, but the number of shops was maintained at four with the opening of a branch in East Hull at 139 Holderness Road. In 1914 both the shop in Jameson Street and those in the Arcade had closed and a new outlet opened at no. 58 Whitefriargate, coincidentally next door to Jacksons Hatters who had left the Arcade three years earlier (see no. 60 Market Place). By 1925 that, too, had closed and was replaced by a branch at 8 Charles Street. The price list pictured would possibly indicate that this was the main branch with Walker Street and Holderness Road being sub-branches although it is equally possible that each shop issued such leaflets giving their own address in bold print. It has not been possible to ascertain the exact date of this price list, but it can be assumed that this would be between 1925 and 1940 as it was in that period that the company operated the three branches mentioned.

Regrettably as the last Hull Directory was published in 1939 and because none of the Althams shops appear in any of the subsequent telephone directories it has not been possible to establish exactly when the company closed their branches in the City. It has, however, been verified that the shop in Walker Street had changed ownership by the early 1940's and that, according to a publication in 1964, both the premises in Charles Street and on Holderness Road were still occupied by the company in that year. It is therefore likely that those two shops, which were by that time listed only as china and glassware dealers, were amongst the final ones to be closed by the company, thus ending a presence in the City of Hull by Althams that had lasted nearly ninety years.

Vernon's Florists, 1924-1925

The name of Vernon's florists appeared in the Hull directories for one year only — 1925 when they occupied no. 5 in the Arcade. Electoral registers for the period show that, in Autumn 1924, the proprietor Arnold Vernon lived at 44 Wellesley Avenue which would have made him a neighbour of Stanley F. Bastow who, at the time had five shops in the Arcade (Stanley lived at no. 9). They also show that his tenancy was a brief one as by the time the Autumn 1925 registers were issued he had gone.

The Radiograph Co., Wireless Dealers, 1925-1926

Following the departure of Mr. Vernon after his brief occupancy of no. 5 came another somewhat 'short lived' stay by the Radiograph Company. In Autumn 1925 the electoral register attributed no. 5 to Frederick William and May Casey of 153 Anlaby Road. By Spring the following year only the name of May Casey appeared on the register and by Autumn 1926 the property is not listed. That fact alone is not sufficient proof that the business had ceased trading by that time as many shops in the Arcade which were known to be occupied were also unlisted, but when the 1929 directory was published the name of the Radiograph Company had disappeared. This shop was reportedly one of the earliest in the city to stock wirelesses which would normally have suggested a brisk trade for the business and it is therefore very feasible that there were probably other reasons than lack of trade that caused the demise of the business.

Thomas Nicholson — Children's Outfitters, 1927-1933

The 'Little Ones Emporium' as the shop was titled was first listed in the directories in 1929 under the name of its owner Thomas Nicholson. However electoral registers have established that the property was first let to Thomas and Mary Elizabeth Nicholson of 19 Clifford Street, Hornsea in 1927. Thomas Nicholson was a clerk in the shipping department at Reckitts and by all accounts a respected and well liked man. The shop was managed by his daughter Evelyn who is pictured outside the premises in around 1929. Evelyn had previously been employed in the grocery trade in Hornsea and returned to that line of business when the 'Little Ones Emporium' closed in 1933, being appointed manageress of the Jackson's food store in her home town. During the Second World War, Evelyn left the retail business completely and went to work in London.

Alan Nicholson recalls:

'Evelyn was my elder sister and when she was working in the Arcade I was still at school. I remember on many occasions calling at the shop at lunchtime and her popping into Hiam's Café and getting a meal for me. In the early days the Arcade was vey busy but as soon as Marks and Spencer closed and moved to Whitefriargate trade fell sharply and I do not think it has ever been as busy since. Eventually trade fell to such a level that my father decided to 'call it a day' and closed the shop.'

Evelyn Nicholson outside 'The Little Ones Emporium' at 5 Hepworth's Arcade.
Courtesy of Alan Nicholson.

Isaac Gardiner, Watchmaker and Jeweller, 1937-1956

See no. 10 Hepworth's Arcade

William's Deacons Bank Ltd., 1957-1966

See no. 9 Silver Street.

Spring Estate Agency, Estate Agents, 1966-1975

See no. 9 Silver Street.

A. Fanthorpe Ltd., 1977-Present Date

See no. 6 Hepworth's Arcade.

NO. 3 HEPWORTH'S ARCADE

Jacob Friedenthal, Music Seller, 1896-1926

Jacob Friedenthal was a Russian jew who came to Hull in the 1880's quite possibly driven out of his homeland by the same anti-semitic regime that forced some two million Jewish refugees to leave Russia in the latter part of the last century. It has not been established if it was in Hull that Jacob and his family first stepped onto British soil, but it was in this city where he made his roots and established the foundations of a business that was still to be in existence over eighty years later.

The first written records of Mr. Friedenthal were in the 1891 census in which he is listed as being 43 years of age and residing at 26 Grimsby Lane, Market

Place with his wife Annie, son Joseph and two daughters Eliza and Rachel. The same census also lists a Harris Friedenthal aged 24 who was more than likely some relative to Jacob, but at the time he was not living with the family but lodging with a tailor, also Russian, at 37 Rodney Street. Both Jacob and Harris Friedenthal were shown as being music book-sellers but no evidence has been found of Harris being involved in the business which Jacob started. It is therefore feasible that he either died young or moved away from the area as in later years it was Joseph who took over the business. The early days in Hull could not have been easy for Jacob settling in a new country, with probably very little grasp of the language whilst still having to support a wife and three children.

It is understood that Jacob began in business in 1887 selling sheet music from a stall on Hull market not far from his home in Grimsby Lane. If that is correct it can safely be assumed that he experienced a certain degree of success as by 1895 when he was first listed in the Hull Directories he was living at 25 Silvester Street, a much more desirable area, and was also attributed with having two shops. He was apparently a close friend of Bert Feldman who was a well-known London music publisher who originated from Hull.

The first of the shops at no. 4 Paragon Arcade (now occupied by Going Places Travel Agency) had been taken over from a John Wilson, music seller, and was originally listed under the name of Jacob's wife Annie. The second was the previously unoccupied shop at no. 3 in the newly opened Hepworth's Arcade. Although the two shops were only small they were both situated in recently built and fashionable arcades probably commanding high rents which would also suggest that the venture was prospering. His neighbour at no. 5 Paragon Arcade was coincidentally Fanny Hiam who later moved her own business to Hepworth's Arcade. By 1897 Jacob had expanded further having also taken over the occupation of no. 3 Paragon Arcade (also now occupied by Going Places Travel Agency).

In 1900 the Friedenthal family increased their presence in Paragon Arcade to four shops when Jacob's son Joseph opened a drapery business at nos. 15 and 16 (now occupied by Hair by Frances), but stayed only three years before moving his venture to 26 Hessle Road.

Jacob continued to trade at both the shop in Hepworth's Arcade and the two in Paragon Arcade until 1905 when, true to the diversification abilities that seemed to attach themselves to the small businessmen of the era, he took over the tobacconist at no. 17 Paragon Arcade (also now occupied by Hair by Frances). He operated that shop alongside his other business which was by that time described as 'music dealer' for three years, but it would appear that the experiment was an unsuccessful one as by 1908 the tobacconist had disappeared and no. 17 was occupied by a Robert Dexter, Bamboo Furniture Dealer.

During the above period Jacob had changed residence twice, first to 21 Wilberforce Street and later, in 1903 to no. 9 Morpeth Street. Joseph meanwhile did not appear to be having the same amount of success and disappeared from the Directories for a three year period after 1905 before being listed again in the 1909 publication as a draper living at 59 Lister Street. By 1912 he was shown as residing at 12 Lansdowne Street, but was described as a warehouseman which would suggest that his own business had failed. He maintained that address and job description until 1919 by which time he had moved to 49 Linnaeus Street and was described, along with his father, as being a music dealer.

In 1921, by which time he had moved to live with his son, Jacob died and it is assumed that, from that year, the business passed to Joseph. It is however possible that, as his father was, at the time of his death, well into his seventies, Joseph had perhaps been operating the business for several years.

By 1925, whilst maintaining the outlet in Hepworth's Arcade, the part of the business which had for nearly thirty years been operated from Paragon Arcade had moved to larger premises in nearby Paragon Street. The new premises at no. 61 Paragon Street which were

Joseph Friedenthal.
Courtesy of Stuart Fredenthal.

near the corner of Chapel Street had for many years previously been used as a public house by the name of The Pavilion and are now occupied by the Bradford and Bingley Building Society. A photograph of the shop circa 1930 with Joseph's eldest son Henry standing outside shows that the business was by that time stocking, in addition to a vast array of sheet music, a variety of musical instruments.

When the Directories for 1929 were published the shop in Hepworth's Arcade had also closed although the

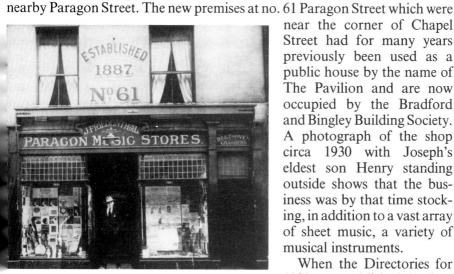

Paragon Music Stores circa 1930
with Henry Friedenthal standing outside.
Courtesy of Philip Fenton.

Louise Friedenthal.
Courtesy of Stuart Fredenthal.

number of outlets was maintained at two with a new branch under the name of Joseph's wife Louise having opened at 352 Hessle Road. The new shop is pictured with Joseph's younger son Lionel standing in the doorway. The number of branches was increased the following year when a third shop was opened at 238 Holderness Road. No alteration to the directory entry was made until 1933 when all three outlets were listed under the title of J. Friedenthal and Sons, music dealers. Joseph had been joined in the business by his two sons, Henry and Lionel, who both left school at 14 in 1918 and 1920 respectively. Mrs. Louise Friedenthal, although known to be still living, was no longer listed in the directories and probably opted to 'take a back seat' and leave the running of the business to her husband and two sons. It is very possible that, considering the Friedenthals had three shops, Joseph, Henry and Lionel took charge of one branch each.

By 1940 although the shop on Holderness Road retained the title of J. Friedenthal and Sons the branch in Paragon Street was renamed Paragon Music Stores and the one on Hessle Road became known as the West Hull Music stores. By 1941 the shop on Hessle Road had closed and just one year later in 1942 the branch on Holderness Road had also ceased trading. Joseph was at the time residing at 247 Spring Bank West near the corner with Hymers Avenue, whilst Lionel had a house at 247 Park Avenue and Henry lived at 203 Cottingham Road.

Although two of the shops operated by the business closed during the war years, possibly due to the lack of sheet music actually available to them because of the paper shortage caused by the War, the main outlet of Paragon Music Stores continued to trade for over thirty years after its sister shops' demise and did not cease trading until 1972.

Joseph Friedenthal died on 17th April 1957 aged 84, having outlived his wife Louise who died on 29th November 1953 aged 75.

By the time of the death of their father the business was being operated by Henry and Lionel and it is known that each of the brothers played a separate roll in the continued operation of the firm. Henry who had in earlier years left the family business for several years to work with Rose, Morris and Company, musical instruments manufacturers in London, was reportedly a talented musician excelling with the flute, saxaphone, piano and clarinet but apparently able to 'turn his hand' to any instrument. This skill proved to be a great asset to the business in later years as he was able to demonstrate to potential customers the capabilities of the various instruments stocked in the shop. Lionel on the other hand had the technical know-how and proficiency to repair practically any musical instrument, a skill which he cleverly adapted during the war years when he served his country by using that expertise in the manufacture and repair of radios for aircraft at the GEC in Bradford. Lionel is pictured in the Paragon Street store in the 1960's.

It has been suggested that a gentleman's agreement made between Joseph Friedenthal and John Scarborough (son of Sydney Scarborough) whereby Paragon Music Stores agreed not to stock gramaphone records in return for Mr. Scarborough's business undertaking not to sell

West Hull Music Stores circa 1930's with Lionel Friedenthal standing outside.
Courtesy of Stuart Fredenthal.

sheet music was perhaps the beginning of the decline in trade for the business. The increase in popularity in gramaphones and records culminating in the boom in the industry in the 1950's and 60's also saw the decline in the popularity of sheet music and a large drop in the number of homes that owned a piano.

Lionel Friedenthal passed away on 10th February 1970 aged 63 and two years later in early 1972 the Paragon Music Stores closed its doors for business for the final time.

The closure of the business after 85 years of trading prompted a report in the *Hull*

Lionel Friedenthal inside Paragon Music Stores.
Courtesy of Stuart Fredenthal.

Daily Mail from which the following extract is taken:

'The last of the old timers in Paragon Street is about to put up the shutters for good. ... Paragon Music Stores, a family business handed down through three generations, is closing within the next few days. Proprietor Mr. Henry Friedenthal (67) has decided to close the business because of ill health. ... 'I am the last of the old-timers in Paragon Street' said Mr. Friedenthal. 'All the old shops have been taken over and changed beyond recognition' ... He remembers the days before the 1939/45 War when the street was virtually full of pubs. 'Only a few doors away were the Windsor, the Neptune, the St. Leger and the Old Brunswick' he said. The firm was sole agents for dances and concerts at the City Hall which, in their heyday, had people like Ted Heath and his band, Harry Gold and his Pieces of Eight and the Squadronnaires performing. For many years they handled tickets for Madeley Street Baths wrestling matches which are now being done by Sydney Scarborough and more recently Locarno dances.'

Henry Friedenthal who was honoured with the life Presidency of the Hull Boys Brigade is pictured in the shop in Paragon Street on the final day of business in 1972. He died on 10th December 1987 aged 82.

Mrs. Winifred Harris (formerly Winifred Robson) who worked with Joseph, Henry and Lionel Friedenthal at the business in Paragon Street recalls:

'I started work for Paragon Music Stores in 1944 when the shop was being operated by Joseph and his elder son Henry. Lionel was away

Henry Friedenthal inside Paragon Music Stores on final day of business.
Courtesy of John Carnazza/Winifred Harris.

working in Bradford at the time and I did not meet him until a couple of years later. I worked for the business for around ten or eleven years, but following that returned on a part-time basis and remember what a really lovely family the Friedenthals were to work for. For many years at the back of the shop where the instruments were sold there was a sign that stated in no uncertain terms. 'THE BLOKE THAT LENDS THE INSTRUMENTS IS OUT' presumably to deter any hopeful customers from even bothering to ask.'

Today, some fifty-one years after starting in the business with Paragon Music Stores, Mrs. Harris is still actively involved in the sale of sheet music in Hull and fondly recalls her days with Joseph Friedenthal and his two sons.

F. D'Arcy Wray, Electrical Engineer, 1928-1933

Francis D'Arcy Wray was born in Beverley in 1898, the son of Alderman Harry Wray, a well known local solicitor and registrar of Hull and Beverley County Courts. His father achieved the distinction of being elected as Mayor of Beverley on no less than eight occasions. Francis obviously opted not to follow in his father's footsteps in the legal profession and was first listed in the Hull Directories in 1926 when he is shown as an electrical engineer operating from Hanover House, Alfred Gelder Street. By 1928, at which time he was living at 55 North Bar, Beverley, he is known to have taken over the tenancy of no. 3 Hepworth's Arcade. He remained in the shop for five years until 1933 having moved residence from Beverley to Hull in 1930 or 1931 presumably to be nearer his business. His new address at 41 Hall Road was given the title 'Raysholme' which would appear to be a play on words. By 1936 he had moved his business to 72 George Street where it was still listed in 1942. Mr. Wray was by all accounts known within the trade as 'a bit of a whizzkid' at the time and apparently had great knowledge in his particular field. After the War his address is given as 'Treetops', Salthouse Road, Sutton an address at which he would stay until the late 1970's. Francis was obviously very proud of his profession and was an Associate Member of the Institute of Electrical Engineers for many years and the letters that signify this (A.M.I.E.E.) were always included after his name in both the town and later the telephone directories. By 1978 Francis had moved to 11 Ness Close, Preston, and received a mention in the local press when he married for the second time at the age of 80. He passed away during the early part of 1983 aged 85.

The Singer Sewing Machine Company, 1934-1939

The Singer Sewing Machine Company was formed in the mid nineteenth century in Boston, U.S.A. by Isaac Merrit Singer who borrowed forty dollars to make his first sewing machine. Although this was the first device to sew continuously it was not the first ever sewing machine. The credit for that goes to a Barthélemy Thimmonier who, some years earlier, had put fifty to work in France making Army Uniforms. Unfortunately for Mr. Thimmonier these were soon smashed by rioting tailors who feared for the loss of their livelihood. In 1846, four years prior to Mr. Singer producing his first machine, an Elia

Howe Junior had patented a machine employing an eye-pointed needle with a shuttle. When Singer and other manufacturers developed their machines Howe sued them. For assistance in the 'Sewing Machine War' Isaac Singer, then based in New York, turned to the law firm Jordan and Clark and an agreement was struck whereby, for a third interest in the company, the junior partner Edward Clark agreed to fight the legal battles. The man who had originally advanced forty dollars, due to ill-health, sold out for six thousand dollars and in 1851 Clark and Singer became equal partners in I. M. Singer and Company. It is from that date that the Singer Organisation traces its history.

The first manufacture of Singer Sewing Machines outside the United States began in Glasgow in 1867. Fifteen years later Edward Clark's successor as head of the company, George Ross McKenzie who had left Scotland some years earlier as a barefoot emigrant boy, returned there and built the biggest of the Singer factories at Clydebank. In the near century and a half since I. M. Singer was formed they have manufactured and sold worldwide in excess of one hundred million sewing machines.

The first appearance of Singer Sewing Machine outlets in Hull was in the 1882 Directory when a branch is listed at 61 Whitefriargate. By 1906 there were four outlets in various parts of the city including one at 21 Beverley Road where the manager was shown as a George Francis Hands. Mr. Hands later became the district manager for Singer in the Hull area and the following year moved his base to the shop at 6 Holderness Arcade, Witham (since demolished but situated at the time around the area to the west of Holborn Street).

In later years George was joined in the shop by two of his daughters daughters Alice Maud Hands and Olive Lillian Hands. Apparently during the time that George and his daughters were working at the shop in Holderness Arcade the family had a pet fox terrier by the name of Snap. Snap was well known around the family home in Morill Street and often paid visits to neighbours and relatives in the nearby area where he would usually be given a titbit or treat. On other occasions when Snap felt in need of some excitement he would pay his owners a visit at the shop knowing that, in the drain which ran nearby on Witham, he could be sure to be able to do some rat catching. However such was the distance from his home in Morill Street to Witham and so often had Snap made the journey, he soon discovered that the trip was quicker and easier by public transport and could regularly be seen riding alone on the tram.

When George Hands died the management of the shop was taken over by Alice aided by her sister Olive and in 1934 when the lease on the premises in Witham ran out they

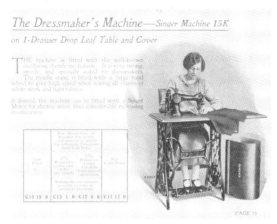

Advert for Singer Sewing machines circa 1930.

Olive and Alice Hands.
Courtesy of Frank Pentith.

moved the business to no. 3 Hepworth's Arcade where they stayed for five years. The sisters are pictured during a visit to Bridlington in 1935. Olive is the second adult from the left and Alice directly to her right. The youngster in the pram incidentally is Mary Booth who later married the nephew of the Hands sisters, Frank Pentith who kindly loaned the photograph.

In 1939 following five years in Hepworth's Arcade the shop closed. Alice married and left the business and Olive was offered a position at the Singer Shop in Princes Avenue. She accepted but did not stay with the company for long after her transfer. Olive recalls:

> 'I had worked for Singer for nearly twenty years and enjoyed my time with the company whilst working with my father and sister, but could not settle at the Princes Avenue branch. That shop was the main store in Hull for all spare parts and opened at 8.30 am each morning which meant a very early start from my home in East Hull. When a friend of mine mentioned that there could be a position at the District Valuer's office because of the extra work being caused by war damage I applied and was given a job as a shorthand typist for which I had originally trained. I stayed with the District Valuers until after the War when I was transferred to the Inland Revenue where I continued to work until my retirement in the mid 1960's.'

During the War Alice was appointed North Holderness organiser for the W.R.V.S. and was later awarded a British Empire Medal for her services to that organisation. She died on 7th October 1982. After retiring Olive moved away

185

from Hull but still resides in a quieter part of Yorkshire. Although now in her nineties she remains in good health and has, despite her age, a remarkable memory and recalls vividly her days in Hepworth's Arcade.

Isaac Gardiner, Watchmaker and Jeweller, 1948-1956

See no. 10 Hepworth's Arcade.

Note: It is quite feasible that Isaac Gardiner, who is known to have occupied the neighbouring property of no.5 from as early as 1937, may have taken over no. 3 earlier than 1948, but it has not been possible to verify positive occupation until that year.

Williams Deacon's Bank, 1956-1966

See no. 9 Silver Street.

Spring Estate Agency, 1966-1975

See no. 9 Silver Street.

A. Fanthorpe Ltd., 1977-Present date

See no. 6 Hepworth's Arcade.

NO. 1 HEPWORTH'S ARCADE

Miss Elizabeth Vergette, Confectioner, 1896-1898

Little information is available on Miss Vergette other than that she was the first tenant of No. 1 and sold sweets. The electoral register for the years 1897/8 confirms that her home address at the time was 69 York Street.

The London Mantle Company, Mantle Makers, 1899-1905

The London Mantle Company is first listed in the Hull Directories in 1899 at No. 1 Hepworth's Arcade when they are described as mantle makers. A mantle in this case is a loose cloak. This name is little used today but was very popular in Victorian England and the Hull Directories at the time listed several mantle makers and mantle warehouses.

Whether the premises in the Arcade were ever actually used as a manufacturing base or merely as a retail outlet is unsure and it is quite possible that, despite the name, this was a local concern merely using the name of London in their title to add some prestige to their business. Around the same time a Mr. F. Walter, a local man, operated a similar business from premises in Prospect Street under the name of the London and Parisian Mantle Warehouse. It can be assumed that the intention of both parties would have been to indicate the origins of the fashions on sale as opposed to that of the business itself.

The 1902/3 electoral register shows a James Oxtoby of 46 Sandringham Street as being the tenant of no. 1 which would indicate that he was either the owner or at least the manager of the business. The register for the following year also lists Mr. Oxtoby as being the tenant, but by this time he had changed his home abode to 111 St. Georges Road. The London Mantle Company was last listed in Hull in the Kelly's Directory for 1905 still at no. 1 Hepworth's

Arcade, after which time they disappeared from the Hull Directories completely.

Thomas Mapplebeck, Umbrella Maker, 1906

The name of Mapplebeck in connection with the manufacture of umbrellas in Hull can be traced back as far as 1823 when a William Mapplebeck is listed in the Directory for the year as a joiner, builder and umbrella maker at no. 34 Lowgate. It certainly appeared to be a peculiar combination of trades, but it can be assumed that the umbrella side of the business must have proved to be the more profitable as by 1842 when the same gentleman is shown as operating from no. 39 Lowgate his profession is plainly listed as umbrella and parasol manufacturer. It has not been established when William's son Thomas first entered the business, but following the death of his father in 1849 the name of the concern still operating from no. 39 Lowgate was changed to his own. For sixty years the name and address of the business did not alter and the premises can be seen in the sketch of Lowgate drawn by F. S. Smith around 1880 shown. From that illustration it would appear that Mr. Mapplebeck's business was on the upper floor of the tobacconist shop occupied by George Stancer, but the directories for the period indicate that Mr. Stancer's premises were next door to those of Mr. Mapplebeck at no. 38. The 1891 census confirms that

Illustration of Lowgate circa 1880 by F. S. Smith.
Courtesy of Hutton Press and Hull City Museums and Art Galleries.

Thomas Mapplebeck, then aged 71, was residing at 220 the Boulevard which was given the name of Rochester House probably in recognition of his father's birthplace which is known to have been Rochester in Kent. He was at the time a widower and lived with his daughters Emma (43) and Ada (35) and his son William (38). The census also verifies that both William (umbrella maker) and Ada (business manager for an umbrella maker) were more than likely also involved in the business.

Thomas Mapplebeck passed away at the end of 1892 and the business which presumably passed to his children continued, under his name, at the same address for a further decade.

In 1903, following over sixty years of occupation at no. 39 Lowgate, the business was moved several doors along the same street to no. 44A but after three years at that address moved again to no. 1 Hepworth's Arcade. That tenancy however was a brief one as by the following year James Meek had taken over the premises and presumably the business because after 1906 the name of Thomas Mapplebeck, Umbrella Manufacturer, was no longer listed in the Hull Directories. It is possible that William also passed away shortly after his father as from 1895 Rochester House is attributed to Thomas's youngest daughter Ada under her married name of Mrs. A. J. Seath, and the name of Thomas Mapplebeck only appears in the directories at the business address.

James Wood Meek, Umbrella Manufacturer, 1907-1916

James Wood Meek was born in Driffield in 1854 and in later years, along with his father, established in the town, a business that was to become well known throughout the East Riding not as umbrella makers but as hairdressers. He apparently came to Hull in the mid 1870's to try to emulate that success in this City. The first listing for Mr. Meek in the Hull Directories was in 1882 as a hairdresser with premises at 25 Paragon Street and by the time the 1885 Directory was published he had added perfumer to his business description. The title of perfumer was dropped by the following directory of 1888, but that of hairdresser remained as did the address of 25 Paragon Street. The advertisement pictured is taken from *The Hull Examiner* in 1890 and would confirm that although James may have

MEEK'S

ALMOND CREAM,
FOR SHAVING.

AN ELEGANT PREPARATION. PRODUCES A RICH CREAMY LATHER.
DEVOID OF ALL IRRITATING PROPERTIES.
IN POTS ONE SHILLING EACH.

The following, among other testimonials, has been received respecting the above :—

High House, Enfield, Highbury,
London, 18th February, 1890.

Dear Sir,
Please send me two more pots of your Almond Shaving Cream. I much prefer it to any preparation of the kind I have yet come across. I find the Perfume pleasant and refreshing.
Yours truly,
CHARLES JENKINSON.
To Mr. J. W. Meek, Perfumer, Hull.

PREPARED BY

J. W. MEEK, Perfumer,
25 AND 26, PARAGON STREET,
HULL.

Advertisement for James Meek from the Hull Examiner circa 1890.

dropped the description of perfumer from his trade description in the directories he was still operating as such. A further advertisement from the same publication proclaims the abilities of the 'Despatch' Umbrella Works to an extent that would suggest that this was more than just a sideline to Mr. Meek's business.

The first connection in the directories between Mr. Meek and umbrellas was in the 1893 Bulmer's Directory when, in addition to his hairdressing business in Paragon Street, James was also credited as being an umbrella manufacturer at 77 and a half Holderness Road. This address for Mr. Meek was apparently only a brief one and although shown again in the Kelly's Directory for 1893 had disappeared by 1895 in which year the Cook's Directory lists him as a hairdresser and umbrella maker at nos. 25 and 26 Paragon Street.

The 1891 census shows that James and his wife Clara were, at the time, also living at nos. 25 and 26 Paragon Street with their two sons, three daughters, a cook, a housemaid and a nurse who presumably took care of the children. By 1897 he is shown as residing at Melrose Villa, The Park, which would be a fair indication that his business or businesses were prospering as this was a prestigious area and probably one of the best addresses in the City at the time. Nothing altered in the descriptions or addresses given for James Meek until 1907 when he is also listed at no. 1 Hepworth's Arcade. It is a reasonable assumption that he either bought out or took over the umbrella business of Thomas Mapplebeck as from that year Mr. Mapplebeck ceases to be mentioned in the directories and Mr. Meek's businesses were listed separately — 1 Hepworth's Arcade — Umbrella Maker and 25/26 Paragon Street —Hairdresser. In 1913 James diversified again from his trade of hairdresser when he took over the neighbouring shop at 27 Paragon Street from John Smith Ridley who was described as a fruiterer. He ran the business which was presumably a fruit shop along with his other two concerns for two years until 1915 by which time the premises at no. 27 were attributed to Mrs. Nellie Miller, fruiterer. The last mention of the umbrella business in Hepworth's Arcade was in 1916 and by the time the 1919 Directory was

Advertisement for James Meek from the Hull Examiner circa 1890.

published James was only listed as a hairdresser at 25/26 Paragon Street, whilst still residing at Melrose Villa. It is, however, known that Meeks the Hairdressers continued to repair umbrellas up until the early 1960's and that just prior to their closure in 1993 still sold walking sticks and rubber ferules. The directory entries for Mr. Meek remain unchanged, other than the substitution of Melrose Villa for no. 44 when the houses in The Park were numbered in the 1920's, until 1937 when Kelly's also credits him, for one year only, with a ladies' hairdressing salon at 15 Anlaby Road. James, who was a freemason being a member of the De La Pole Lodge, died on 13th March 1938 aged 82. He was a member of the Baptist Church in George Street and, according to a *Hull Daily Mail* report at the time of his death, was often referred to as 'the man who made Paragon Street' because his business attracted so many people. James left a widow and three daughters, both of his sons having died fighting for their country in the First World War. He had retired from the concern some thirteen years earlier and a company had been formed to continue the business.

The 1939 Kelly's Directory lists the business in Paragon Street as Meek Ltd. which continued to trade from the same premises (although the number was changed to 91 when the street was re-numbered in the 1950's) until 1966 when it moved to Storey Street.

Meeks the Hairdresser was known throughout the City by the public and in the trade as the best hairdresser in Hull to quote from Geoff Matchett, himself a hairdresser (see no. 10 Hepworth's Arcade). The company was not at the time of removal owned by the Meek family, but by a local businessman and continued to operate from the first floor of 13 Storey Street until February 1993 when it closed its doors for the final time ending an era of hairdressing in Hull by Meeks spanning over a century.

Following the departure from no. 1 of James Meek circa 1916 the premises were not listed in any directories until 1959 when they were shown as being occupied by Williams Deacon's Bank along with no. 9 Silver Street. It is known that the dividing wall between the two shops had, some time prior to 1934, been removed to form larger premises and it is conceivable that this had been done as early as 1917 to extend the premises of the occupiers of 9 Silver Street at the time – H. Samuel Ltd. (See no. 9 Silver Street).

Williams Deacon's Bank, 1946-1965
See no. 9 Silver Street.

Spring Estate Agency, 1965-1975
See no. 9 Silver Street.

Williams and Glyn's Bank / The Royal Bank of Scotland PLC., 1975-Present Date
See no. 9 Silver Street.

Note: *The upper floors of nos. 1, 3 and 5 Hepworth's Arcade had at some time between 1956 and 1966 been knocked through to join with the premises above nos. 8 and 9 Silver Street which were, at the time, used as offices. The staircases from nos. 3 and 5 were removed and that belonging to no. 1 was separated from the* *ground floor of that shop and formed an additional entrance to the offices on the first floor. Between 1966 and 1981 the first floors of nos. 1, 3 and 5 Hepworth's Arcade were occupied by H. Gore Atkinson, a firm of chartered accountants who had been established in Silver Street since 1910.*

NO. 9 SILVER STREET

As was the case with its 'twin' shop across the Arcade at no. 8, number 9 Silver Street, when first built, had additional accommodation on the first, second and third floors above the shop and a 'half share' of the three storeys that spanned the Arcade. In later years although the ground floor was extended to include the shop at no. 1 Hepworth's Arcade the upper floors were altered to become, along with the corresponding part of no. 8 Silver Street, part of the premises allocated to and accessed through no. 2 Hepworth's Arcade.

J. Forrester and Co., Jewellery and Fancy Goods, 1895-1906

John Forrester commenced in business in Clayton Street, Newcastle upon Tyne in 1888 dealing in jewellery and fancy goods. By 1894 he had opened two further branches at Sunderland and South Shields and had expanded his original range of products to include such diverse items as spectacles, small musical instruments and rocking chairs. He had also established a brisk trade in toys and novelties many of which were imported from the Continent.

In 1895 the business expanded further opening at no. 9 Silver Street, Hull at the corner of Hepworth's Arcade, the first stage of which had recently been completed. A 'Christmas at the Shops' article published in the *Hull Daily Mail* later that year contained a tribute to the business from which the following extract is taken:

> 'At Messrs. J. Forrester and Co.'s establishment in Silver Street the Manager (Mr. Henderson) brought to the notice of our represent-ative goods of almost every description suitable for all classes and tastes. The most interesting probably was, we think, that where children's toys of every conceivable shape and make (mechanical, musical and automatic) were on view. This section struck one as being a perfect 'baby dreamland'. Well worth inspection too were the articles of jewellery, watches, clocks, electro-plated goods etc. Ladies' engagement rings, gentlemen's rings and rings in precious stones are a speciality at this establishment and may be had from one shilling to fifteen guineas. A leading line also is in electro-plated and leather goods and cutlery. There are enough Tea and Coffee Services, Cruets, Tea Pots, Coffee Pots, Butter Coolers, Prize Cups etc. to select from, that would furnish probably every house in town. Other departments too were those where China and Leather Goods, Musical Instruments, Music Boxes etc. were to be seen in large quantities and at prices that appeal to all classes.'

By the following year the shop's trade in toys appeared to have really taken off with 'Dreamland' as the toy department of Forrester and Co. had been Christened the year before by the *Mail* being the subject of large adverts placed

Advertisement for Forrester and Co. from the Hull Daily Mail.
Courtesy of the Hull Daily Mail.

Advertisement for Forrester and Co. from the Hull Daily Mail.
Courtesy of the Hull Daily Mail.

regularly in the *Hull Daily Mail* by the company.

By 1902 another tribute to the business in the 'Christmas at the Shops' article in the *Hull Daily Mail* proclaimed that Forrester's seemed to have made provision for the classes and masses and that toys could be purchased from a penny to a pound.

A further advert was also placed in the *Mail* in December 1902 and although the lists of gifts available are impressive to say the least the question must be asked. What about Mother?

In 1905 Forrester and Co. informed the public of Hull of the Greatest of Great Sales with everything half price before their removal to more central premises on January 8th the following year.

Although the shop did almost certainly close in the early part of 1906 no evidence has been found of the business ever re-appearing either in more central premises or indeed in any other part of Hull. It has also been noted that the company branch in Sunderland closed in 1906 and those in Newcastle and South Shields had both disappeared by 1908, and it could therefore be speculated that it was indeed never the intention to re-open in Hull and that the closure of Silver Street was possibly the first step in the winding down of the business before either retirement or insolvency. Although H. Samuel, who were also jewellers moved into the vacated premises only two months after the departure of J. Forrester and Co., no evidence has been found to suggest a take-over by Samuels. Further investigation shows that although the Forrester shops in Newcastle and South Shields were also later occupied by jewellers neither of these were H. Samuel and the outlet in Sunderland later became a dairy.

H. Samuel, Watchmakers and Jewellers, 1906-1934

The origins of H. Samuel can be traced back to Liverpool, where in 1821, two brothers Moses and Lewis Samuel ran a successful clock making business.

Following the death of the two gentlemen the family concern passed to the son of Lewis. Unfortunately he only outlived his father by eighteen months and when he died the control of the business passed to his widow — Harriet Samuel. It was Harriet who, in 1862, gave the company the name by which it is known today.

Harriet Samuel moved to Manchester setting up in business as a mail order company in Market Street in the city and for many years advertised nationally offering extensive catalogues to potential customers.

It was Harriet's son Edgar who developed the retail side of the business opening the first branch in Preston, Lancashire in 1890 followed by a second in Rochdale and numerous others throughout the North of England. In later years, for reasons probably better known only to himself, Edgar changed his surname to Edgar thus becoming known as Edgar Edgar.

In 1912 the company headquarters which were still on the site of the mail order business in Manchester were moved to Birmingham which was considered at the time to be the centre of the jewellery manufacturing industry. The first factory was also built on Hunters Road in the city, opened in 1935 and

Advertisement for Forrester and Co. from the Hull Daily Mail. Courtesy of the Hull Daily Mail.

Harriet Samuel.
Courtesy of The Signet Group Plc.

continued to manufacture rings solely for H. Samuel shops until 1986, although during the war years it served a very different function when it was utilised for the manufacture of tank parts.

Following the Second World War the company embarked on a programme of expansion under the leadership of Harriet Samuel's grandsons Gilbert and Robert Edgar. The brothers had joined the company in 1918 and 1920 respectively.

In 1948 H. Samuel became a limited company having shares quoted on the London, Birmingham and Liverpool Stock Exchanges. The business continued to flourish during the post-war years with many new branches being opened. The increase in turnover resulted in the existing factory, offices and warehouse proving inadequate and by acquisition of land on the opposite side of Hunters Road a new building was erected and opened in 1958.

In 1984 whilst under the guidance of Anthony Edgar, the great-grandson of Harriet Samuel, the company acquired the James Walker Group giving H. Samuel Ltd. nearly 450 retail outlets and extensive national coverage.

During 1986 the group of H. Samuel Companies was acquired by the Ratner Group PLC headed by Gerald Ratner.

Following further acquisitions of the Ernest Jones Group in 1987, the Ratner Group became the market leaders in jewellery in the United Kingdom and in May the following year opened an H. Samuel branch in Shaftesbury Avenue, London — the one thousandth branch in the Group. In October 1988 the Group also acquired Zales UK, Salisburys, Collingwood and J. Weir and Sons bringing the Group share of UK jewellery sales to 30 per cent.

In November 1992 Gerald Ratner left the company and his successor James McAdam perceived one of his first tasks was to re-name the Group to disassociate itself with the bad publicity that Ratners had attracted.

In September 1993 the Group was relaunched as the Signet Group which now trades under three names within the Group — H. Samuel, Ernest Jones and Leslie Davis and can boast of having a branch or branches in every major town or city in the country.

Some twelve years after establishing their original outlet in Preston, Lanchashire H. Samuel opened their doors to the public of Hull for the first time having taken over the premises of no. 5 Silver Street previously occupied by George Dove, Fancy Draper.

The business remained at that address until early 1906 when the outlet was moved just four doors along Silver Street to no. 9 recently vacated by J. Forrester.

Illustration of no. 9 Silver Street circa early 1900's.
Courtesy of The Signet Group Plc.

The pencil drawing of the premises was used by the company, along with those of their various other branches, in advertisements and on stationery.

It should be noted at this point that, following the departure of J. Meek from no. 1 Hepworth's Arcade in 1916, the shop is unlisted in the directories for a period of 43 years. It is therefore very probable that from that date H. Samuel extended their shop at no. 9 Silver Street into those premises.

Throughout the early 1900's the company advertised extensively nationwide promoting their shops and the H. Samuel Big Book of Bargains. As the following letter which was sent with the catalogue confirms, the company was keen to leave all potential customers without any doubts about the benefits that could be gained by making purchases from themselves rather than their competitors.

The company also advertised locally, regularly placing large advertisements in the *Hull Daily Mail* an example of which is included. Taken from the *Mail* in mid December the advert explains that 'It's Getting Urgent' and encourages the reader to purchase Xmas Gifts at Next To Factory Prices from the company outlet at 9 Silver Street. In some advertisements H. Samuel offered to refund train fares to purchasers spending 25 shillings upwards presumably in an attempt to attract those travelling to Hull from further afield.

A tribute to the H. Samuel shop in Silver Street taken from the ever popular *Hull Daily Mail* article 'Christmas at the Shops' congratulated the company on

195

H. Samuel letterheading.
Courtesy of The Signet Group Plc.

Advertisement for H. Samuel from the Hull Daily Mail. Courtesy of the Hull Daily Mail.

its Christmas illuminations and informed their readers 'What Samuels have in their extensive stock is enumerated in a catalogue of the size of a foolscap sheet with as many pages as a novel. There generally seems to be someone in the shop buying something from a wedding ring down to a clock that plays a musical selection as the hours come around. Here is variety, novelty and quality. These words would make a good motto over the door. The public can easily test if what we have written can be justified.'

On 14th April 1928 the company opened a second outlet in Hull at no. 28 in nearby Whitefriargate and in usual Samuel's style included a picture of the new shop, although now in photograph form, in adverts promoting the business.

Both outlets continued to operate until the 5th May 1934 when the branch in Silver Street closed. A few years later the clock which had hung outside those premises for nearly thirty years was moved to the newer shop. It was for many years seen as a necessity by the company for all branches to have a clock bearing the name of H. Samuel at the front of their premises and a ruling that this must be kept correctly set at all times was strictly adhered to. The company no doubt thought that any inaccuracy in a timepiece advertising the company name would reflect badly on both H. Samuel and their merchandise. It is interesting to note that the repairs and maintenance of these clocks, many of which are still prominent outside Samuel's outlets all over the country, is not, despite their many years experience as clock and watch makers, carried out by the company themselves but by a firm who are specialists in the field of exterior clocks — John Smiths of Derby. That company have been caring for the Samuel's clocks for over sixty years and although not responsible for the movement of the clock from Silver Street to Whitefriargate did install a replacement clock at those premises in 1959 and were later, in 1981, entrusted with its removal to the current site outside the premises on Monument Bridge.

In the early 1950's H. Samuel again returned to two shops in the city taking over new premises at no. 9 King Edward Street which they maintained, along with 28 Whitefriargate, for over a decade before returning to just one shop in the mid 1960's.

When the newly built Prospect Centre opened in 1974 H. Samuel was one of the original tenants moving into the prestigious premises on the corner of the Centre Entrance and Prospect Street which, it could be said, was a very similar site to the one they had occupied nearly seventy years earlier on the corner of Hepworth's Arcade and Silver Street.

The branch in Whitefriargate closed in 1977 but the name of H. Samuel was maintained on two shops in the city when the outlet at no. 2 Alfred Gelder Street which, although occupied by the company since 1952, and had

H. Samuel premises at 28 Whitefriargate circa early 1930's.
Courtesy of The Signet Group Plc.

previously traded under a different title, also became known as H. Samuel.

Both the branch in the Prospect Centre and that in Alfred Gelder Street (or on Monument Bridge as it is known locally) continue to operate in the city to this day no doubt serving some customers whose ancestors had been served at the shop in Silver Street nearly ninety years before.

S. C. Bastow, Hosiers, Hatter and Glovers, 1934-1939

See no. 6 Hepworth's Arcade.

Williams Deacon's Bank / Williams & Glyn's Bank / The Royal Bank of Scotland PLC., 1946-1966 and 1976-Present Date

Williams Deacon's Bank was founded in London in 1771 and in 1890 amalgamated with Manchester and Salford Bank which had a growing network of branches in the North West of England.

Expansion continued in both London and Northern England until the 1920's when the depression in Lancashire, where the bank's business was concentrated, severely affected its stability and by the end of that decade it urgently needed the support of a larger partner.

In 1929 through the offices of the Bank of England, The Royal Bank of Scotland made an offer for the company's entire share capital which was finally accepted the following year. The English branch network of the business continued to trade separately under the name of Williams Deacon's and following the Second World War began to expand into new geographical areas, the first of which was Hull.

In 1970 The Royal Bank of Scotland's English constituents were merged to form Williams & Glyn's Bank and fifteen years later, in 1985, that group and The Royal Bank of Scotland merged fully to become a single bank under the name of The Royal Bank of Scotland PLC.

As previously mentioned the Group, under the name of Williams Deacon's Bank first opened in Hull shortly after the Second World War occupying the premises at 9 Silver Street and 1 Hepworth's Arcade from 3rd March 1947.

The premises which had previously been occupied by H. Samuel were actually leased to the bank in 1946 but such was the extent of the alterations required to alter the shop units into premises suitable for use as a bank that it took several months to complete the renovation. Indeed when the branch did eventually open for business the refurbishment of the public area and the manager's office had been completed but not the rest of the office. The picture shows the bank premises in the 1950's and from this it is easy to understand why the renovation took so long as the complete shop fronts facing both Silver Street and the Arcade had been replaced. At some point either prior to or during their occupation of 9 Silver Street and 1 Hepworth's Arcade the bank also secured the leases on nos. 3 and 5 in the Arcade occupied at the time by Isaac Gardiner, jewellers and following the departure of that business in 1956 extended their offices into the vacant shops.

In 1962 it was felt that the Silver Street frontage was too small and when the

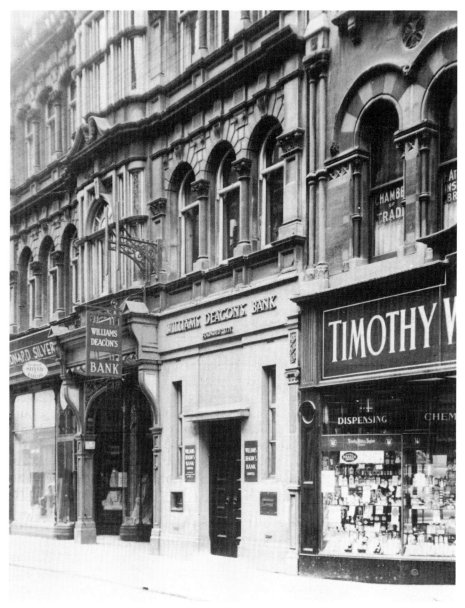

Williams Deacon's Bank, 9 Silver Street circa 1950's.
See demolished site page 202. Courtesy of The Royal Bank of Scotland Plc.

neighbouring premises of 10 and 11 Silver Street were vacated by Timothy White and Taylors the bank purchased the property.

Williams Deacon's demolished the existing properties replacing them with a new four-storey building which was completed on 31st January 1966. The second photograph showing the site following the demolition of the old premises gives an unusual and somewhat unique view of the rear of the shops on the North Western side of the Arcade. This view would have been seen for the first time ever in the early 1960's and is very unlikely to be seen again for many many years.

Following their removal to 10/11 Silver Street the bank did, for a short period, vacate both 9 Silver Street and the three shops in the Arcade sub-letting the premises to the Spring Estate Agency but later, in 1976, returned to the refurbished premises of 9 Silver Street and 1 Hepworth's Arcade by extending their new premises.

The shop fronts facing both Silver Street and the Arcade have now been restored to their former appearance and are currently used by the bank as part of their public area.

Spring Estate Agency, 1966-1975

Spring Estate Agency was formed in 1963 by Ronald Bannister and his wife Janet and originally operated from premises at 90 Spring Bank which consisted of a single room and one telephone. Within two years of its formation the company had expanded to such an extent that the original office was unsuitable and new premises in a more central location were sought.

In November 1965 an agreement was made between Mr. Bannister and the Williams and Glyn's Bank that, following the removal of the bank to its newly built premises next door at

Advertisement for Williams Deacon's Bank from the Hull Daily Mail.
Courtesy of the Hull Daily Mail.

numbers 10 and 11, Spring Estate Agency would take over the vacated property of no. 9 Silver Street together with the office space accommodated in nos. 1, 3 and 5 Hepworth's Arcade.

Within four years the company had expanded to include branches in Brough, Cottingham and Hedon in addition to their premises in Silver Street which became their head office. In 1971 they added to these an office in the Square, Willerby the design of which attracted a glowing report from the *Hull Daily Mail* from which the following extract is taken...

> '... When the premises were first purchased last summer the original notice in the window read 'Spring will be here in the Autumn' but due to a complete re-design of the ground floor the Agency were not able to open the doors to the general public until, ironically, the

200

second day of Spring — the first day being a Sunday... The Georgian oak bay window is a work of art and a credit to the main contractor. It would be well worth a ride to view this unusual modern office...'

Advertisement for Spring Estate Agency from the Hull Daily Mail.
Courtesy of The Hull Daily Mail.

The article went on to point out that Spring Estate Agency was at the time, the only local agency advertising regularly on television a formula that no doubt proved successful as by 1975 the company had out-grown their headquarters in Silver Street and purchased and renovated no. 2 Land of Green Ginger.

Their new premises which stood on the corner of Land of Green Ginger and Manor Street were once owned and occupied by Hull leather merchants, Tesseymans, and dated back over a century.

The company expanded to a total of six branches before being merged with Wm. H. Brown Estate Agents in 1987. The name of Spring Estate Agency was, however, kept until 1990 following which time the name above the various branches was changed to that of Wm. H. Brown.

The advertisement is taken from a 1966 edition of the *Hull Daily Mail* and highlights the increase in house prices during the past thirty years.

The Royal Bank of Scotland PLC. 1975-Present Date

See earlier reference.

To conclude the chapter on the tenants of Hepworth's Arcade it is probably appropriate to attempt to answer two questions which have been posed on many occasions during the course of the research for this book —

Which is the oldest shop/business in the Arcade now?   and
Which business stayed in the Arcade for the longest period?

In order to answer those questions it is necessary to establish what should be taken as being the starting date for any concern and whether a change in ownership, name or type of business being conducted constitutes the formation

*The vacant site created by the demolition of
nos. 10 and 11 Silver Street.*
Courtesy of The Royal Bank of Scotland Plc.

of a new venture. Because of the alternatives available which could easily be disagreed upon by different individuals the three possible candidates are listed below.

1.   George William Dinsdale commenced in business in the Arcade in 1930 as a dealer in gramophones and records. The business is still in the Arcade today 65 years later but has, during

that time, not only changed to a joke and magic shop but has also changed ownership passing from George Senior to his son.

2.   The premises at nos. 9 and 11 have been listed as being a café since 1899 but during the 96 years that have passed the business has had five different owners.

3.   Brantons Jewellers have only been at no. 13 since 1967 but that business now forms part of the same operation as Gardiners Jewellers who were listed in the Arcade between 1900 and 1956. Total 84 years.

The answers are therefore, to say the least, debatable but it cannot be disputed that the above mentioned businesses and the many more who have occupied the Arcade over the last one hundred years have all contributed, in one way or another, to the colourful history and continued popularity of Hepworth's Arcade.

SUMMARY

Throughout the past century Hepworth's Arcade has had a chequered history and an ever-changing string of tenants experiencing varying degrees of success.

In the early days when Market Place, Silver Street and Whitefriargate were considered to be the centre for shopping in Hull the Arcade was obviously very popular with its shops proving to be in great demand by both local and national businesses. The fashion-conscious ladies of the Victorian Era would no doubt have found it to be a shoppers' paradise with a wide variety of establishments allied to the clothing and footwear industry.

By the early 1930's the popularity of the Arcade, along with the Old Town itself as a shopping area, had diminished and from that period, which also marked the beginning of the Recession, until the end of the Second World War many of the shops in the Arcade remained empty for long periods. The structure itself, although avoiding any direct hits from attacks by enemy forces, sustained a substantial amount of damage from the bombs dropped on nearby Market Place. It is reported that, at times during the six years that the country was at war, the floor of the Arcade was often covered in broken glass from the roof which had been shattered by the blasts from nearby explosions.

Following the end of the hostilities in 1945 the Arcade was given a new lease of life with many of the shops being occupied by new businesses started by ex-servicemen who had returned from fighting for their country and were keen to make a fresh start. Some of those businesses failed in the early years but several, although now under the management of the next generation of the family, survive to this day.

The 1950's and early 60's brought mixed fortunes for the Arcade and whilst some new names did appear over the shops and a few of the existing businesses expanded within the Arcade others turned their back on the Old Town heading for pastures new in the premises rapidly being built and refurbished in the newer part of the City Centre.

The Arcade itself suffered and by the late 1960's and 1970's, although often described as having plenty of character, began to look shabby and in need of refurbishment.

The 1980's brought a revival of interest in the Old Town with many old buildings being converted for use as offices, shops and living accommodation. New houses and flats were built in that area of the City for the first time in many years and, following the development of the Marina and the refurbishment of the Market Hall, the City Council began a project of renovation in the Arcade.

The shop fronts of number 9 Silver Street and numbers 1, 3 and 5 in the Arcade which had, for many years, been partially bricked up were restored and the rest of the Arcade given a complete face-lift. By the latter part of that decade most of the shops had been refurbished, a new floor laid and fresh interest generated in the area as a place to shop.

Numbers 1, 3 and 5 Hepworth's Arcade whilst shop front partially bricked up.
Courtesy of Hull City Council Planning Department.

By the early 1990's a link-through leading to both the Indoor Market Hall and the beer garden of Ye Old Blue Bell had been established, a new shop at no. 21 built and the café extended. The premises at nos. 15 and 17 were again divided into two units and, following their occupation by the present tenants, the Arcade was once again fully occupied.

Although still somewhat adrift from the fashionable shopping areas of Whitefriargate and the New Town the Arcade is becoming very popular offering several types of retail outlets which cannot be found elsewhere in the City Centre. Because of its historical value the Arcade has always proved to be a tourist attraction and the floral display on the balcony, which is provided through contributions from the tenants themselves, has received recognition on several occasions in the competitions held yearly in the Old Town.

Today, as throughout the past one hundred years, the majority of the tenants in the Arcade are local businesses operated by local people and it is a common belief, amongst those traders, that it is that quality which makes the Arcade a unique part of Hull's City Centre and a contrast to those throughout the country which, it is often noted, vary very little from one to the other being home to the same string of national names and businesses.

The Arcade remains, as in the early days of its existence, a pleasant place to visit and shop unaffected by the weather. It offers the citizens of Hull the opportunity to appreciate a part of the history of this great City of ours whilst supporting their local businesses and will hopefully continue to do so for a good few centuries to come.

ACKNOWLEDGEMENTS

I would like to thank the following individuals and organisations for the assistance and encouragement they have given me during the past two and a half years as without that support the publication of this book would not have been possible.

Sam Allon Ltd., Edna Anderson, *The Ashton-under-Lyne Reporter*, Chris Aspin, Kathleen Banks, Ronald Bannister, Rosa Barker, Frank Bastow, Jack Stanley Bastow, David Baxter, Chris Beasley, Fran Beasley, Mr. Beaver, Eric Beckwith, Janice Bell — Burnley Central Library, Marjorie Bennion, Mim Benson, Marjorie Bolton, Bowden Holdings, the late Thomas Branton Junior, British Shoe Corporation, Anne Brittain, Angela Burns, Anne Burrell, Dorothy Carmody, John Carnazza, Selwyn Clark, Blanch Cleveland, Jill Crowther, Judi Crumpton, Margaret Dibb, Shirley Dinsdale, George Dinsdale, Judy Dolman, Sara Donaldson, Ada Drake, Nick Duddy, Malcolm Dufton, Mike Fanthorpe, Laura Fanthorpe, Eleanor Farmer, Joan Farmer, Jenny Featherstone, Philip Fenton, Mrs. Figg, Graham Frall, Susan Fraser, Stuart Fredenthal, Steve Frost, Ken Furmage, Anthony Furmage, Pamela Gardam, Gelder and Kitchen, David Gibson, Arnold Girling, Rosemary Glusick, Chas. E. Goad Ltd., David Gordon, Debbie Gowans, Robert Graham, Gavin Gray, Eric Greaves, Joanne Green — Ashton-under-Lyne Town Hall, Mrs. Hainsworth, Olive Hands, Peggy Harding, Mrs. Harman, Winifred Harris, Margaret Harrison, Richard Hayton, Angela Heard, Mr. Henrikson, Kathleen Hiam, Hill's Biscuits Ltd., Mary Hodges, Fred Hodgson, Miss Hodgson, Helen Holford, Kathleen Holgate, Jeremy Holmes, Mrs. Hope, Gill Horsley, Geoffrey Hubbard, Hull Local History Library, Hull Business Centre, Hull Civic Society, *The Hull Daily Mail*, Humberside County Council Archives Office, Beverley, Humberside Libraries, Janet Hunter, Peter Jackson, Paul Jackson, Richard Jenkinson, Ian Johnson, Mike Johnson, Betty Joplin, Patricia Jorna, Jim Kane, Raymond Kauffman, Barry Kaye, Marion Kendall, Chris Ketchell, Tony Kettlewell, Basil King, Kingston Communications, Graeme Knox — Hull City Council, Chas. Latter, Leeds Central Library, Stan Leeman, Michael Leslie, Peter Leslie, Charlie Linford, Louise, Manchester Central Library, Marks and Spencer Plc. London, Mary Marrington, Christine Martin, David Martin, Mr. Martin, Geoff Matchett, Mrs. Mathieson, Mrs. Matthews, Andrew McDowell, *Middlesbrough Evening Gazette*, Middlesbrough Central Library, Dudley C. D. Moore, Kathleen Mowthorpe, Councillor Jim Mulgrove, Maureen Murphy, Kim Napper, Newcastle Central Library, Rob Nicholson, Alan Nicholson, Bob North, Mr. Oxley and his staff at Hull City Records Office, Johnny Pat, Mr. Pearson, Frank Pentith, Sharron Peschke, Mrs. Phillips, Honor Platten, Mike Plaxton, Phillip Rackham, Mrs. Rand, Jim Richardson, Lillian Robson, C. B. Robson,

Roy Sangwin, Colin Shakespeare, Sheila Shephard, Norman Shuttleworth, Eric Silver, Singer U.K. Ltd., Kathy Slingoe — *Burnley Express*, Nicky Smit, Eva Smith, John Smith, Pat Smith, Geoffrey Smith, Tony Smith, Peter Spencer, Gillian Spokes, South Shields Library, Helen Stinson, Stockton-on-Tees Library, Ron Storey, Mrs. Stubbs, Mrs. D. Sugarman, Mr. L. Sugarman, Anna Sullivan, Sunderland Central Library, Alice Sutton, Tameside Local Studies Library, Peter Tarbotten, Mary Taylor, John Taylor, The Royal Bank of Scotland Plc., the *Hull Daily Mail*, The Signet Group Plc., Mrs. Toby, John W. Todd, Topcolour, Audrey Townend, Brian Tozer Sally Tozer, Alison Turton, Pat Tuxworth, Ted Tuxworth, Mr. Waller, Cliff Wallis, Tony Ward, Pat Ward, Pat Webster, Tony Westoby, Ida Whincup, John Whittaker and Hull City Council Planning Department, Larry Willby, Edith Williams, Graham Williams, Jane Wilshere, Muriel Wilson, Margaret Wingfield, Phillip Winterbottom, Roy Woodcock, Angela Wright, Vicki Wyatt, Keith Yeomans.

And finally but by no means least, my wife Debbie for her support and patience during the past two and a half years.

SELECTED BIBLIOGRAPHY

1891 Census.

A History of Leeds Clothing Industry.

A Centenary History of Marks and Spencer.

Atkinson's Directories of Hull.

Brown's Directories of Hull.

Bulmer's Directories of Hull and the East Riding.

Burnley Express.

Burnley Gazette.

Contemporary Biographies.

Cook's Directories of Hull.

Country Coppers.

Heavysides Almanac.

Hull Electoral Registers.
Hull Topic.

Hull District Telephone Directory.

Hull Daily Mail.

Hull Examiner.

Illustrated Hull.

Images of Victorian Hull: F. S. Smith's Drawings of the Old Town.

Industries of Yorkshire.

Kelly's Directories of Hull.

Leeds and Yorkshire Mercury.

Leeds Illustrated.

Men of the Period.

Policemen of Hull.

Rivers of the North.

Surprising Lancashire.

The History of the Spread Eagle, Market Place by Richard Hayton (Unpublished).

The House of Kings.

The History of Hills Biscuits.

The Ashton-under-Lyne Reporter.

Tyneside Industries (1890).

Yorkshire Post.

Yorkshire Evening Post.

Yorkshire Evening News.

Phoenix

FREIGHT INTERNATIONAL LTD.

6/7 COELUS STREET
GREAT UNION STREET,
HULL HU9 1AX

TEL: 01482 215645
FAX: 01482 215646

**GROUPAGE, FULL AND PART LOAD
TRAILER SERVICES TO ALL PARTS OF
SCANDINAVIA & EUROPE**

OFFICES AT BASILDON, PARIS & CANNES